ERIK H. ERIKSON

ERIK H. ERIKSON, by training a psychoanalyst, is now Professor of Human Development and lecturer on psychiatry at Harvard. His clinical practice has included the treatment of children of all ages and he has participated in the study of growing up in a variety of cultural and social settings. In his first book, *Childhood and Society,* he summarized a decade and a half of his clinical and applied work; it is being read widely and has appeared in seven foreign languages. For another decade, Erikson worked in the Austen Riggs Center for treatment and research, primarily on problems of young adulthood. In *Young Man Luther,* he investigates the relationship of youth and history in the emergence of a great innovator. He has since extended his studies to problems of productivity in middle age.

ERIK H. ERIKSON

Childhood and Society
Young Man Luther
Insight and Responsibility
Identity: Youth and Crisis
Gandhi's Truth

ERIK H. ERIKSON

Young Man Luther

A Study in Psychoanalysis and History

The Norton Library

W · W · NORTON & COMPANY · INC ·

NEW YORK

W. W. Norton & Company, Inc., Edition
Published October, 1958: four printings

Norton Library Edition
Published July 1962: nine printings

Austen Riggs Monograph No. 4

W. W. Norton & Company Inc. is also the publisher of
the works of Otto Fenichel, Karen Horney and Harry Stack
Sullivan, and the principal works of Sigmund Freud.

PRINTED IN THE UNITED STATES OF AMERICA

90

Contents

Contents

Preface

THIS STUDY of Martin Luther as a young man was planned as a chapter in a book on emotional crises in late adolescence and early adulthood. But Luther proved too bulky a man to be merely a chapter. His young manhood is one of the most radical on record: whatever he became part of, whatever became part of him, was eventually destroyed or rejuvenated. The clinical chapter became a historical book. But since clinical work is integral to its orientation, I will, in this preface, enlarge briefly on my colleagues and my patients, and our common foci of preoccupation.

During the last five years a grant from the Field Foundation has enabled me to concentrate on the study of emotional disturbances of people in their late teens and early twenties. The clinical work with acutely disturbed young people was done mainly at the Austen Riggs Center in Stockbridge, Massachusetts, and at intervals at the Western Psychiatric Institute in the School of Medicine of the University of Pittsburgh. Austen Riggs is a small, open (*i.e.*, with no closed facilities), research-minded private hospital in a small residential town in New England. The Western Psychiatric Institute is a skyscraper with closed floors, on one of the fastest-growing medical campuses in the world, in the center of the capital of steel. In Pittsburgh, under the generous direction of Dr. Henry W. Brosin and of Dr. Frederik Weniger, I was able to test my hypotheses on patients who came from backgrounds altogether different from those of the patients at Austen Riggs Center, where, thanks to Dr.

Robert P. Knight's vision, selective smallness permits a joint and
systematic awareness of the therapeutic factors in all the areas of a
patient's life. Within the safe outlines of the diagnostic facilities and
the therapeutic practices of both hospitals I could study the afflictions of young patients as variations on one theme, namely, a life
crisis, aggravated in patients, yet in some form normal for all youth.
I could identify those acute life tasks that would bring young people
to a state of tension in which some would become patients; I could
study their initial symptoms and the emergence of a psychiatric
syndrome. I could explore possible similarities in their childhood experiences and discover what kinds of parents and what kinds of
backgrounds would be apt to prejudice development in such a way
that the life crisis of adolescence might prove insurmountable without special help or exceeding good fate, in the form of the opportunity to deploy special gifts under favorable conditions. Joan
Erikson's work in transforming at Riggs what once was occupational
therapy into a meaningful "activities program" helped me to understand the curative as well as the creative role of work which, as we
shall see, is so prominent in young Luther's life, and in his views
about work—and "works."

Each new clinical experience supports and is supported by developments in theory. This book will more or less explicitly take account
of recent thinking about the ego's adaptive as well as its defensive
functions. Sigmund Freud's monumental work is the rock on which
such exploration and advancement must be based. Anna Freud, with
her book on the ego, opened a whole new theoretical area for study,[1]
and August Aichhorn opened a therapeutic frontier in work with
young people.[2] What I have learned from them, from the writings of
Heinz Hartmann,[3] and in recent years from joint work with David
Rapaport,[4] I have tried to expand in line with new observations, first
in a preliminary paper,[5] and now in this book; a clinical monograph
is to follow. Here I will say only that any comparison made between
young man Luther and our patients, is, for their sake as well as his,
not restricted to psychiatric diagnosis and the analysis of pathological dynamics, but is oriented toward those moments when young
patients, like young beings anywhere, prove resourceful and insightful beyond all professional and personal expectation. We will
concentrate on the powers of recovery inherent in the young ego.

I must also acknowledge another kind of professional experience which helped focus my thoughts on a controversial figure in the history of ideas. In 1956, I gave the Yale Centenary address in honor of Sigmund Freud [6] and also spoke on the hundredth anniversary of his birthday at the University of Frankfurt.[7] I spoke of dimensions of lonely discovery, as exemplified in Freud the beginner, the first, and for a decade the only, psychoanalyst. I compared Freud with Darwin, and noted that neither man had come upon his most decisive contribution as part of an intended professional design; both lived through an extended intellectual "moratorium"; and, in both, neurotic suffering accompanied the breakthrough of their creativity. The address on Freud, of course, bridged the clinical study of disturbances in youth which I was observing and treating with the method created by him, and conflicts of early adulthood which men like him fight through to the creativity of their manhood. Moreover, it seemed to me that Luther's specific creativity represented a late medieval precursor of some aspects of Freud's determined struggle with the father complex; even as Luther's emancipation from medieval dogma was one of the indispensable precursors both of modern philosophy and of psychology.

Whatever references are made in this book to analogies in Luther's and Freud's lives are not derived from any impression of a personal likeness between these two men; far from it. But both men illustrate certain regularities in the growth of a certain kind of genius. They had, at any rate, one characteristic in common: a grim willingness to do the dirty work of their respective ages: for each kept human conscience in focus in an era of material and scientific expansion. Luther referred to his early work as *"im Schlamm arbeiten,"* "to work in the mud," and complained that he had worked all alone for ten years; while Freud, also a lone worker for a decade, referred to his work as labor *in der Tiefe,* calling forth the plight of a miner in deep shafts and wishing the soft-hearted *eine gute Auffahrt,* "a good ascent."

I have attempted in this preface to give a brief rationale for writing this book; I doubt, though, that the impetus for writing anything but a textbook can ever be rationalized. My choice of subject forces me to deal with problems of faith and problems of Germany, two enigmas which I could have avoided by writing about some other young great man. But it seems that I did not wish to avoid them.

When speaking about Freud to the students at Frankfurt and at Heidelberg, I remembered an event in my own early years, a memory which had been utterly covered by the rubble of the cities and by the bleached bones of men of my kind in Europe. In my youth, as a wandering artist I stayed one night with a friend in a small village by the Upper Rhine. His father was a Protestant pastor; and in the morning, as the family sat down to breakfast, the old man said the Lord's Prayer in Luther's German. Never having "knowingly" heard it, I had the experience, as seldom before or after, of a wholeness captured in a few simple words, of poetry fusing the esthetic and the moral: those who have once suddenly "heard" the Gettysburg Address will know what I mean.

On occasion we should acknowledge emotional debts other than traumatic ones. Perhaps, then, this study is a tribute to a spring morning in that corner of Europe from which Schweitzer came; and an attempt to grasp something essential in that reformation which stands at the beginning of our era, something which we have neither completely lived down nor successfully outlived. Such is the material of psychoanalysis.

This book was made possible by a grant from the Foundation's Fund for Research in Psychiatry which freed me for a year of all clinical and academic responsibilities.

The manuscript was read and criticized at various stages by David Rapaport, and also by Scott Buchanan, John Headley, Robert P. Knight, Margaret Mead, Gardner and Lois Murphy, Reinhold Niebuhr, and David and Evelyn Riesman. Both for the suggestions which I accepted and for those which I had to overrule, my heartfelt thanks.

Larry Hartmus read some of the medieval Latin with me in Ajijic. Edith Abrahamsen of Copenhagen checked my translation of Kierkegaard's Danish.

Dorothy F. Hoehn ably assembled the pieces in a final typescript.

My wife, Joan Erikson, lived with me through the reading and the writing and sealed the experience by editing the manuscript.

ERIK HOMBURGER ERIKSON

Stockbridge, Massachusetts

Young Man Luther

CHAPTER

I

Case and Event

THE LITERATURE on Luther, and by Luther, is stupendous in volume. Yet it adds up to very few reliable data on his childhood and youth. His role in history, and above all his personality, remain ambiguous on a grandiose scale. Luther has been both vilified and sanctified, and both by sincere and proven scholars, who have spent a good portion, if not all, of their lifetimes reconstructing him from the raw data—only to create, whenever they tried to encompass him with a formula, a superhuman or a suprahuman robot, a man who could never have breathed or moved or least of all spoken as Luther spoke. In writing this book, did I intend to do better?

Soeren Kierkegaard—the one man who could judge Luther with the compassionate objectivity of a kindred *homo religiosus*—once made a remark which sums up the problem which I felt I could approach with the means at my disposal. He wrote in his diary: "Luther. . . . is a patient of exceeding import for Christendom" (*en for Christenheden yderst vigtig Patient*).[1] In quoting this statement out of context, I do not mean to imply that Kierkegaard intended to call Luther a patient in the sense of a clinical "case"; rather, he saw in him a religious attitude (patienthood) exemplified in an archetypal and immensely influential way. In taking this statement as a kind of motto for this book, we do not narrow our perspective to the clinical; we expand our clinical perspective to include a life style of patienthood as a sense of imposed suffering, of an intense need for cure, and (as Kierkegaard adds) a "passion for expressing and describing one's suffering."

Kierkegaard's point was that Luther overdid this subjective, this "patient," side of life, and in his old age failed to reach "a doctor's commanding view" (*Laegen's Overskuelse*). The last question we must leave open for the present.

"A patient" . . . . I expected to have access to this wider meaning of patienthood from my work with gifted but acutely disturbed young people. I did not wish merely to reduce young Luther to his diagnosis (which, within limits, could be done rather convincingly); I wished to delineate in his life (as I had done in the lives of young contemporaries) one of those life crises which make conscious or unconscious, diagnosed or unofficial, patients out of people until they find a cure—and this often means a cause.

I have called the major crisis of adolescence the *identity crisis;* it occurs in that period of the life cycle when each youth must forge for himself some central perspective and direction, some working unity, out of the effective remnants of his childhood and the hopes of his anticipated adulthood; he must detect some meaningful resemblance between what he has come to see in himself and what his sharpened awareness tells him others judge and expect him to be. This sounds dangerously like common sense; like all health, however, it is a matter of course only to those who possess it, and appears as a most complex achievement to those who have tasted its absence. Only in ill health does one realize the intricacy of the body; and only in a crisis, individual or historical, does it become obvious what a sensitive combination of interrelated factors the human personality is—a combination of capacities created in the distant past and of opportunities divined in the present; a combination of totally unconscious preconditions developed in individual growth and of social conditions created and recreated in the precarious interplay of generations. In some young people, in some classes, at some periods in history, this crisis will be minimal; in other people, classes, and periods, the crisis will be clearly marked off as a critical period, a kind of "second birth," apt to be aggravated either by widespread neuroticisms or by pervasive ideological unrest. Some young individuals will succumb to this crisis in all manner of neurotic, psychotic, or delinquent behavior; others will resolve it through participation in ideological movements passionately concerned with religion or politics, nature or art. Still others, although suffering and deviating dangerously through what appears to be a prolonged adolescence, eventually come to contribute an original bit to an emerging style of life: the very danger which they have sensed has forced them to mobilize capacities to see and say, to dream and plan, to design and construct, in new ways.

Luther, so it seems, at one time was a rather endangered young man, beset with a syndrome of conflicts whose outline we have learned to recognize, and whose components to analyse. He found a spiritual solution, not without the well-timed help of a therapeutically clever superior in the Augustinian order. His solution roughly bridged a political and psychological vacuum which history had created in a significant portion of Western Christendom. Such coincidence, if further coinciding with the deployment of highly specific personal gifts, makes for historical "greatness." We will follow Luther through the crisis of his youth, and the unfolding of his gifts, to the first manifestation of his originality as a thinker, namely, to the emergence of a new theology, apparently not immediately perceived as a radical innovation either by him or his listeners, in his first Lectures on the Psalms (1513). What happened to him after he had acquired a historical identity is more than another chapter; for even half of the man is too much for one book. The difference between the young and the old Luther is so marked, and the second, the sturdy orator, so exclusive a Luther-image to most readers, that I will speak of "Martin" when I report on Luther's early years, which according to common usage in the Luther literature include his twenties; and of "Luther" where and when he has become the leader of Lutherans, seduced by history into looking back on his past as upon a mythological autobiography.

Kierkegaard's remark has a second part: ". . . of very great import for Christendom." This calls for an investigation of how the individual "case" became an important, an historic "event," and for formulations concerning the spiritual and political identity crisis of Northern Christendom in Luther's time. True, I could have avoided those methodological uncertainties and impurities which will undoubtedly occur by sticking to my accustomed job of writing a case history, and leaving the historical event to those who, in turn, would consider the case a mere accessory to the event. But we clinicians have learned in recent years that we cannot lift a case history out of history, even as we suspect that historians, when they try to separate the logic of the historic event from that of the life histories which intersect in it, leave a number of vital historical problems unattended. So we may have to risk that bit of impurity which is inherent in the hyphen of the psycho-historical as well as of all other hyphenated approaches. They are the compost heap of today's interdisciplinary efforts, which may help to fertilize new fields, and to produce future flowers of new methodological clarity.

Human nature can best be studied in the state of conflict; and human conflict comes to the detailed attention of interested recorders mainly under special circumstances. One such circumstance is the clinical encounter, in which the suffering, for the sake of securing help, have no other choice than to become case histories; and another special circumstance is history, where extraordinary beings, by their own self-centered maneuvers and through the prodding of the charismatic hunger of mankind, become (auto)biographies. Clinical as well as historical scholars have much to learn by going back and forth between these two kinds of recorded history. Luther, always instructive, forces on the workers in both fields a special awareness. He indulged himself as he grew older in florid self-revelations of a kind which can make a clinical biographer feel that he is dealing with a client. If the clinician should indulge himself in this feeling, however, he will soon find out that the imaginary client has been dealing with him: for Luther is one of those autobiographers with a histrionic flair who can make enthusiastic use even of their neurotic suffering, matching selected memories with the clues given to them by their avid public to create their own official identities.

2

I intend to take my subtitle seriously. This "Study in Psychoanalysis and History" will re-evaluate a segment of history (here the youth of a great reformer) by using psychoanalysis as a historical tool; but it will also, here and there, throw light on psychoanalysis as a tool of history. At this point I must digress for a few pages from the subject of my main title in order to attend to the methodological subtitle.

Psychoanalysis, like all systems, has its own inner history of development. As a method of observation it takes history; as a system of ideas it makes history.

I indicated in the preface that whenever a psychoanalyst shifts the focus of his interest to a new class of patients—be they of the same age, of similar background, or the victims of the same clinical syndrome—he is forced not only to modify his therapeutic technique, but also to explain the theoretical rationale of his modification. Thus, from a gradual refinement of therapeutic technique, the perfection of a theory of the mind is expected to result. This is the historical idea psychoanalysis lives by.

The treatment of young patients who are neither children, adolescents, nor adults is characterized by a specific exaggeration of trends met with in all therapies. Young patients (as well as extraordinary young people) make rather total demands on themselves and on their environment. They insist on daily confirming themselves and on being confirmed either in their meaningful future or in their senseless past; in some absolute virtue or in a radical state of vice; in the growth of their uniqueness or in abysmal self-loss. Young people in severe trouble are not fit for the couch: they want to face you, and they want you to face them, not as a facsimile of a parent, or wearing the mask of a professional helper, but as the kind of over-all individual a young person can live by or will despair of. When suddenly confronted with such a conflicted young person the psychoanalyst may learn for the first time what facing a face, rather than facing a problem, really means—and I daresay, Dr. Staupitz, Martin's spiritual mentor, would know what I have in mind.

In the treatment of young people, furthermore, it is impossible to ignore what they are busy doing or not doing in their work life or in their unofficial avocations. Probably the most neglected problem in psychoanalysis is the problem of work, in theory as well as in practice: as if the dialectic of the history of ideas had ordered a system of psychological thought which would as resolutely ignore the way in which the individual and his group make a living as Marxism ignores introspective psychology and makes a man's economic position the fulcrum of his acts and thoughts. Decades of case histories have omitted the work histories of the patients or have treated their occupation as a seemingly irrelevant area of life in which data could be disguised with the greatest impunity. Yet, therapeutic experiments with the work life of hospitalized young patients indicate that patients in a climate of self-help, of planful work, and of communal association can display an adaptive resourcefulness which seemed absent only because our theories and beliefs decreed that it be absent.

This is part of the wider problem, now being discussed in a large part of the psychiatric and sociological literature, of how much psychiatry has tended to make patienthood a self-defining, self-limiting role prison, within which the development of the patient's stunted capacities is as clearly prevented, by the mere absence of systematic stimulation and opportunity, as if it were professly forbidden.

Such discoveries make it obvious that clinical methods are subject to a refinement of technique and a clarification of theory only to a point; beyond this point they are subject to ideological influences. The emergence in different countries and cities of intensely divergent schools of clinical thought corroborates the idea that an evolving clinical science of the mind is colored and often darkened by ideological trends even as it inadvertently influences the intellectual and literary climate, if and when and where history makes use of it. Maybe, then, a clinical science of the human mind will eventually demand a special historical self-awareness on the part of the clinical worker and scholar. As the historian Collingwood put it: "History is the life of mind itself which is not mind except so far as it both lives in the historical process and knows itself as so living." [2]

Of all the habits of thought which the historically self-conscious psychoanalyst is apt to detect in his work, one is most important for our book. In its determination to be sparing with teleological assumption, psychoanalysis has gone to the opposite extreme and developed a kind of *originology*—a term which I hope is sufficiently awkward to make a point without suggesting itself for general use. I mean by it a habit of thinking which reduces every human situation to an analogy with an earlier one, and most of all to that earliest, simplest, and most infantile precursor which is assumed to be its "origin."

Psychoanalysis has tended to subordinate the later stages of life to those of childhood. It has lifted to the rank of a cosmology the undeniable fact that man's adulthood contains a persistent childishness: that vistas of the future always reflect the mirages of a missed past, that apparent progression can harbor partial regressions, and firm accomplishment, hidden childish fulfillment. In exclusively studying what is repetition and regression and perseveration in human life, we have learned more about the infantile in the adult than was ever before known. We have thus prepared an ethical reorientation in human life which centers on the preservation of those early energies which man, in the very service of his higher values, is apt to suppress, exploit, or waste. In each treatment, and in all our applications, this reorientation governs our conscious intentions. To formulate them on an historically valid scale, however, it is necessary to realize that the psychopathologist, called upon to treat in theory and practice the passions, anxieties, and rages of the race, will always have to make some kind of convincing philosophy out of a state of partial knowledge; while neurotic patients and panicky people in general are so starved for beliefs that they will fanatically spread among the unbelievers what are often as yet quite shaky convictions.

Because we did not include this fact in our awareness, we were shocked at being called pansexualists when our interest (that is, the affects of curiosity and confirmation) was selectively aroused by the minutest references to sexual symbolism. We were distressed when we saw ourselves caricatured in patients who, in social life, spread a compulsive attitude of mutual mental denuding under the guise of being alert to the defensive tricks of the ego. And we were dismayed when we saw our purpose of enlightenment perverted into a widespread fatalism, according to which man is nothing but a multiplication of his parents' faults and an accumulation of his own earlier selves. We must grudgingly admit that even as we were trying to devise, with scientific determinism, a therapy for the few, we were led to promote an ethical disease among the many.

The existence and the multiplicity of defensive regressive mechanisms in adolescence were systematically demonstrated in Anna Freud's *The Ego and the Mechanisms of Defence*.[3] Her book defines inner defense in the widest sense; but it does not foreclose the psychoanalysis of adolescent development. When she states: "The abstract intellectual discussions and speculations in which young people delight are not genuine attempts at solving the tasks set by reality. Their mental activity is rather an indication of a tense alertness for the instinctual processes and the translation into abstract thought of that which they perceive," [4] she presents the defensive half of the story of adolescent rumination, the other half being its adaptive function,[5] and its function in the history of changing ideas. In this book we will add to this formulation the historical concomitance which teaches us how, in the period between puberty and adulthood, the resources of tradition fuse with new inner resources to create something potentially new: a new person; and with this new person a new generation, and with that, a new era. The question of what happens to persons, generations, and eras because guiding ideologies are of postadolescent origin, will be discussed in conclusion, although it transcends the frame of this study, which is dedicated rather to the proposition that what we have learned as pathologists must become part of an ecology of the mind before we can take full responsibility for the ideological implications of our knowledge.

We cannot even begin to encompass the human life cycle without learning to account for the fact that a human being under observation has grown stage by stage into a social world; this world, always for worse *and* for better, has step by step prepared for him an outer reality made up of human traditions and institutions which utilize and thus nourish his developing capacities, attract and modulate his drives, respond to and delimit his fears and phantasies, and assign to him a position in life appropriate to his psychosocial powers. We cannot even begin to encompass a human being without indicating for each of the stages of his life cycle the framework of social influences and of traditional institutions which determine his perspectives on his more infantile past and on his more adult future. In this sense, we can learn from patients only to the extent that we realize (and the patient realizes) that what is said and done in treatment is based on a formal contract between healer and patient and must be carefully transposed before being applied to the general human condition. This is the reason why the fragments of case histories or psychoanalytic interpretations which flutter around in increasing numbers in our newspapers and magazines seem lost like bats in the daytime.[6]

On the other hand, we cannot leave history entirely to nonclinical observers and to professional historians who often all too nobly immerse themselves into the very disguises, rationalizations, and idealizations of the historical process from which it should be their business to separate themselves. Only when the relation of historical forces to the basic functions and stages of the mind has been jointly charted and understood can we begin a psychoanalytic critique of society as such without falling back into mystical or moralistic philosophizing.

Freud warned against the possible misuse of his work as an ideology, a *"Weltanschauung;"* [7] but as we shall see in Luther's life and work, a man who inspires new ideas has little power to restrict them to the area of his original intentions. And Freud himself did not refrain from interpreting other total approaches to man's condition, such as religion, as consequences of man's inability to shake off the bonds of his prolonged childhood, and thus comparable to collective neuroses.[8] The psychological and historical study of the religious crisis of a young great man renews the opportunity to review this assertion in the light of ego-psychology and of theories of psychosocial development.

3

As to the dichotomy of psychoanalysis and religion, I will not approach it like a man with a chip on each shoulder. Psychology endeavors to establish what is demonstrably true in human behavior, including such behavior as expresses what to human beings seems true and feels true. I will interpret in psychological terms whatever phenomena clinical experience and psychoanalytic thought have made me recognize are dependent on man's demonstrable psychic structure. This is my job, as a clinician and as a teacher—a job which (as I have pointed out) includes the awareness that psychoanalysis for historical reasons often occupies a position on the borderline of what is demonstrably true and of what demonstrably *feels* true. The fact that each new vital focus of psychoanalytic research inadvertently leads to a new implied value system obliges us to ask ourselves whether or not we mean what we seem to be saying. It obligates us, as well as our critics, to differentiate psychoanalysism from psychoanalysis, and to realize that ours is not only a profession recognized among professions, but also a system of thought subject to fashionable manipulation by molders of public opinion. Our very success suggests that our partisanship be judicial.

Religion, on the other hand, elaborates on what feels profoundly true even though it is not demonstrable: it translates into significant words, images, and codes the exceeding darkness which surrounds man's existence, and the light which pervades it beyond all desert or comprehension. This being a historical book, however, religion will occupy our attention primarily as a source of ideologies for those who seek identities. In depicting the identity struggle of a *young* great man I am not as concerned with the validity of the dogmas which laid claim to him, or of the philosophies which influenced his systematic thought, as I am with the spiritual and intellectual milieu which the isms of his time—and these isms *had* to be religious—offered to his passionate search.

My focus, then, is on the "ideological." In modern history, this word has assumed a specifically political connotation, referring to totalitarian systems of thought which distort historical truth by methods ranging from fanatic self-deception to shrewd falsification and cold propaganda. Karl Mannheim has analyzed this word and the processes for which it stands from the sociological point of view.[9] In this book, *ideology* will mean an unconscious tendency underlying religious and scientific as well as political thought: the tendency at a given time to make facts amenable to ideas, and ideas to facts, in order to create a world image convincing enough to support the collective and the individual sense of identity. Far from being arbitrary or consciously manageable (although it is as exploitable as all of man's unconscious strivings), the total perspective created by ideological simplification reveals its strength by the dominance it exerts on the seeming logic of historical events, and by its influence on the identity formation of individuals (and thus on their "ego-strength"). In this sense, this is a book on identity and ideology.

In some periods of his history, and in some phases of his life cycle, man needs (until we invent something better) a new ideological orientation as surely and as sorely as he must have air and food. I will not be ashamed then, even as I analyze what is analyzable, to display sympathy and empathy with a young man who (by no means lovable all of the time) faced the problems of human *existence* in the most forward terms of his era. I will use the word *existential* in this simplest connotation, mindful that no school of thought has any monopoly on it.

The Fit in the Choir

THREE OF young Luther's contemporaries (none of them a later follower of his) report that sometime during his early or middle twenties, he suddenly fell to the ground in the choir of the monastery at Erfurt, "raved" like one possessed, and roared with the voice of a bull: "*Ich bin's nit! Ich bin's nit!*"[1] or "*Non sum! Non sum!*"[2] The German version is best translated with "It isn't me!" the Latin one with "I am *not!*"

It would be interesting to know whether at this moment Martin roared in Latin or in German; but the reporters agree only on the occasion which upset him so deeply: the reading of Christ's *ejecto a surdo et muto daemonio*—Christ's cure of a man possessed by a *dumb spirit*.[3] This can only refer to Mark 9:17: "And one of the multitude answered and said, Master, I have brought unto thee my son, which hath a dumb spirit." The chroniclers considered that young Luther was possessed by demons—the religious and psychiatric borderline case of the middle ages—and that he showed himself possessed even as he tried most loudly to deny it. "I am *not*," would then be the childlike protestation of somebody who has been called a name or has been characterized with loathsome adjectives: here, dumb, mute, possessed.

We will discuss this alleged event first as to its place in Luther's life history, and then, as to its status in Luther's biography.

The monk Martinus entered the Black Monastery of the Augustinians in Erfurt when he was twenty-one years old. Following a vow made in an attack of acute panic during a severe thunderstorm, he had abruptly and without his father's permission left the University of Erfurt, where had had just received with high honors the degree of a master of arts. Behind the monk lay years of strict schooling supported only with great sacrifice by his ambitious father, who wanted him to study the law, a profession which at that time was becoming the springboard into administration and politics. Before him lay long years of the most intense inner conflicts and frequently morbid religious scruples; these eventually led to his abandonment of monasticism and to his assumption of spiritual leadership in a widespread revolt against the medieval papacy. The fit in the choir, then, belongs to a period when his career, as planned by his father, was dead; when his monastic condition, after a "godly" beginning, had become problematic to him; and when his future was as yet in an embryonic darkness. This future could have been divined by him only in the strictest (and vaguest) term of the word, namely, as a sense of a spiritual mission of some kind.

It is difficult to visualize this young man, later to become so great and triumphant, in the years when he took that chance on perdition which was the very test and condition of his later greatness. Therefore, I shall list a few dates, which may be of help to the reader.

EVENTS OF MARTIN'S YOUTH

Born in 1483, Martin Luther	1483
entered the University of Erfurt at seventeen;	1501
received his master's degree at twenty-one, and entered the monastery, having vowed to do so during a thunderstorm.	1505
Became a priest and celebrated his first Mass at the age of twenty-three; then fell into severe doubts and scruples which may have caused the "fit in the choir."	1507 +
Became a doctor of theology at the age of twenty-eight; gave his first lectures on the Psalms at the University of Wittenberg, where he experienced the "revelation in the tower."	1512 +
At thirty-two, almost a decade after the episode in the choir, he nailed his ninety-five theses on the church door in Wittenberg.	1517

The story of the fit in the choir has been denied as often as it has been repeated; but its fascination even for those who would do away with it seems to be great. A German professor of theology, Otto Scheel, one of the most thorough editors of the early sources on Luther's life, flatly disavows the story, tracing it to that early hateful biography of Luther written by Johannes Cochläus in 1549.[4] And yet, Scheel does not seem to be able to let go of the story. Even to him there is enough to it so that in the very act of belittling it he grants it a measure of religious grandeur: "Nicolaus Tolentinus, too," he writes "when he knelt at the altar and prayed, was set upon by the Prince of Darkness. But precisely in this visibly meaningful (*sinnfaellig*) struggle with the devil did Nicolaus prove himself as the chosen armour of the Lord. . . . Are we to count it to Luther's damnation if he, too, had to battle with the devil in a similarly meaningful way?"[5] He appeals to Catholic detractors: "Why not measure with the same yardstick?" And in a footnote he asks the age-old question: "Or was Paul's miraculous conversion also pathological?" Scheel, incidentally, in his famous collection of documents on Luther's development, where he dutifully reprints Cochläus' version, makes one of his very rare mistakes by suggesting that the biblical story in question is Mark 1:23, where a "man with an unclean spirit . . . *cried out*" and was *silenced* by Christ.[6] However, the *surdus* and *mutus daemonius* can hardly refer to this earlier passage in Mark.

Scheel is a Protestant professor of theology. For him the principal task is explaining as genuinely inspired by a divine agency those attacks of unconsciousness and fits of overwhelming anxiety, those delusional moments, and those states of brooding despair which occasionally beset young Luther and increasingly beset the aging man. To Scheel they are all *geistlich*, not *geistig*—spiritual, not mental. It is often troublesome to try to find one's way through the German literature on Luther, which refers to various mental states as "*Seelenleiden*" (suffering of the soul) and "*Geisteskrankheit*," (sickness of the spirit)—terms which always leave it open whether soul or psyche, spirit or mind, is afflicted. It is especially troublesome when medical men claim that the reformer's "suffering of the soul" was mainly *biologically* determined. But the *professor*—as we will call Scheel when we mean to quote him as the representative of a particular academic-theological school of Luther biography—the professor insists, and in a most soberly circumstantial biography, that all of Luther's strange upsets came to him straight down from heaven: *Katastrophen von Gottes Gnaden.*

The most famous, and in many ways rightly infamous, detractor of Luther's character, the Dominican Heinrich Denifle, Sub-Archivar of the Holy See, saw it differently. For him such events as the fit in the choir have only an inner cause, which in no way means a decent conflict or even an honest affliction, but solely an abysmal depravity of character. To him, Luther is too much of a psychopath to be credited with honest mental or spiritual suffering. It is only the Bad One who speaks through Luther. It is, it must be, Denifle's primary ideological premise, that nothing, neither mere pathological fits, nor the later revelations which set Luther on the path to reformation, had anything whatsoever to do with divine interference. "Who," Denifle asks, in referring to the thunderstorm, "can prove, for himself, not to speak of others, that the alleged inspiration through the Holy Ghost really came from above . . . and that it was not the play of conscious or unconscious self-delusion?"[7] Lutheranism, he fears (and hopes to demonstrate) has tried to lift to the height of dogma the phantasies of a most fallible mind.

With his suspicion that Luther's whole career may have been inspired by the devil, Denifle puts his finger on the sorest spot in Luther's whole spiritual and psychological make-up. His days in the monastery were darkened by a suspicion, which Martin's father expressed loudly on the occasion of the young priest's first Mass, that the thunderstorm had really been the voice of a *Gespenst,* a ghost; thus Luther's vow was on the borderline of both pathology and demonology. Luther remained sensitive to this paternal suspicion, and continued to argue with himself and with his father long after his father had no other choice than to acknowledge his son as a spiritual leader and Europe's religious strong man. But in his twenties Martin was still a sorely troubled young man, not at all able to express either what inspired or what bothered him; his greatest worldly burden was certainly the fact that his father had only most reluctantly, and after much cursing, given his consent (which was legally dispensable, anyway) to the son's religious career.

With this in mind, let us return to Mark 9:17-24. It was a father who addressed Christ: "Master I have brought unto Thee my son, which hath a dumb spirit. . . . and he asked his father, how long

is it ago since this came unto him? And he said, Of a child.
. . . Jesus said unto him, If thou canst believe, all things are possible
to him that believeth. . . . And straightway the father of the child
cried out, and said with tears, Lord, I believe; help thou mine un-
belief." Two cures, then, are suggested in the Bible passage: the
cure of a son with a dumb spirit, after a father has been cured of a
weak faith. The possibility of an "inner-psychological" kernel in
Martin's reaction to this passage will thus deserve to be weighed
carefully, although with scales other than those used by Father
Denifle—to whom we will refer as the *priest*, whenever we quote
him as a representative of a clerical-scholastic school in Luther
biography.

But now to another school of experts. An extremely diligent
student of Luther, the Danish psychiatrist, Dr. Paul J. Reiter,
decides unequivocally that the fit in the choir is a matter of severest
psychopathology. At most, he is willing to consider the event as a
relatively benign hysterical episode; even so, he evaluates it as a
symptom of a steady, pitiless, "endogenous" process which, in
Luther's middle forties, was climaxed by a frank psychosis. *Endogenous* really means biological; Reiter feels that Luther's attacks
cannot "with the best of will" be conceived of as links "in the chain
of meaningful psychological development." [8] It would be futile,
then, to try to find any "message," either from a divine or an inner
source, in Luther's abnormalities other than indications of erratic
upsets in his nervous system. Reiter considers the years in which we
are most interested—when Luther was twenty-two to thirty—as
part of one long *Krankheitsphase*, one drawn-out state of nervous
disease, which extended to the thirty-sixth year; these years were
followed by a period of "manic" productivity, and then by a severe
breakdown in the forties. In fact, he feels that only a pitifully small
number of Luther's years were really characterized by the reformer's famous "robust habitual state"—which means that Luther
was like himself only very rarely, and most briefly. Reiter considers
at least Luther's twenties as a period of neurotic, rather than of
psychotic, tension, and he acknowledges the crisis of this one period
as the only time in Luther's life when his ideological search remained meaningfully related to his psychological conflicts; when
his creativity kept pace with his inner destructive processes; and
when a certain "limited intellectual balance" was reached.

We will make the most of the license thus affirmed by the *psychiatrist,* as we shall call Reiter when we quote him as the representative of a medical-biological school in Luther-biography. This class of biographers ascribes Luther's personal and theological excesses to a sickness which, whether "seated" in brain, nervous system, or kidneys, marks Luther as a biologically inferior or diseased man. As to the event in the choir, Reiter makes a strange mistake. Luther, he says, could not have been conscious, for he called out with "utmost intentionality . . . 'That's me!' " (*Ich bin's*)[9]—meaning, the possessed one of the evangelium. Such a positive exclamation would do away with a good part of the meaning which we will ascribe to the event in the choir; however, three hundred pages earlier in the same book, Reiter, too, tells the story in the traditional way, making Martin call out: "That's *not* me."[10]

And how about a psychoanalyst? The professor and the psychiatrist frequently and most haughtily refer to a representative of the "modern Freudian school"—Professor Preserved Smith, then of Amherst College, who, beside writing a biography of Luther,[11] and editing his letters,[12] wrote, in 1915, a remarkable paper: "Luther's Early Development in The Light of Psychoanalysis."[13] I use the word "beside" deliberately, for this paper impresses one as being a foreign body in Smith's work on Luther; it is done, so to speak, with the left hand, while the right and official hand is unaware. "Luther," Smith claims, "is a thoroughly typical example of the neurotic quasi-hysterical sequence of an infantile sex-complex; so much so, indeed, that Sigismund [sic] Freud and his school could hardly have found a better example to illustrate the sounder part of their theory than him."[14] Smith musters the appropriate data to show (what I, too, will demonstrate in detail) that Luther's childhood was unhappy because of his father's excessive harshness, and that he was obsessively preoccupied with God as an avenger, with the Devil as a visible demon, and with obscene images and sayings. Smith unhesitatingly characterizes "the foundation-stones of early Protestantism . . . as an interpretation of Luther's own subjective life." Outstanding in Luther's morbid subjectivity is his preoccupation with "concupiscence" which Smith, contrary to all evidence, treats as if to Luther it had been a mere matter of sexual "lust." Smith in fact (while conceding that "it is to his great credit that there is good reason to believe he never sinned with women") attributes Luther's great preoccupation with concupiscence to his losing battle with masturbation.

It is instructive to see what an initial fascination and temporary indoctrination with "Freudian" notions can do to a scholar, in particular perhaps to one with a Puritan background: the notions remain in his thinking like a foreign body. In order to make the masturbation hypothesis plausible, Smith, obviously a thorough student of the German sources, flagrantly misinterprets a famous statement of Luther's. Luther reported repeatedly that at the height of his monastic scruples he had confessed to a trusted superior, "not about women, but about *die rechten Knotten*." [15] This phrase means "the real knots"; in the language of the peasant, it means the knotty part of the tree, the hardest to cut. This reference to real hindrances Smith suspects is a hint at masturbation, although the sound of the words does not suggest anything of the kind, and although at least on one occasion Luther specifies the knots as transgressions against *die erste Taffel* [16] that is, the first commandment concerning the love of God the Father. This would point to Luther's increasing and obsessive-blasphemous ambivalence toward God, partially a consequence (and here Smith is, of course, correct and is seconded by the psychiatrist) of a most pathological relationship to his father; which, in turn provides the proper context for Luther's sexual scruples. Professor Smith, incidentally, translates the reported outcry in the choir as "It is not I!"—words which I doubt even a New Englander would utter in a convulsive attack.

Although the professor, the priest, and the psychiatrist refer to Smith as "the psychoanalyst," I myself cannot characterize him in this way, since his brilliant but dated contribution appears to be an isolated exercise of a man who, to my knowledge, never systematically pursued psychoanalysis either in practice or in theory.

2

Why did I introduce my discussion of Luther with this particular event in the choir, whose interpretation is subject to so many large and small discrepancies?

As I tried to orient myself in regard to Luther's identity crisis by studying those works which promised to render the greatest number of facts and references for independent study, I heard him, ever again, roar in rage, and yet also in laughter: *Ich bin's nit!* For with the same facts (here and there altered, as I have indicated, in details precisely relevant to psychological interpretation), the professor, the priest, the psychiatrist, and others as yet to be quoted each concocts his own Luther; this may well be the reason why they all agree on one point, namely, that dynamic psychology must be kept away from the data of Luther's life. Is it possible that they all agree so that each may take total and unashamed possession of him, of the great man's charisma?

Take the professor. As he sifts the sources minutely and masterfully establishes his own versions, a strange belligerence (to judge from Freud's experience not atypical of the German scientific scene of the early part of this century) leads him to challenge other experts as if to a duel. He constantly imputes to them not only the ignorance of high school boys, but also the motives of juveniles. This need not bother us; such duels spill only ink and swell only footnotes. But the emerging image of Luther, erected and defended in this manner, assumes, at decisive moments, some of the military qualities of the method; while otherwise it remains completely devoid of any psychological consistency. At the conclusion of the professor's first volume, only a soldierly image suffices to express his hopes for sad young Martin behind whom the gates of the monastery have just closed: "Out of the novice Luther," he writes, "the warrior shall be created, whom the enemy can touch neither with force nor with cunning, and whose soul, after completion of its war service, will be led to the throne of the judge by archangel Michael." [17] *Kriegsdienst* is the metallic German word for war service, and the professor makes the most of the biblical reference to God as El Zebaoth, the master of the armies of angels; he even makes God share the Kaiser's title *Kriegsherr*. Everything extraordinary, then, that happens to Luther is *befohlen*, ordered from above, without advance notice or explanation and completely without intention or motivation on Luther's part; consequently, all psychological speculation regarding motivation is strictly *verboten*. No wonder that Luther's "personality" seems to be put together from scraps of conventional images which do not add up to a workable human being. Luther's parents and Luther himself are pasted together; their ingredients are the characteristics of the ordinary small-town German: simple, hardworking, earnest, straightforward, dutiful folk (*bieder, tuechtig, gehorsam,* and *wacker*). The myth to be created, of course, is that God selects just such folk to descend on in a sudden "catastrophic" decision.

Boehmer,[18] whom I would place in the same school, although equally well-informed, is milder and more insightful. Yet for him, too, Luther's father is a harsh, but entirely well-meaning, sturdy, and healthy type, until suddenly, without any warning whatsoever, he behaves "like a madman" when his son enters the monastery. Boehmer acts as if such a childish explosion were a German father's prerogative and above any psychologizing.

Scheel's book is a post-World War I heir of two trends in the Lutheran writing of history, initiated by two men and never surpassed by others: the universalistic-historical trend of the great von Ranke,[19] the "priestly historian," whose job it was to find in the conflicting forces of history "the holy hieroglyph of God"; the other, a theological-philosophical trend (sometimes fusing, sometimes sharply separating philosophy and religion) begun by the elder Harnack.[20] We will return to this last point of view when we come to the emergence of Luther's theology.

Denifle the Dominican priest, also an acknowledged scholar and authority on late medieval institutions of learning (he died a few days before he was to receive an honorary degree from the University of Cambridge), as well as a most powerful detective of Luther's often rather free quotations from and reinterpretations of theological doctrine, feels obliged to create a different image of Luther. To him he is an *Umsturzmensch*, the kind of man who wants to turn the world upside down without a plan of his own. To Denifle, Luther's protestant attitude introduced into history a dangerous kind of revolutionary spirit. Luther's special gifts, which the priest does not deny, are those of the demagogue and the false prophet—falseness not only as a matter of bad theology, but as a conscious falsification from base motives. All of this follows from the priest's quite natural thesis that war orders from above, such as the professor assumes to have been issued to Luther, could only be genuine if they showed the seal and the signature of divinity, namely, signs and miracles. When Luther prayed to God not to send his miracles, so that he would not become proud and be deflected from the Word by Satan's delusions, he only discarded grapes which were hanging as high as heaven itself: for the faintest possibility of any man outside the Church receiving such signs had been excluded for all eternity by the verification of Jesus as God's sole messenger on earth.

Denifle is only the most extreme representative of a Catholic school of Luther biography, whose representatives try hard to divorce themselves from his method while sharing his basic assumption of a gigantic moral flaw in Luther's personality. The Jesuit Grisar [21] is cooler and more dissecting in his approach. Yet he too ascribes to Luther a tendency for "egomanic self-delusion," and suggests a connection between his self-centeredness and his medical history; thus Grisar puts himself midway between the approaches of the priest and of the psychiatrist.

Among all of Luther's biographers, inimical or friendly, Denifle seems to me to resemble Luther most, at least in his salt-and-pepper honesty, and his one-sided anger. "Tyrolean candor," a French biographer ascribes to him.[22] The Jesuit is most admirable in his scholarly criticism of Luther's theology; most lovable in his outraged response to Luther's vulgarity. Denifle does not think that a true man of God would ever say "I gorge myself (*fresse*) like a Bohemian and I get drunk (*sauff*) like a German. God be praised. Amen," [23] although he neglects the fact that Luther wrote this in one of his humorous letters to his wife at a time when she was worried about his lack of appetite. And he seriously suggests that the sow was Luther's model of salvation. I cannot refrain from translating here the quotation on which Denifle bases this opinion, which offers a contrast to Scheel's martial image and as such, is an example of a radically different and yet equally scholarly suggestion for the real core of Luther's personality.

In an otherwise hateful pamphlet written in his middle forties, Luther relaxes into that folksy manner which he occasionally also used in his sermons. What he wants to make clear is that there is a prereligious state of mind. "For a sow," he writes, "lies in the gutter or on the manure as if on the finest feather bed. She rests safely, snores tenderly, and sleeps sweetly, does not fear king nor master, death nor hell, devil or God's wrath, lives without worry, and does not even think where the clover (*Kleien*) may be. And if the Turkish Caesar arrived in all his might and anger, the sow would be much too proud to move a single whisker in his honor. . . . And if at last the butcher comes upon her, she thinks maybe a piece of wood is pinching her, or a stone. . . . The sow has not eaten from the apple, which in paradise has taught us wretched humans the difference between good and bad." [24] No translation can do justice to the gentle persuasiveness of these lines. The priest, however, omits the argument in which they appear: Luther is trying to persuade his readers that the as yet expected Messiah of the Jews could not make a man's life a tenth as good as that of a sow, while the coming of Christ has done more, has put the whole matter of living on a higher plane. And yet one cannot escape the fact that in Luther's rich personality there was a soft spot for the sow so large that Denifle correctly considers it what I will call one of Luther's identity elements. Oftentimes when this element became dominant, Luther could be so vulgar that he became easy game for the priest and the psychiatrist, both of whom quote with relish: "Thou shalt not write a book unless you have listened to the fart of an old sow, to which you should open your mouth wide and say 'Thanks to you, pretty nightingale; do I hear a text which is for me?' " [25] But what writer, disgusted with himself, has not shared these sentiments —without finding the right wrong words?

The Danish psychiatrist, in turn, offers in his two impressive volumes as complete an account of Luther's "environment, character, and psychosis" as I have come across. His study ranges from the macrocosm of Luther's times to the microcosm of his home and home town, and includes a thorough discussion of his biological make-up and of his lifelong physical and emotional symptoms. But the psychiatrist lacks a theory comprehensive enough for his chosen range. Psychoanalysis he rejects as too dogmatic, borrowing from Preserved Smith what fragments he can use without committing himself to the theory implied. He states his approach candidly: it is that of a psychiatrist who has been consulted on a severe case of manifest psychosis (diagnosis: manic-depressive, à la Kraepelin) and who proceeds to record the presenting condition (Luther's acute psychosis in his forties) and to reconstruct the past history, including the twenties. He shows much insight in his asides; but in his role of bedside psychiatrist, he grimly sticks to his central view by asserting that a certain trait or act of Luther's is "absolutely typical for a state of severe melancholia" and "is to be found in every psychiatric textbook." The older Luther undoubtedly approached textbook states, although I doubt very much that his personal meetings with the devil were ever true hallucinations, or that his dramatic revelations concerning his mental suffering can be treated on the same level as communications from a patient.

Furthermore, when it comes to the younger Luther and the psychiatrist's assertion that his *tentationes tristitiae*—that sadness which is a traditional temptation of the *homo religiosus*—is among the "classical traits in the picture of most states of depression, especially the endogenous ones," [26] we must be decidedly more doubtful. For throughout, this psychiatric textbook version of Luther does not compare him with other examples of sincere religious preoccupation and corresponding genuine giftedness, but with some norm of *Ausgeglichenheit*—an inner balance, a simple enjoyment of life, and an ordinary decency and decided direction of effort such as normal people are said to display. Though the psychiatrist makes repeated allowances for Luther's genius, he nevertheless demands of him a state of inner repose which, as far as I know, men of creative intensity and of an increasing historical commitment cannot be expected to be able to maintain. At any rate, he points out that even in his last years Luther's "psychic balance was not complete," his inner state only "relatively harmonious." Using this yardstick of normality, the psychiatrist considers it strange that Luther could not accept his father's reasonable plans and go ahead and enjoy the study of law; that he could not be relaxed during his ordination as other young priests are; that he could not feel at home in as sensible and dignified a regime as that of an Augustinian monastery; and that he was not able, much later, to sit back and savor with equanimity the fruits of his rebellion. The professor, too, finds most of this surprising; but he assumes that God, for some divine reason, needled Luther out of such natural and sensible attitudes; the psychiatrist is sure that the needling was done from within, by endogenous mental disease.

I do not know about the kind of balance of mind, body, and soul that these men assume is normal; but if it does exist, I would expect it least of all in such a sensitive, passionate, and ambitious individual as young Luther. He, as many lesser ones like him, may have had good inner reasons to escape premature commitments. Some young people suffer under successes which, to them, are subjectively false, and they may even shy away as long as they possibly can from what later turns out to be their true role. The professor's and the psychiatrist's image of normality seems an utterly incongruous measure to use on a future professional reformer. But then the psychiatrist (with the priest) not only disavows God's hand in the matter, he also disregards, in his long list of character types and somatotypes, the existence of a *homo religiosus* circumscribed and proved not necessarily by signs and miracles, but by the inner logic of his way of life, by the logic of his working gifts, and by the logic of his effect on society. To study and formulate this logic seems to me to constitute the task at hand, if one wishes to consider the total existence of a man like Luther.

I will conclude this review of a few of the most striking and best-informed attempts at presenting prejudiced versions of Luther's case with one more quotation and one more suggested Luther image. This image comes from sociology, a field certainly essential to any assessment of the kind to which our authors aspire. I could not, and would not, do without *The Social Basis of the German Reformation* although its author, R. Pascal, a social scientist and historical materialist, announces with the same flatness which we have encountered in the other biographers how well he could manage without me and my field. "The principle underlying [Luther's contradictions]," he states, "is not logical, it is not psychological. The consistency amid all these contradictions is the consistency of class-interest." [27]

This statement is, perhaps, the most Marxist formulation in the economic-political literature of Luther's personality and his influence on the subsequent codevelopment of protestantism and capitalism. (The most encompassing book with this economic-political point of view is by Ernst Troeltsch [28]; the most famous, at least in this country, those of Weber [29] and of Tawney.[30]) I am not smiling at it in superiority, any more than I am smiling at the statements of the dogmatic professor of theology, the Dominican scholar, or the "constitutional" psychiatrist. For each cites valid data, all of which, as we shall see, complement each other. It is necessary, however, to contemplate (if only as a warning to ourselves) the degree to which in the biography of a great man "objective study" and "historical accuracy" can be used to support almost any total image necessitated by the biographer's personality and professed calling; and to point out that biographers categorically opposed to systematic psychological interpretation permit themselves the most extensive psychologizing—which they can afford to believe is common sense only because they disclaim a defined psychological viewpoint. Yet there is always an implicit psychology behind the explicit antipsychology.

One of the great detractors of Luther, Jacob Burckhardt, who taught Nietzsche to see in Luther a noisy German peasant who at the end waylaid the march of Renaissance man, noted: "Who are we, anyway, that we can ask of Luther . . . that [he] should have fulfilled *our* programs? . . . This concrete Luther, and no other, existed; he should be taken for what he was" (*Man nehme ihn wie er gewesen ist*).[31]

But how does one take a *great* man "for what he was"? The very adjective seems to imply that something about him is too big, too awe-ful, too shiny, to be encompassed. Those who nonetheless set out to describe the whole man seem to have only three choices. They can step so far back that the great man's contours appear complete, but hazy; or they can step closer and closer, gradually concentrating on a few aspects of the great man's life, seeing one part of it as big as the whole, or the whole as small as one part. If neither of these works, there is always polemics; one takes the great man in the sense of appropriating him and of excluding others who might dare to do the same. Thus a man's historical image often depends on which legend temporarily overcomes all others; however, all these ways of viewing a great man's life may be needed to capture the mood of the historical event.

3

The limitations of my knowledge and of the space at my disposal for this inquiry preclude any attempt to present a new Luther or to remodel an old one. I can only bring some newer psychological considerations to bear on the existing material pertaining to one period of Luther's life. As I indicated in Chapter I, the young monk interests me particularly as a young man in the process of becoming a great one.

It must have occurred to the reader that the story of the fit in the choir attracted me originally because I suspected that the words "I am *not!*" revealed the fit to be part of a most severe identity crisis— a crisis in which the young monk felt obliged to protest what he was *not* (possessed, sick, sinful) perhaps in order to break through to what he was or was to be. I will now state what remains of my suspicion, and what I intend to make of it.

Judging from an undisputed series of extreme mental states which attacked Luther throughout his life, leading to weeping, sweating, and fainting, the fit in the choir could well have happened; and it could have happened in the specific form reported, under the specific conditions of Martin's monastery years. If some of it is legend, so be it; the making of legend is as much part of the scholarly rewriting of history as it is part of the original facts used in the work of scholars. We are thus obliged to accept half-legend as half-history, provided only that a reported episode does not contradict other well-established facts; persists in having a ring of truth; and yields a meaning consistent with psychological theory.

Luther himself never mentioned this episode, although in his voluble later years he was extraordinarily free with references to physical and mental suffering. It seems that he always remembered most vividly those states in which he struggled through to an insight, but not those in which he was knocked out. Thus, in his old age, he remembers well having been seized at the age of thirty-five by terror, sweat, and the fear of fainting when he marched in the Corpus Christi procession behind his superior, Dr. Staupitz, who carried the holy of holies. (This Dr. Staupitz, as we will see, was the best father figure Luther ever encountered and acknowledged; he was a man who recognized a true *homo religiosus* in his subaltern and treated him with therapeutic wisdom.) But Staupitz did not let Luther get away with his assertion that it was Christ who had frightened him. He said, "*Non est Christus, quia Christus non terret, sed consolatur.*" (It couldn't have been Christ who terrified you, for Christ consoles.) [32] This was a therapeutic as well as a theological revelation to Luther, and he remembered it. However, for the fit in the choir, he may well have had an amnesia.

Assuming then that something like this episode happened, it could be considered as one of a series of seemingly senseless pathological explosions; as a meaningful symptom in a psychiatric case-history; or as one of a series of religiously relevant experiences. It certainly has, as even Scheel suggests, *some* marks of a "religious attack," such as St. Paul, St. Augustine, and many lesser aspirants to saintliness have had. However, the inventory of a total revelation always includes an overwhelming illumination and a sudden insight. The fit in the choir presents only the symptomatic, the more pathological and defensive, aspects of a total revelation: partial loss of consciousness, loss of motor coordination, and automatic exclamations which the afflicted does not know he utters.

In a truly religious experience such automatic exclamations would sound as if they were dictated by divine inspiration; they would be positively illuminating and luminous, and be intensely remembered. In Luther's fit, his words obviously expressed an overwhelming inner need to deny an accusation. In a full religious attack the positive conscience of faith would reign and determine the words uttered; here negation and rebellion reign: "I am *not* what my father said I was and what my conscience, in bad moments, tends to confirm I am." The raving and roaring suggest a strong element of otherwise suppressed rage. And, indeed, this young man, who later became a voice heard around the world, lived under monastic conditions of silence and meditation; at this time he was submissively subdued, painfully sad, and compulsively self-inspective—too much so even for his stern superiors' religious taste. All in all, however, the paroxysm occurred in a holy spot and was suggested by a biblical story, which places the whole matter at least on the borderline between psychiatry and religion.

If we approach the episode from the psychiatric viewpoint, we can recognize in the described attack (and also in a variety of symptomatic scruples and anxieties to which Martin was subject at the time) an intrinsic ambivalence, an inner two-facedness, such as we find in all neurotic symptoms. The attack could be said to deny in its verbal part ("I am not") what Martin's father had said, namely, that his son was perhaps possessed rather than holy; but it also proves the father's point by its very occurrence in front of the same congregation who had previously heard the father express his anger and apprehension. The fit, then, is both unconscious obedience to the father and implied rebellion against the monastery; the words uttered both deny the father's assertion, and confirm the vow which Martin had made in that first known anxiety attack during a thunderstorm at the age of twenty-one, when he had exclaimed, "I want to be a monk." [33] We find the young monk, then, at the crossroads of obedience to his father—an obedience of extraordinary tenacity and deviousness—and to the monastic vows which at the time he was straining to obey almost to the point of absurdity.

We may also view his position as being at the crossroads of mental disease and religious creativity and we could speculate that perhaps

Luther received in three (or more) distinct and fragmentary experiences those elements of a total revelation which other men are said to have acquired in one explosive event. Let me list the elements again: physical paroxysm; a degree of unconsciousness; an automatic verbal utterance; a command to change the over-all direction of effort and aspiration; and a spiritual revelation, a flash of enlightenment, decisive and pervasive as a rebirth. The thunderstorm had provided him with a change in the over-all direction of his life, a change toward the anonymous, the silent, and the obedient. In fits such as the one in the choir, he experienced the epileptoid paroxysm of ego-loss, the rage of denial of the identity which was to be discarded. And later in the experience in the tower, which we will discuss in Chapter V, he perceived the light of a new spiritual formula.

The fact that Luther experienced these clearly separate stages of religious revelation might make it possible to establish a psychological rationale for the conversion of other outstanding religionists, where tradition has come to insist on the transmission of a total event appealing to popular faith. Nothing, to my mind, makes Luther more a man of the future—the future which is our psychological present—than his utter integrity in reporting the steps which marked the emergence of his identity as a genuine *homo religiosus*. I emphasize this by no means only because it makes him a better case (although I admit it helps), but because it makes his total experience a historical event far beyond its immediate sectarian significance, namely, a decisive step in human awareness and responsibility. To indicate this step in its psychological coordinates is the burden of this book.

Martin's general mood just before he became a monk, a mood into which he was again sliding at the time of the fit in the choir, has been characterized by him and others as a state of *tristitia*, of excessive sadness. Before the thunderstorm, he had rapidly been freezing into a melancholy paralysis which made it impossible for him to continue his studies and to contemplate marriage as his father urged him to do. In the thunderstorm, he had felt immense anxiety. Anxiety comes from *angustus*, meaning to feel hemmed in and choked up; Martin's use of *circumvallatus*—all walled in—to describe his experience in the thunderstorm indicates he felt a sudden constriction of his whole life space, and could see only one way out: the abandonment of all of his previous life and the earthly future it implied for the sake of total dedication to a new life. This new life, however, was one which made an institution out of the very configuration of being walled in. Architecturally, ceremonially, and in its total world-mood, it symbolized life on this earth as a self-imposed and self-conscious prison with only one exit, and that one, to eternity. The acceptance of this new frame of life had made him, for a while, peaceful and "godly"; at the time of his fit, however, his sadness was deepening again.

As to this general veil of sadness which covered the conflicts revealed so explosively in the choir, one could say (and the psychiatrist has said it) that Martin was sad because he was a melancholic; and there is no doubt that in his depressed moods he displayed at times what we would call the clinical picture of a melancholia. But Luther was a man who tried to distinguish very clearly between what came from God as the crowning of a worthwhile conflict, and what came from defeat; the fact that he called defeat the devil only meant he was applying a diagnostic label which was handy. He once wrote to Melanchthon that he considered him the weaker one in public controversy, and himself the weaker in private struggles—"if I may thus call what goes on between me and Satan." [34] One could also say (and the professor has said it) that Martin's sadness was the traditional *tristitia*, the melancholy world mood of the *homo religiosus;* from this point of view, it is a "natural" mood, and could even be called the truest adaptation to the human condition. This view, too, we must accept to a point—the point where it becomes clear that Martin was not able in the long run to embrace the monastic life so natural to the traditional *tristitia;* that he mistrusted his sadness himself; and that he later abandoned this melancholic mood altogether for occasional violent mood swings between depression and elation, between self-accusation and the abuse of others. Sadness, then, was primarily the over-all symptom of his youth, and was a symptom couched in a traditional attitude provided by his time.

4

Youth can be the most exuberant, the most careless, the most self-sure, and the most unselfconsciously productive stage of life, or so it seems if we look primarily at the "once-born." This is a term which William James adopted from Cardinal Newman; he uses it to describe all those who rather painlessly fit themselves and are fitted into the ideology of their age, finding no discrepancy between its formulation of past and future and the daily tasks set by the dominant technology.

James [35] differentiates the once-born from those "sick souls" and "divided selves" who search for a second birth, a "growth-crisis" that will "convert" them in their "habitual center of . . . personal energy." He approvingly quotes Starbuck to the effect that "conversion is in its essence a normal adolescent phenomenon" and that "theology . . . brings those means to bear which will intensify the normal tendencies" and yet also shorten "the period by bringing the person to a definite crisis." James (himself apparently the victim in his youth of a severe psychiatric crisis) does not make a systematic point of the fact that in his chapters on the Sick Soul, the Divided Self, and Conversion, his illustrations of spontaneous changes in the "habitual center of personal energy" are almost exclusively people in their late teens and early twenties—an age which can be most painfully aware of the need for decisions, most driven to choose new devotions and to discard old ones, and most susceptible to the propaganda of ideological systems which promise a new world-perspective at the price of total and cruel repudiation of an old one.

We will call what young people in their teens and early twenties look for in religion and in other dogmatic systems an *ideology*. At the most it is a militant system with uniformed members and uniform goals; at the least it is a "way of life," or what the Germans call a *Weltanschauung*, a world-view which is consonant with existing theory, available knowledge, and common sense, and yet is significantly more: an utopian outlook, a cosmic mood, or a doctrinal logic, all shared as self-evident beyond any need for demonstration. What is to be relinquished as "old" may be the individual's previous life; this usually means the perspectives intrinsic to the life-style of the parents, who are thus discarded contrary to all traditional safeguards of filial devotion. The "old" may be a part of himself, which must henceforth be subdued by some rigorous self-denial in a private life-style or through membership in a militant or military organization; or, it may be the world-view of other castes and classes, races and peoples: in this case, these people become not only expendable, but the appointed victims of the most righteous annihilation.

The need for devotion, then, is one aspect of the identity crisis which we, as psychologists, make responsible for all these tendencies and susceptibilities. The need for repudiation is another aspect. In their late teens and early twenties, even when there is no explicit ideological commitment or even interest, young people offer devotion to individual leaders and to teams, to strenuous activities, and to difficult techniques; at the same time they show a sharp and intolerant readiness to discard and disavow people (including, at times, themselves). This repudiation is often snobbish, fitful, perverted, or simply thoughtless.

These constructive and destructive aspects of youthful energy have been and are employed in making and remaking tradition in many diverse areas. Youth stands between the past and the future, both in individual life and in society; it also stands between alternate ways of life. As I pointed out in "The Problem of Ego-Identity," [36] ideologies offer to the members of this age-group overly simplified and yet determined answers to exactly those vague inner states and those urgent questions which arise in consequence of identity conflict. Ideologies serve to channel youth's forceful earnestness and sincere asceticism, as well as its search for excitement and its eager indignation, toward that social frontier where the struggle between conservatism and radicalism is most alive. On that frontier, fanatic ideologists do their busy work and psychopathic leaders their dirty work; but there, also, true leaders create significant solidarities.

In its search for that combination of freedom and discipline, of adventure and tradition, which suits its state, youth may exploit (and be exploited by) the most varied devotions. Subjecting itself to hardship and discipline, it may seek sanctioned opportunities for spatial dispersion, follow wandering apprenticeships, heed the call of frontiers, man the outposts of new nations, fight (almost anybody's) holy wars, or test the limits of locomotive machine-power. By the same token it is ready to provide the physical power and the vociferous noise of rebellions, riots, and lynchings, often knowing little and caring less for the real issues involved. On the other hand, it is most eager to adopt rules of physical restriction and of utter intellectual concentration, be it in the study of ancient books, the contemplation of monkhood, or the striving for the new—for example, in the collective "sincerity" of modern thought reform. Even when it is led to destroy and to repudiate without any apparent cause, as in delinquent gangs, in colonies of perverts and addicts, or in the circles of petty snobs, it rarely does so without some obedience, some solidarity, some hanging on to elusive values.

Societies, knowing that young people can change rapidly even in their most intense devotions, are apt to give them a *moratorium*, a span of time after they have ceased being children, but before their deeds and works count toward a future identity. In Luther's time the monastery was, at least for some, one possible psychosocial moratorium, one possible way of postponing the decision as to what one is and is going to be. It may seem strange that as definite and, in fact, as eternal, a commitment as is expressed in the monastic vow could be considered a moratorium, a means of marking time. Yet in Luther's era, to be an ex-monk was not impossible; nor was there necessarily a stigma attached to leaving a monastic order, provided only that one left in a quiet and prescribed way—as for example, Erasmus did, who was nevertheless offered a cardinalate in his old age; or that one could make cardinals laugh about themselves, as the runaway monk Rabelais was able to do. I do not mean to suggest that those who chose the monastery, any more than those who choose other forms of moratoria in different historical coordinates (as Freud did, in committing himself to laboratory physiology, or St. Augustine to Manichaeism) *know* that they are marking time before they come to their crossroad, which they often do in the late twenties, belated just because they gave their all to the temporary subject of devotion. The crisis in such a young man's life may be reached exactly when he half-realizes that he is fatally overcommitted to what he is not.

As a witness to the predicament of over-commitment let me quote an old man who, looking back on his own youth, had to admit that no catastrophe or failure stopped him in his tracks, but rather the feeling that things were going meaninglessly well. Somehow events in his life were coming to a head, but he felt that he was being lived by them, rather than living them. A man in this predicament is apt to choose the kind of lonely and stubborn moratorium which all but smothers its own creative potential. George Bernard Shaw describes his crisis clearly and unsparingly.[37]

"I made good in spite of myself, and found, to my dismay, that Business, instead of expelling me as the worthless imposter I was, was fastening upon me with no intention of letting me go. Behold me, therefore, in my twentieth year, with a business training, in an occupation which I detested as cordially as any sane person lets himself detest anything he cannot escape from. In March, 1876 I broke loose."

Breaking loose meant to leave family and friends, business and Ireland, and to avoid the danger of success without identity, of a success unequal to "the enormity of my unconscious ambition." He thus granted himself a prolongation of the interval between youth and adulthood. He writes: ". . . when I left my native city I left this phase behind me, and associated no more with men of my age until, after about eight years of solitude in this respect, I was drawn into the Socialist revival of the early eighties, among Englishmen *intensely serious* and *burning with indignation* at *very real* and *very fundamental evils* that affected *all the world*." (The words I have italicized in this statement are almost a list of the issues which dominate Martin's history.) In the meantime, Shaw apparently avoided opportunities, sensing that "Behind the conviction that they could lead to nothing that I wanted, lay the unspoken fear that they might lead to something I did not want." We have to grant some young people, then, the paradoxical fear of a negative success, a success which would commit them in a direction where, they feel, they will not "grow together."

Potentially creative men like Shaw build the personal fundament of their work during a self-decreed moratorium, during which they often starve themselves, socially, erotically, and, last but not least, nutritionally, in order to let the grosser weeds die out, and make way for the growth of their inner garden. Often, when the weeds are dead, so is the garden. At the decisive moment, however, some make contact with a nutriment specific for their gifts. For Shaw, of course, this gift was literature. As he dreamt of a number of professional choices, "of literature I had no dreams at all, any more than a duck has of swimming."

He did not dream of it, but he did it, and with a degree of ritualization close to what clinicians call an "obsessive compensation." This often balances a temporary lack of inner direction with an almost fanatic concentration on activities which maintain whatever work habits the individual may have preserved. "I bought supplies of white paper, demy size, by sixpence-worths at a time; folded it in quarto; and condemned myself to fill five pages of it a day, rain or shine, dull or inspired. I had so much of the schoolboy and the clerk still in me that if my five pages ended in the middle of a sentence I did not finish it until the next day. On the other hand, if I missed a day, I made up for it by doing a double task on the morrow. On this plan I produced five novels in five years. It was my professional apprenticeship. . . ." We may add that these five novels were not published for over fifty years, at which time Shaw, in a special introduction, tried to dissuade the potential buyer from reading them, while recommending to his attention their biographical importance. To such an extent was Shaw aware of their true function and meaning; although his early work habits were almost pathological in their compulsive addictiveness, they were autotherapeutic in their perseverance: "I have risen by sheer gravitation, too industrious by acquired habit to stop working (I work as my father drank)." There is a world of anguish, conflict, and victory in this small parenthesis; for to succeed, Shaw had to inwardly defeat an already outwardly defeated father some of whose peculiarities (for example, a strange sense of humor) contributed to the son's unique greatness, and yet also to that specific failure that is in each greatness. Shaw's autobiographical remarks do not leave any doubt about the true abyss which he, one of the shyest of religious men, faced in his youth before he had learned to cover his sensitivities by appearing on the stage of history as the great cynic ("in this I succeeded only too well"), while using the theatre to speak out of the mouth of the Maid of Orleans.

As was indicated in the preface, Freud and Darwin are among the great men who came upon their most decisive contribution only after a change of direction and not without neurotic involvement at the time of the breakthrough to their specific creativity. Darwin failed in medicine, and had, as if accidentally, embarked on a trip which, in fact, he almost missed because of what seem to have been psychosomatic symptoms. Once aboard the *Beagle*, however, he found not only boundless physical vigor, but also a keen eye for unexplored details in nature, and a creative discernment leading straight to revolutionary insights: the law of natural selection began to haunt him. He was twenty-seven years old when he came home; he soon became an undiagnosed and lifelong invalid, able only after years of concentrated study to organize his data into a pattern which convincingly supported his ideas. Freud, too, was already thirty when, as if driven to do so by mere circumstance, he became a practicing neurologist and made psychiatry his laboratory. He had received his medical degree belatedly, having decided to become a medical scientist rather than a doctor at the age of seventeen. His moratorium, which gave him a basic schooling in method while it delayed the development of his specific gift and his revolutionary creativity, was spent in (then physicalistic) physiology. And when he at last did embark on his stupendous lifework, he was almost delayed further by neurotic suffering. However, a creative man has no choice. He may come across his supreme task almost accidentally. But once the issue is joined, his task proves to be at the same time intimately related to his most personal conflicts, to his superior selective perception, and to the stubbornness of his one-way will: he must court sickness, failure, or insanity, in order to test the alternative whether the established world will crush him, or whether he will disestablish a sector of this world's outworn fundaments and make a place for a new one.[38]

Darwin dealt with man's biological origins. His achievement, and his sin, was a theory that made man part of nature. To accomplish this, and only for this, he was able to put his neurosis aside. Freud, however, had to "appoint his own neurosis that angel who was to be wrestled with and not to be let go, until he would bless the observer." Freud's wrestling with the angel was his working through of his own father complex which at first had led him astray in his search for the origins of the neuroses in childhood. Once he understood his own relationship to his father, he could establish the existence of the universal father image in man, break through to the mother image as well, and finally arrive at the Oedipus complex, the formulation of which made him one of the most controversial figures in the history of ideas. In *The Interpretation of Dreams*,[39] Freud gave psychoanalysis its orientation as the study of unconscious motivation in the normal as well as the pathological, in society as well as the individual. At the same time he freed his own creativity by self-analysis and was able to combine strict observation with disciplined intuition and literary craftsmanship.

This general discussion of the qualities of that critical area between neurosis and creativity will introduce the state of mind which engulfed Martin at the time of the fit in the choir. Even the possibly legendary aspects of this fit reflect an unconscious understanding on the part of the legend-makers, here Martin's monastic brothers, as to what was going on inside him. In the next chapter we will analyze what little is known of Martin's childhood. Then we will trace the subsequent personality change which made it possible for the young man who in the choir was literally felled by the power of the need to negate to stand before his emperor and before the Pope's emissary at the Diet of Worms twelve years later and affirm human integrity in new terms: "My conscience is bound by God's words. Retract anything whatsoever I neither can nor will. For to act against one's conscience is neither safe nor honorable." [40]

God's words: he had, by then, become God's "spokesman," preacher, teacher, orator, and pamphleteer. This had become the working part of his identity. The eventual liberation of Luther's voice made him creative. The one matter on which professor and priest, psychiatrist and sociologist, agree is Luther's immense gift for language: his receptivity for the written word; his memory for the significant phrase; and his range of verbal expression (lyrical, biblical, satirical, and vulgar) which in English is paralleled only by Shakespeare.

The development of this gift is implicit in the dramatic outcry in the choir of Erfurt: for was it not a "dumb" spirit which beset the patient before Jesus? And was it not muteness, also, which the monk had to deny by thus roaring "like an ox"? The theme of the Voice and of the Word, then, is intertwined with the theme of Luther's identity and with his influence on the ideology of his time.

We will therefore concentrate on this process: how young Martin, at the end of a somber and harsh childhood, was precipitated into a severe identity crisis for which he sought delay and cure in the silence of the monastery; how being silent, he became "possessed"; how being possessed, he gradually learned to speak a new language, *his* language; how being able to speak, he not only talked himself out of the monastery, and much of his country out of the

Roman Church, but also formulated for himself and for all of mankind a new kind of ethical and psychological awareness: and how,
at the end, this awareness, too, was marred by a return of the
demons, whoever they may have been.

III

Obedience—To Whom?

AT ITS height, Luther's rebellion centered in the question of man's differential debt of obedience to God, to the Pope, and to Caesar—or rather, to the multitude of Caesars then emerging. At the beginning of his career another and, as it were, preparatory dichotomy preoccupied him: that between the obedience owed to his natural father, whose views were always brutally clear, and the obedience owed to the Father in heaven, from whom young Luther had received a dramatic but equivocal call.

The earlier dichotomy actually followed Luther far into the manhood of his theological struggles; as late as in his thirty-eighth year, having defied emperor and Pope, and having become the spokesman of God's word, Luther appealed to his natural father in a preface to the work in which he justifies the abandonment of his monastic vows (*De Votis Monasticis*): "Would you not rather have lost a hundred sons than miss this glory? . . . For who can doubt that I stand in the service of the Word?" [1] When he had found a new agency to disobey, namely, the Pope, he had to tell his father publicly that he had finally obeyed him; but we cannot overlook the ambivalent wish to be right at all costs, for he adds: "Would you still want to tear me out [of the monastery]? . . . In order to save you from a sense of vainglory, God outdistanced you and took me out himself. . . ." [2] Thus Luther stated to all the world (for his works were then best-sellers) not only that his father had opposed the monastic career, but also that the son had belatedly made this opposition his own—to God's glory, not the father's. At the same time, we can only wonder at the naïveté with which Luther insisted on airing, to the widest possible public, conflicts which seem too ordinary for a man of his stature. Or are they so ordinary? Perhaps only a man of such stature could be sufficiently sensitive to the personal conflicts that contributed to his theological decisions, and would have enough honesty to talk about them. Being a rebellious theologian, not an armchair psychologist, Luther described his conflicts in surprising, sometimes blustering, and often unreliable words. But one cannot help feeling that Luther often publicly confessed just those matters which Freud, more than three hundred years later (enlightenment having reached the psychological point of no return) faced explicitly, and molded into concepts, when, studying his dreams, he challenged and disciplined the neurotic component of his intellectual search.

But now it is time for facts. There are only a few facts about Luther's childhood: his father was a miner who had left the farm; his parents were hard, thrifty, and superstitious, and beat their boy; and school was monotonous and cruel. Martin gleaned from the combined harshness of home, school, and what he considered the Church's exclusive preoccupation with the last judgment, a world-mood of guilt and sadness which "drove him into monkishness."

Except for bits of often questionable amplification here or there, and some diligent background study by the biographers (especially Scheel), these are all the facts we have. If any determining insight had to be drawn from this material alone, it would be better not to begin. But a clinician's training permits, and in fact forces, him to recognize major trends even where the facts are not all available; at any point in a treatment he can and must be able to make meaningful predictions as to what will prove to have happened; and he must be able to sift even questionable sources in such a way that a coherent predictive hypothesis emerges. The proof of the validity of this approach lies in everyday psychoanalytic work, in the way that a whole episode, a whole life period, or even of a whole life trend is gradually clarified in therapeutic crises leading to decisive advances or setbacks sufficiently circumscribed to suggest future strategies. In biography, the validity of any relevant theme can only lie in its crucial recurrence in a man's development, and in its relevance to the balance sheet of his victories and defeats. In discussing the first and less well-documented half of Luther's life, I can do no better by my readers than to consider them participants or auditors in a seminar in which a first batch of material has been presented; I shall try to formulate, on the basis of my experience, what the material suggests we should be watching for in our search for further material. In this book, we can deal with Luther's later life only in conclusion; but the older Luther is so well-known to so many that a follow-up on my thesis will not depend on my own contribution.

We should realize, however, that in work such as this the law of parsimony can guide us only if adjusted to historical material. This adjustment was made by Freud in his concept of "over-determination." Any historical and personological item is always determined by many more forces and trends working with and upon each other than a sparing explanation can cover. Often a certain extravagance in searching for all possible relevances is the only way to get an inkling of the laws which determine the mutual influence upon each other of some factors, and the mutual exclusion of others.

Real peasants, *rechte Bauern*, Luther calls his father and grand-father; and it has become customary to call Luther a peasant or a peasant's son. Even quite modern works speak of Luther's lifelong nostalgia for a peasant's life, such as he is said to have enjoyed as a child. Yet Luther's father, in Luther's memory, never lived the life of a peasant; and Martin as a child never knew whatever homogeneity the life of the German peasant may have had to offer at that time. On the contrary, he was a second-generation ex-peasant; and we in America have learned a few things about second-generation migrants. Martin's father, in *his* early twenties, had to leave the grandfather's farm in Thuringia. The law was that older sons yielded a paternal farm to the youngest brother; an older son could either become the youngest brother's sharecropper, marry into another farm, or leave and seek work elsewhere. Hans Luder decided to work in the mines, and moved to Eisleben with his wife, who was then pregnant with Martin. Half a year after Martin's birth they moved again, this time to Mansfeld, a thriving copper and silver mining center.

Whatever such enforced migration meant to the rest of those oldest sons, it is, I think, possible to trace in Martin that split about ancestral images which is apt to occur in the second generation of migrating families. Sometimes to be "a peasant" meant to him to be *rusticus et durus*—the kind of hard simplicity he was pleased to call his own; at other times he felt a nostalgia for the muddy paradise of the village, which was expressed in the sermon on the sow; but in his later years, with increasing frequency and vehemence, he divorced himself from the German peasant whom he condemned for being vulgar, violent, and animal-like. During the great Peasants' War, he used his efficient propaganda machine to suggest the ruthless extermination of all rebellious peasants—those same peasants who, at the beginning, had looked to him as one of their natural leaders. Yet toward the end of his life he accused himself of having the blood of these peasants on his head—the brow of which had never known a peasant's sweat. (Possibly he overstated things; yet the peasants might never have gone as far as they did in challenging their masters had it not been for their faith in Luther, and, because of him, their faith in a new image of man. We will come back to this.) The main point is that the second-generation ex-peasant Luther was highly ambivalent about his ancestry.

The sociologist might see in Luther's turning against the German peasants a reflection of the inexorable class war; and he would be quite right as far as his theory and his historical curiosity go. However, this interpretation ignores the pivotal role of childhood and youth in the transfer of positive or negative values from generation to generation. Luther's childhood illustrates the fact that adherence to an occupation, or rather an "estate," such as that of peasant, cannot remain a reliable factor in one's inner sense of continuity unless one is involved in the common hardships, hopes, and hates of that estate. These alone keep an ideology relevant. Luther's father not only abandoned a peasant's identity, he also turned against it, developing and imposing on his children in the shortest possible time those virtues which would serve the pursuit of new goals: the negative goal of avoiding the proletarization which befell many ex-peasants; and the positive goal of working himself up into the managerial class of miners. Incidentally, Martin's mother was of urban origin; it is not clear how she came to marry a disinherited peasant, but it stands to reason that she supported his fight upward. In Martin's upbringing, then, the image of a peasant may have become what we call a negative identity fragment, *i.e.*, an identity a family wishes to live down—even though it may sentimentalize it at moments—and the mere hint of which it tries to suppress in its children. As a matter of fact, the literature on Luther abounds in the same ambivalence. In one place a reference to his peasant nature is made to underline his sturdiness; in another, to explain his vulgarity and blockheadedness; and Nietzsche, for example, calls him a *Bergmannssohn*, a miner's son (literally, the son of a man of the mountain) when he wants to do him honor.

The life of a miner in those days was hard, but honorable and well-regulated. Roman law had not penetrated to it; far from being slave-labor, it had a self-regulating dignity, with maximum hours, sanitation laws, and minimum wages. By succeeding in it at the time when he did, Hans Luder not only escaped the proletarization of the landless peasant and unskilled laborer, he also made a place for himself in the managerial class of mine shareholders and foundry co-leasers; he thus became one of the "masters," who, increasingly well-organized, were able to establish through their guilds a kind of closed succession in that they decided about the admission and the advancement of apprentices. To call Hans Luder a peasant, therefore, shows either sentimentality or contempt. He was an early small industrialist and capitalist, first working to earn enough to invest, and then guarding his investment with a kind of dignified ferocity. When he died he left a house in town and 1250 *Goldgulden*.

In order to achieve all this, young Hans and his wife undoubtedly had to work extremely hard and be meticulously thrifty. It was this aim-conscious self-denial which Luther in later years—when he was sitting at his well-appointed meals, practically dictating his famous *Tischreden* to the openmouthed children and busily-writing students, boarders, and friends—was fond of glamorizing as a poverty-ridden childhood, in the same breath denouncing his teacher's beastliness and the monastery's corruption. The image of a very poor and intensely unhappy childhood is thus based on Luther's own later reports.

It cannot be stated too emphatically that Luther, the public figure, is not a very reliable reporter on Martin, the child, or the struggling young man. Reporter of facts, I mean. But then, any autobiographical account of a person's childhood requires a key for the unconscious motto guiding the repression of some items and the special selection of others. Psychoanalysis realized early that all memories must pass through a number of screens; because of these screens, earlier years appear in a haze which distorts form and modifies color. The period of language development forms one screen; going to school (the post-oedipal period) another. To these we must add the period of the completion of identity development at adolescence, which results in a massive glorification of some of the individual's constituent elements, and repudiation of others. In the life of a man like Luther (and in lesser ways in all lives), another screen is strongly suggested: the beginning of an official identity, the moment when life suddenly becomes biography. In many ways, life began for Luther all over again when the world grabbed eagerly at his ninety-five theses, and forced him into the role of rebel, reformer, and spiritual dictator. Everything before that then became memorable only insofar as it helped him to rationalize his disobediences. Maybe this motivation is behind most attempts at historifying the past.

Luther's parents *were* simple folk, to be sure: hard, thrifty, and superstitious—but most of all, Hans Luder was an ambitious man. This ex-peasant, who had to yield his father's farm and fortune, made his wife go and gather firewood in the forest—one of the items which has impressed biographers. But anybody who has wandered in a German forest knows that when Luther's mother carried firewood from the feudal forest she was exercising a customary privilege which did not mark her as destitute. He also made his son go to Latin school and to a university, and expected him to become a jurist and, maybe, a *Buergermeister*. For this, no price was too high, and money was available. In this family framework— a past to be lived down and a future to be started then and there, and at any cost—we must view the scant data on Luther's upbringing, sometimes surer of the forces than of the facts.

It is always difficult to ascertain from historical works which of the over-all political and economic changes that stand out so clearly in retrospect were central to a particular individual in a particular region—central to his conscious hopes and worries, and central to his unconscious aspirations and adaptations. The Holy Roman Empire and the medieval papacy of Hans Luder's time were invigorated and threatened by the same combination of technological and political developments which beset the empires of today. These were and are: *Mastery over geographic space:* then the globe was being circumnavigated by water routes which opened new continents; now the conquest is by air and space-ship. *Communication:* then printing was being developed; now we have television and face the problems involved in the amplified and cheapened power of the image and the voice. *Holy wars:* then the attempts to contain or destroy the world of Islam, and the struggle against the gradual penetration of medieval learning by the philosophical and scientific ideas of the Arabic thinkers; today the wars of economic ideologies, with a similar interpenetration of scientific ideas and social values. *Technology:* then the transition from feudal land ownership to the accumulation of money by an international banking and business class, and the involvement of the Church itself in international finance; now the emergence of an industrial civilization, and the involvement of government itself in the race for atomic power. *Armament:* then the supersession of chivalry and man-to-man combat by fire-power; now armed services made obsolete by the technicians of space war. This brief list characterizes some of the horizons of the medieval world as we recognize them now; every one of these developments had ramifications for the course of Luther's life. How little he was aware of some of them is indicated in his table talk.

The communication of news by its very methods of legendizing and advertising tends to make universal news unreal for the individual—until universal change hits the marketplace, Main Street, and the home. The comman man is apt to set his faith on what he can encompass with his provincial mind and do something about in his daily chores. This is the source of his search for smaller and often reactionary entities which will keep the world together, maintain sensible values, and make action rewarding. Of the late medieval world in which Hans Luder lived, Tawney says:

Its primary unit had been the village; and the village, a community of agrarian shareholders fortified by custom, had repressed with a fury of virtuous unanimity the disorderly appetites which menaced its traditional routine with the evil whose name is Change. Beyond the village lay the greater, more privileged, village called the borough, and the brethren of borough and guild had turned on the foreign devil from upland and valley a face of flint. Above both were the slowly waking nations. Nationalism was an economic force before nationality was a political fact, and it was a sound reason for harrying a competitor that he was a Florentine or a man of the Emperor. The privileged colony with its depot, the Steel-yard of the Hanseatic League, the Fondaco Tedesco of the south Germans, the Factory of the English Merchant Adventurers, were but tiny breaches in a wall of economic exclusiveness. Trade, as in modern Turkey or China, was carried on under capitulations.

This narrow framework had been a home. In the fifteenth century it was felt to be a prison. Expanding energies pressed against the walls; restless appetites gnawed and fretted wherever a crack in the surface offered room for erosion.[3]

Mining was one of the breaches in the wall, and it prospered during the fifteenth century as a source of wealth storable as money and durable household goods. The mining industry, although prosperous, also reflected the enormous disparities in the distribution of wealth; and its workers were subject to the same danger that large classes of people (including most of the clergy) then faced: proletarization. Social units structured themselves more tightly to withstand the shifts of the times. Territorial princes asserted their borders, free cities their walls and their intersection of the trade routes, and guilds their monopoly of economic pursuits. One might speak of a search for territorial identity, and of autonomies increasingly guarded by explicit law, while implicit laws of the universal—the Roman—identity crumbled.

What Hans Luder realized of all this, we do not know; but I think it is fair to assume that he employed his personal idiosyncrasies in the service of certain overwhelming apprehensions and hopes fed by the world situation. He wanted his son to be a lawyer, that is, one who would understand and profit by the new secular laws which were replacing those of the Roman commonwealth. He wanted his son to serve princes and cities, merchants and guilds, and not priests and bishoprics and papal finance—an economic attitude which at that time did not preclude a devout Christian sentiment. Most of all he wanted, as did millions of other ex-peasants and miners, to see his son employ his mind in higher matters, instead of dulling it with miners' superstitions, and to enjoy the wealth unearthed by others instead of dirtying his hands in shafts sunk into the earth. This, then, was what the history books call the "peasant" father of a "peasant" son.

A clinician can and should make a connection between global occurrences and certain small town items recorded in the records of Mansfeld. Hans Luder had a brother in Mansfeld who was called Little Hans. The brothers had been baptized *Gross-Hans* and *Klein-Hans*, which paired them in a possibly significant way for Martin. At any rate, Little Hans followed Big Hans to Mansfeld, while their other two brothers stayed in Thuringia; one took a landed wife, and the other, the father's farm. Little Hans was a drunkard, and when drunk, violent and quick with the knife. Some sources suggest that his court record is blackest when Martin was between five and ten years old, usually years of heightened values in a boy with a sensitive conscience. Other sources add that the uncle arrived in town just when Martin left for boarding school. In any case, his infamy must have preceded him; and the very existence of such a brother whom scandal (maybe even murder) eventually brought to town must have underlined for Big Hans the danger of losing his own hard-won position—and this especially because he himself apparently had a towering temper, and was, in fact, supposed to have killed a shepherd before coming to Mansfeld. Any such killing must be viewed in the light of a then greater leeway for a citizen's taking the law in his own hands; yet it must also reflect a feeling which Luder the home-owner would want to contain, which means that he would have to express some of his native fury, thus diverted from potential enemies, in the home itself.

Martin, as we know from his outbursts in later life, had inherited his father's temper with interest, *mit Zins und Zinseszinsen*. And yet, in his childhood and youth this temper was strangely dormant. Had his father beaten or scared it out of him? Much speaks for this assumption. At any rate, we must add Little Hans to the concept of "dirty peasant" in the list of possible negative identities: as an evil uncle (who according to his name was a minor edition of the righteous father), he was a constant reminder of a possible inherited curse which potentially could lead to proletarization if there were any relaxation of watchfulness, any upsurge of self-indulgent impulse. Every clinician has seen over and over again how a parent's fear that his child may turn out to be just like a particular uncle or aunt can drive the child in that very direction, especially if the warning parent himself is not an especially good model. Luther's father became a model citizen, but at home he seems to have indulged in a fateful two-facedness. He showed the greatest temper in his attempts to drive temper out of his children. Here, I think, is the origin of Martin's doubt that the father, when he punishes you, is really guided by love and justice rather than by arbitrariness and malice. This early doubt later was projected on the Father in heaven with such violence that Martin's monastic teachers could not help noticing it. "God does not hate you, you hate him," one of them said; and it was clear that Martin, searching so desperately for his own justification, was also seeking a formula of eternal justice which would justify God as a judge.

Peasants they were not. But miners are by no means released from soil, dirt, and earth. In fact, they attack the earth more directly and more deeply. They rape and rob it of its precious substance without cultivating its fertile cooperation through care, work and prayer. This rapacious activity, plus the constant danger of being crushed by a mere squeeze of the earth's insides, make miners prone to primitive superstition, for they are, at all times, exposed to individual chance, both lucky and disastrous. The miners of Thuringia thus are reported to have been even more superstitious than the peasants; and the Thuringian peasant to this day remains the most superstitious in Germany. Into this kind of miner's world Hans Luder was forced to go in his early twenties; the work-ideology and cosmology he acquired there dominated Martin's early years. The saying that all is not gold that glitters has a fateful meaning for the miner; it is his job to look for that which glitters, look for it with avaricious but disciplined attention which allows him to avoid wrong leads and recover quickly from disappointment. In those days, of course, the avarice which might make the miner look too eagerly and so doubly fail was attributed to the devil. "In the mines the devil vexes and fools people, and makes apparitions before their eyes so that they are quite sure they see a big pile of ore and of solid silver where there is nothing." [4] The feeling that some glistening pile might turn out to be dirt or worse may have been such a basic and constant superstition that we may have to learn to recognize it in the father's general suspiciousness, and even in his later admonitions to his ordained son that in the most resplendent manifestations of divinity he had better be on the lookout for "ghosts." And Martin, having almost literally absorbed such superstitions with his mother's milk (for the mother is said to have been the more superstitious parent, though she put greater emphasis on benevolent magic), may never have been able *not* to believe his father when he invoked the sinister wisdom of those who worked in the bowels of the earth. Even a few days before his death, Luther saw the devil sitting on a rainpipe outside of his window, exposing his behind to him. Such "reality" always existed for him alongside Aristotle and St. Augustine, St. Paul and the Scriptures.

Luther praised radical suspiciousness as a guarantor of a man's "work, sense, and reason." Ideological distortion is fraught with unfathomable danger; this, plus his background of the miner's constant fear of catastrophe, gave Luther's work an orientation toward sudden death, and thus a constant alertness toward the judgment which might have to be faced at any moment. Kierkegaard once said that Luther always spoke and acted as if lightning were about to strike behind him the next moment. He was referring, of course, to the mysterious thunderstorm considered the revelatory cause of Luther's decision to become a monk. Yet an excessive expectation of catastrophe, an all-too-anxious wish to be ready for the judgment, was part of Martin's world long before that thunderstorm, and it may have made that storm what it became.

Rather late in his life, Luther could say, "Many regions are inhabited by devils; Prussia is full of them"—one of his few contributions to the study of national character. The fact is that Luther, like all children of his time, was deeply imbued with the idea of the universal presence of spirits in concrete form. One may assume a certain melée of contending spirits on that social frontier on which he grew up: the frontier of transition from the agrarian preoccupation with mud, soil, and fertility to the miner's preoccupation with rock, dirt, and the chances of a haul; and beyond this, the mercantile aim of amassing metal and money, shiny and yet "dirty," and all subject to a new adventurous and boundless avarice which the Church tried to crush with all her might—and at the same time to monopolize.

In his childhood, strange noises made by wind and water, and strange sights seen in the traitorous twilight and in the dark, were as a matter of course taken as evidence of that population of demons sent by sorcerers and witches which were peaceable only as long as one kept an eye on them—that is, as long as one was cautious and suspicious enough. The belief in demons permitted a persistent externalization of one's own unconscious thoughts and preconscious impulses of avarice and malice, as well as thoughts which one suspected one's neighbor of having. The externalization of a neighbor's thoughts probably more often than not involved a fusion of the subjective and the objective: if a neighbor, whose public personality and activities are known—although, of course, not his secret thoughts—seems intent on being harmful, it means that with the entirely unfair help of some spirits, he will find a way of doing to me those things which harmless I may only impotently *wish* to do to him. In all magic thinking, the unknown and the unconscious meet at a common frontier: murderous, adulterous, or avaricious wishes, or sudden moods of melancholy or friskiness are all forced upon me by evil-wishing neighbors. Sexual phantasies, too, can thus be treated as extraterritorial. Even sexual events, such as an all-too-vivid dream, or a neighbor in one's bed, can be blamed on the devil's sneaky habit of lying underneath sleeping men, or on top of sleeping women: *Unter oder oblegen*, in Luther's words; *succubus et incubus* in those of theology.

All this is quite handy if your conscience and your reason are primitive or foxy enough to let it pass. If they are too developed, the scruple appears which came to bother Luther: how could you know (once you were incautious enough to want to know) whether you had desired and abetted what thus afflicted you when you were not conscious—well, not quite conscious? Or, on the other hand, in those rare moments when you were quite conscious, fervently alert and full of good conscience, how did you ever know that this very excess of goodness was not a *Trugbild*, a mirage of the devil?

It is tempting to treat these superstitions as primitive obsessions, and to pity the people who did not know any better and who must have felt haunted. But we should not overlook the fact that within reason—that is, to the extent that the superstitions were not exploited by mass panic and neurotic anxiety—they were a form of collective mastery of the unknown. In a world full of dangers they may even have served as a source of security, for they make the unfamiliar familiar, and permit the individual to say to his fears and conflicts, "I see you! I recognize you!" He can even tell others what he saw and recognized while remaining reasonably free, by a contract between like-minded, of the aspersion that he imagined things out of depravity or despair, or that he was the only one to be haunted. What else do we do today when we share our complexes, our coronaries, and our communists?

Nor was the world entirely left to evil spirits by any means. Corresponding to the population of demonic middlemen between man and the worldly underground was an ever-increasing number of mediators between him and heaven: the angels and the saints, the heavenly aunts and uncles, more human, more accessible, and more understandable than the forbidding Trinity. As every man had his angel, so every disease and misfortune had its saint who, strangely enough, was often assumed to create the very disease which he could cure—maybe in order to maintain himself in an increasingly competitive market, for all those saints had their separate altars where, for a price, their services could be solicited. The miners had one major and several ancillary saints. St. Anne, the mother of the mother of God, was Hans', as well as Martin's, *Abgott*—a strange term, for it means "idol," and indicates the persistent trend in Catholic communities to focus florid idolatry on a saint and a solid image in a solid church, and leave the rest of religion to the professionals. St. Anne watched over the miners' health, and protected them against sudden accidents; but she "is especially dear because she does not come with empty hands, brings mighty goods and money." We will hear of St. Anne in the hour of Martin's revelatory decision.

According to the characterology established in psychoanalysis, suspiciousness, obsessive scrupulosity, moral sadism, and a preoccupation with dirtying and infectious thoughts and substances go together. Luther had them all. One of Martin's earliest reported remarks (from his student days) was a classical obsessive statement: "the more you cleanse yourself, the dirtier you get." [5] On the other hand, we have already quoted his victoriously humorous treatment of the sow in her bed of manure. Some understanding of this part of his personality can be gained on the basis of a hypothesis I would like to offer, which is founded on work with obsessive patients and also on the study of preliterate societies. That the devil can be completely undone if you manage to fart into his nostrils is only one of those, shall we say homeopathic, remedies which Luther, undoubtedly on the basis of a homegrown demonology, advocated all of his life. His method is based on beating the devil with his own weapons; and it suggests the hypothesis, which cannot be substantiated at this point, that the devil and his home, and feces and the recesses of their origin, are all associated in a common underground of magic danger. To this common underground, then, we may assign both the bowels of the earth, where dirt can become precious metal (by means of a magic process which the alchemists tried to repeat experimentally in their laboratories above ground), and also that innermost self, that hidden "soul ground" (*Seelengrund*) where a mystical transformation of base passions can be effected.

In dealing with this layer of primitive thought, and also with the people among whom it has created a living folklore, it is necessary to re-evaluate the meanings of dirt in its mineral and vegetable forms. It is less necessary (although it helps) to study so-called primitives, or those among us who fall victim to our common but usually unconscious proclivity for equating dirt and preciousness which is expressed in many neurotic symptoms and in such colloquialisms as "paydirt." Anyone who has worked in mining areas or in coal- and steel-minded communities like Pittsburgh must be aware of the double evaluation of "smog" for instance; I am speaking of the honest productive black smog of concentrated industry, not the smog thrown off by automobile exhausts. The older Pittsburghers were originally east- and south-European peasants, and in their old country mud turned into ground, and ground into mud, and the process assured fertility. In this country smog, or at any rate, smoke, meant productivity; not only employment, but also the continuous manufacture by which the nation's steel was produced. The sky was blue and the rivers were clean only during shutdowns and strikes: the cleanliness was a reminder of a deadly vacuum and a possible final stoppage of production. Those modern Pittsburghers who undertook to make Pittsburgh clean had much support from applauding strangers who pitied Pittsburgh as a national Cinderella; they had little support from those immigrant families to whom smoke and grime had become an aspect of home.

One of the psychiatrist's observations throws some light on the particular milieu in which Luther's basic infantile experiences took place. "Luther's family," he writes, obviously on the basis of his background studies, "occupied a narrow dark house with a few small and low rooms, badly lighted and badly aired, in which parents and children were huddled together; it is also probable that all or most of the family, that is, of both sexes, slept together, naked, in one broad alcove." [6] Reiter suggests that the boy Martin, already made sleepless by corporal punishment—a point which we will discuss presently—thus had ample opportunity to receive bodily stimulation and to witness sexual acts—and, we may add, birth, sickness, and death. Those who wish to belittle the contribution of infantile traumata to Luther's personality usually at this point invoke the statistical repudiation that this circumstance was typical for all similar households, and, therefore, is unspecific. Yet this observant and imaginative boy, inclined to rumination about the nature of things and God's justification in having arranged them thus, may well have suffered—call it neurotically, call it sensitively—under observations which leave (or, indeed, make) others dull. At any rate whatever happened in this boy's dreams and in his half-dreams, and was sensed and heard in sleep and half-sleep, became richly associated with the sinister dealings of demons and of the devil himself; while some of the observations made at night may have put the father's moralistic daytime armour into a strange sadistic light.

Some biographers state without hesitation that Luther's father beat into him that profound fear of authority and those pervading streaks of stubbornness and rebelliousness which allegedly caused Luther to be sickly and anxious as a boy, "sad" as a youth, scrupulous to a fault in the monastery, and beset with doubts and depressions in later life; and which finally made him pursue the question of God's justice to the point of unleashing a religious revolution. The professor will have none of this. To him, "prayer and work, discipline and the fear of God" are the four pillars of wisdom; and while Luther's father may have been a bit less discerning in the choice of means and a bit more hot-blooded than he might have been, his motives were those of Proverbs 13:24, and his aim the son's moral well-being, intellectual perfection, and civic advancement. *Wacker Gestrichen* is the professor's term for what we might call a lusty caning. He is right, of course, in pointing out that other boys were caned as Luther was; and, indeed, Luther himself seems to emphasize the universality of such discipline when he frequently refers to the monotonous drumming of canes in his home and in school.

However, the professor's statistical approach to a given effect—the assertion that the cause was too common to have an uncommon effect on one individual—is neither clinically nor biographically valid. We must try to ascertain the relationship of caner and caned, and see if a unique element may have given the common event a specific meaning.

Two statements of Luther's are frequently quoted: "My father once whipped me so that I ran away and felt ugly toward him until he was at pains to win me back." "My mother caned me for stealing a nut until the blood came. Such strict discipline drove me to a monastery although she meant it well." [7] In spite of this last remark, Bainton, whose translation is quoted, does not think that these whippings aroused more than a "flash of resentment." Many authorities on Luther, making no attempt at psychological thinking, judge this matter of punishment either to be of no importance, or on the contrary, to have made an emotional cripple of Martin. It seems best however, to outline a framework within which we may try to evaluate these data.

In my profession one learns to listen to exactly what people are saying; and Luther's utterances, even when they are reported secondhand, are often surprises in naïve clarification. The German text of Luther's reference to the whipping incidents of which I quoted Bainton's translation, adds, to the report of the whipping: "*dass ich ihn flohe und ward ihm gram, bis er mich wieder zu sich gewoehnte.*" [8] These words are hard to render in another language, and Bainton, from his point of view, saw no reason to ponder them. He translated them into what an American boy might have said: "I ran away . . . I felt ugly." But a more literal translation would be, "I fled him and I became sadly resentful toward him, until he gradually got me accustomed (or habituated) to him again." Thus, "*ich ward ihm gram*" describes a less angry, sadder and more deeply felt hurt than "I felt ugly toward him." A child can feel ugly toward somebody for whom he does not specially care; but he feels sadly resentful toward somebody he loves. Similarly, a parent could be "at pains to win back" almost anybody, and for any number of reasons; but he would try to *reaccustom* somebody to himself only for the purpose of restoring an intimate daily association. The personal quality of that one sentence thus reveals two trends which (I believe) characterized Hans' and Martin's relationship. Martin, even when mortally afraid, *could not really hate his father*, he could only be sad; and Hans, while he could not let the boy come close, and was murderously angry at times, *could not let him go for long*. They had a mutual and deep investment in each other which neither of them could or would abandon, although neither of them was able to bring it to any kind of fruition. (The reader may feel this interpretation places too big a burden on one sentence; but we will find further support in the whole story as we proceed.)

I know this kind of parent-child relationship all too well from my young patients. In the America of today it is usually the mother whose all-pervasive presence and brutal decisiveness of judgment—although her means may be the sweetest—precipitate the child into a fatal struggle for his own identity: the child wants to be blessed by the one important parent, not for what he does and accomplishes, but for what he *is*, and he often puts the parent to mortal tests. The parent, on the other hand, has selected this one child, because of an inner affinity paired with an insurmountable outer distance, as the particular child who must *justify the parent*. Thus the parent asks only: What have you *accomplished?* and what have you done for *me?* It is my contention that Luther's father played this role in Martin's life, and so jealously that the mother was eclipsed far more than can be accounted for by the mere pattern of German house-wifeliness.

I said that Luther could not hate his father openly. This statement presumes that he did hate him underneath. Do we have any proof of this? Only the proof which lies in action delayed, and delayed so long that the final explosion hits nonparticipants. In later life Luther displayed an extraordinary ability to hate quickly and persistently, justifiably and unjustifiably, with pungent dignity and with utter vulgarity. This ability to hate, as well as an inability to forgive those who in his weaker years had, to his mind, hindered him, he shares with other great men. However, as we follow his tortured obediences and erratic disobediences in later life, we cannot help asking what made it impossible for him to at least evade this father (as another brutalized son and later emancipator, Lincoln, did, sadly yet firmly), and even within the paternalistic system of those days eventually leave him aside, make compromises, and get his way. Erasmus, and Calvin, and many lesser people, met their crises in defying their father's wills, but settled them somehow without making their rebellion the very center of their self-justification.

I have so far mentioned two trends in the relationship between Hans and Martin: 1) the father's driving economic ambition, which was threatened by something (maybe even murder) done in the past, and by a feeling close to murder which he always carried inside; and 2) the concentration of the father's ambition on his oldest son, whom he treated with alternate periods of violent harshness and of habituating the son to himself in a manner which may well have been somewhat sentimental—a deadly combination.

I would add to these trends the father's display of righteousness. Hans seems to have considered himself the very conception, the *Inbegriff*, of justice. After all, he did not spare himself, and fought his own nature as ruthlessly as those of his children. But parents are dangerous who thus take revenge on their child for what circumstances and inner compulsion have done to them; who misuse one of the strongest forces in life—true indignation in the service of vital values—to justify their own small selves. Martin, however, seems to have sensed on more than one occasion that the father, behind his disciplined public identity, was possessed by an angry, and often alcoholic, impulsiveness which he loosed against his family (and would dare loose *only* against his family) under the pretense of being a hard taskmaster and righteous judge.

The fear of the father's anger, described as constant by some biographers, included the absolute injunction against any back-talk, any *Widerrede*. Here again the fact that only much later, and only after an attempt to screw down the lid with the rules of monastic silence, did Martin become one of the biggest and most effective back-talkers in history, forces us to ask what kept him silent for so long. But this was Martin: in Latin school he was caned for using the German language—and later he used that language with a vengeance! We can deduce from what burst forth later that which must have been forced to lie dormant in childhood; this may well have included some communality of experience with the mother, whose spontaneity and imagination are said to have suffered at the side of Hans Luder.

This much, I think, one can say about the paternal side of Martin's childhood dilemma. Faced with a father who made questionable use of his brute superiority; a father who had at his disposal the techniques of making others feel morally inferior without being quite able to justify his own moral superiority; a father to whom he could not get close and from whom he could not get away—faced with such a father, how was he going to submit without being emasculated, or rebel without emasculating the father?

Millions of boys face these problems and solve them in some way or another—they live, as Captain Ahab says, with half of their heart and with only one of their lungs, and the world is the worse for it. Now and again, however, an individual is called upon (called by *whom*, only the theologians claim to know, and by *what*, only bad psychologists) to lift his individual patienthood to the level of a universal one and to try to solve for all what he could not solve for himself alone.

Luther's statement of the maltreatment received at the hands of his mother is more specific; however, whatever resentment he felt against her was never expressed as dramatically as was his fatherhate, which took the form of a burning doubt of divine righteousness. The Madonna was more or less gently pushed out of the way. What lack in Martin and what void in religion were thus created, we will discuss later.

To return to the statement quoted, it says that the mother beat him "until the blood came"; that this was for "one nut" which he presumably stole; and that such discipline "drove him into the monastery." Actually, the German text of this statement does not say "into the monastery"—and, indeed, Luther never relinquished the conviction that it was God who made him go into the monastery. *In die Moencherei* literally means "into monkery," into the monk-business, so to speak, and refers to his exaggeration of the ascetic and the scrupulous. He implies strongly, then, that such treatment was responsible for the excessive, the neurotic side of the religionism of his early twenties. "Such discipline," however, also refers to the general disciplinary methods of his time, not just to those of his mother; while "for one nut" may well cover, although we must not make too much of it, a complaint with many ramifications: it is one of a whole series of incidents which he cited even into old age to support a certain undertone of grievance in his self-justification.

We may add that if he was being punished for a breach of property rights, he may well have found the severity puzzling. Many children through the ages, like the juvenile delinquents of today have found incomprehensible the absolutism of an adult conscience that insists that a little theft, if not pounced upon with the whole weight of society's wrath, will breed many big ones. Criminals are thus often made; since the world treats such small matters as a sure sign of potential criminality, the children may feel confirmed in one of those negative identity fragments which under adverse circumstances can become the dominant identity element. Luther all his life felt like some sort of criminal, and had to keep on justifying himself even after his revelation of the universal justification through faith had led him to strength, peace, and leadership.

"Until the blood came" (often translated as "flowed") has become a biographical stereotype which, in reading, one passes over as lightly as news about a widespread famine in China, or the casualties of an air raid. However, in regard to these larger news items, one would, if one stopped to think, detect some subliminal horror in oneself; but in regard to the blood thus exacted from children there seems to exist a widespread ambivalence. Some readers feel a slight revulsion in reading about it, others (and so the users of the stereotype seem to know), suspect it of being one of those factors which *made* the victim a sturdy personality worthy of a biography. Actually, in Martin's case, the German text only says that "afterwards there was blood," which at least takes out of the story that element of determined bloodthirstiness which the stereotype implies by the intentional "until." This whole disciplinary issue calls for a more general discussion before we send Martin to school and to further beatings.

The caning and whipping of children was as typical of Martin's time as the public torture of criminals. But since we are not making a zoological survey of human behavior, we are not obliged to accept what everybody does as natural. Nor do we have to agree with those hardy souls who, looking us straight in the eye, assure us that a good caning never did them any harm, quite the contrary. Since they could not escape the punishment when they were children, and can not undo it now, their statement only indicates their capacity to make the best of what cannot be helped. Whether or not it did them any harm is another question, to answer which may call for more information about the role they have come to play in adult human affairs.

It is well to remember that the majority of men have never invented the device of beating children into submission. Some of the American Plains Indian tribes were (as I had an opportunity to relate and to discuss twenty years ago [9]) deeply shocked when they first saw white people beat their children. In their bewilderment they could only explain such behavior as part of an over-all missionary scheme—an explanation also supported by the white people's method of letting their babies cry themselves blue in the face. It all must mean, so they thought, a well-calculated wish to impress white children with the idea that this world is not a good place to linger in, and that it is better to look to the other world where perfect happiness is to be had at the price of having sacrificed this world. This is an ideological interpretation, and a shrewd one: it interprets a single typical act not on the basis of its being a possible cause of a limited effect, but as part of a world view. And indeed, we now beat our children less, but we are still harrying them through this imperfect world, not so much to get them to the next one as to make them hurry from one good moment to better ones, to climb, improve, advance, progress.

It takes a particular view of man's place on this earth, and of the place of childhood within man's total scheme, to invent devices for terrifying children into submission, either by magic, or by mental and corporeal terror. When these terrors are associated with collective and ritual observances, they can be assumed to contain some inner corrective which keeps the individual child from facing life all by himself; they may even offer some compensation of belongingness and identification. Special concepts of property (including the idea that a man can ruin his own property if he wishes) underlie the idea that it is entirely up to the discretion of an individual father when he should raise the morality of his children by beating their bodies. It is clear that the concept of children as property opens the door to those misalliances of impulsivity and compulsivity, of arbitrariness and moral logic, of brutality and haughtiness, which make men crueler and more licentious than creatures not fired with the divine spark. The device of beating children down—by superior force, by contrived logic, or by vicious sweetness—makes it unnecessary for the adult to become adult. He need not develop that true inner superiority which is naturally persuasive. Instead, he is authorized to remain significantly inconsistent and arbitrary, or in other words, childish, while beating into the child the desirability of growing up. The child, forced out of fear to pretend that he is better when seen than when unseen, is left to anticipate the day when he will have the brute power to make others more moral than he ever intends to be himself.

Historically, the increasing relevance of the Roman concepts of law in Luder's time helped to extend the concept of property so that fatherhood took on the connotation of an ownership of wife and children. The double role of the mother as one of the powerless victims of the father's brutality and also as one of his dutiful assistants in meting out punishment to the children may well account for a peculiar split in the mother image. The mother was perhaps cruel only because she had to be, but the father because he wanted to be. From the ideology inherent in such an arrangement there is— as we will see in Luther's punitive turn against the peasant rebels— only one psychological and a few political steps to those large-scale misalliances among righteousness, logic, and brutality that we find in inquisitions, concentration camps, and punitive wars.

The question, then, whether Martin's fears of the judgment day and his doubts in the justice then to be administered were caused by his father's greater viciousness, or by his own greater sensitivity, or both, pales before the general problem of man's exploitability in childhood, which makes him the victim not only of overt cruelty, but also of all kinds of covert emotional relief, of devious vengefulness, or sensual self-indulgence, and of sly righteousness—all on the part of those on whom he is physically and morally dependent. Some day, maybe, there will exist a well-informed, well-considered, and yet fervent public conviction that the most deadly of all possible sins is the mutilation of a child's spirit; for such mutilation undercuts the life principle of trust, without which every human act, may it feel ever so good and seem ever so right, is prone to perversion by destructive forms of conscientiousness.

For the sake of the instructive illustration with which Luther's life may provide us, it is necessary to keep away from all-too-simple causal alternatives such as whether or not, in Luther's case, a brutal father beat a sickly or unstable son into such a state of anxiety and rebellion that God and even Christ became for him revengers only—

Stockmeister und Henker—and not redeemers. As Luther puts it: "From childhood on, I knew I had to turn pale and be terror-stricken when I heard the name of Christ; for I was taught only to perceive him as a strict and wrathful judge." [10] The psychiatrist and the priest—each for reasons of his own approach—consider this statement the quirk of an excessively gifted but unstable individual; and they bolster their contention with references to dozens of theologians of the time, none of whom exclusively emphasizes Christ's role as a revenger. And it is obvious that Luther's statement is most personal, influenced as it was by his upbringing and by his later decision to tackle that aspect of the disciplinary and religious atmosphere of his day which had almost crushed him, and which he felt was enslaving, not, of course, the professional religionists, but the common people of whom God had made so many.

We will hear more about the father; we have now all but exhausted the available references to the mother. We had better prepare ourselves, right here, for an almost exclusively masculine story: Kierkegaard's comment that Luther invented a religion for the adult man states the limitation as well as the true extent of Luther's theological creation. Luther provided new elements for the Western male's identity, and created for him new roles; but he contributed only one new feminine identity, the parson's wife—and this solely perhaps because his wife, Katherine of Bora, created it with the same determined unself-consciousness with which she made the great Doktor marry her. Otherwise, the Lutheran revolution only created ideals for women who wanted to be like parsons if they couldn't be like parsons' wives.

And in spite of Katherine and her children, wherever Luther's influence was felt, the Mother of God (that focus of women's natural religion-by-being-and-letting-be) was dethroned. Luther refers to her almost sneeringly as one of the female saints who might induce a man to "hang on their necks," or "hold on to their skirts": "And because we could never do enough penance and holy works, and in spite of it all remained full of fear and terror of [God's] anger, they told us to look to the saints in heaven who should be the mediators between Christ and us; and they taught us to pray to the dear mother of Christ and reminded us of the breasts which she had given to her son so that she might ask him to go easy with his wrath toward us, and make sure of his grace." [11] The sneer, it is true, is not for Mary but for those who suggested that he speak through her to Him to whom he "wanted to speak directly."

All of this comes to mind as one scans the thousands of pages of the literature on Luther; one comes to ask, over and over again, didn't the man have a mother?

Obviously, not much to speak of. The books repeat: of Luther's mother we know little. Didn't she stand between the father and the son whom she had suckled? Whose agent was she when she beat him "for one nut"? Did she disavow him on her own when he became a monk—a disavowal responsible for her one rather sandwiched mention in the *Documents of Luther's Development*: "I became a monk," Luther is quoted as saying, "against the wishes of my father, of my mother, of God, and of the Devil." [12] And what did she feel when she bore and lost so many children that their number and their names are forgotten? Luther does mention that some of her children "cried themselves to death," which may have been one of his after-dinner exaggerations; and at any rate, what he was talking about then was only that his mother had considered these children to have been bewitched by a neighbor woman. And yet, a friend of Luther's who visited her in her old age reported that Luther was her "spit and image."

The father seems to have been standoffish and suspicious toward the universe; the mother, it is said, was more interested in the imaginative aspects of superstition. It may well be, then, that from his mother Luther received a more pleasurable and more sensual attitude toward nature, and a more simply integrated kind of mysticism, such as he later found described by certain mystics. It has been surmised that the mother suffered under the father's personality, and gradually became embittered; and there is also a suggestion that a certain sad isolation which characterized young Luther was to be found also in his mother, who is said to have sung to him a ditty: "For me and you nobody cares. That is our common fault." [13]

A big gap exists here, which only conjecture could fill. But instead of conjecturing half-heartedly, I will state, as a clinician's judgment, that nobody could speak and sing as Luther later did if his mother's voice had not sung to him of some heaven; that nobody could be as torn between his masculine and his feminine sides, nor have such a range of both, who did not at one time feel that he was like his mother; but also, that nobody would discuss women and marriage in the way he often did who had not been deeply disappointed by his mother—and had become loath to succumb the way she did to the father, to fate. And if the soul is man's most bisexual part, then we will be prepared to find in Luther both some horror of mystic succumbing and some spiritual search for it, and to recognize in this alternative some emotional and spiritual derivatives of little Martin's "pre-historic" relation to his mother.

Preserved Smith (as pointed out, not a psychoanalyst) introduced the Oedipus complex into the literature on Luther. The psychiatrist picks it up, not without (quite figuratively speaking) crossing himself before the clinical world: "Maybe an orthodox psychoanalyst will phantasy into Luther's life the trivial outline of a deep and firmly anchored Oedipus complex which was aroused by a forceful and libidinal attachment to the vivacious and, as far as we know, gifted and imaginative mother, and accentuated by the sinister harshness of the father toward him, toward the siblings and maybe also to the mother." [14] To this, we would reply that most certainly we would ascribe to Luther an Oedipus complex, and not a trivial one at that. We would not wish to see any boy—much less an imaginative and forceful one—face the struggles of his youth and manhood without having experienced as a child the love and the hate which are encompassed in this complex: love for the maternal person who awakens his senses and his sensuality with her ministrations, and deep and angry rivalry with the male possessor of this maternal person. We would also wish him with their help to succeed, in his boyhood, in turning resolutely away from the protection of women to assume the fearless initiative of men.

Only a boy with a precocious, sensitive, and intense conscience would *care* about pleasing his father as much as Martin did, or would subject himself to a scrupulous and relentless form of self-criticism instead of balancing the outer pressure with inventive deviousness and defiance. Martin's reactions to his father's pressure are the beginnings of Luther's preoccupation with matters of individual conscience, a preoccupation which went far beyond the requirements of religion as then practised and formulated. Martin took unto himself the ideological structure of his parents' consciences: he incorporated his father's suspicious severity, his mother's fear of sorcery, and their mutual concern about catastrophes to be avoided and high goals to be met. Later he rebelled: first against his father, to join the monastery; then against the Church, to found his own church—at which point, he succumbed to many of his father's original values. We can only surmise to what extent this outcome was prepared for in childhood by a cumulative rebelliousness and by an ever-so-clandestine hate (for our conscience, like the medieval God, knows everything and registers and counts everything).

This biographical problem overlaps an historical one: Did Luther have a right to claim that his own fear, and his feeling of being oppressed by the image of an avenging God, were shared by others? Was his attitude representative of a pervasive religious atmosphere, at least in his corner of Christendom? The psychiatrist and the priest answer definitely not; the professor can dispense with this historical discussion altogether, since for him, God chose the moment of his word to Martin.

These questions can only be answered by a survey like the one Huizinga made of the waning middle ages in France and the Netherlands, in which he described the disintegration of the medieval identity and the emergence of the new burgher identity on evidence derived from literature and documentary art. In a general way, Huizinga's description must also apply to Martin's time and place:

At the close of the Middle Ages, a sombre melancholy weighs on people's souls. Whether we read a chronicle, a poem, a sermon, a legal document even, the same impression of immense sadness is produced by them all. It would sometimes seem as if this period had been particularly unhappy, as if it had left behind only the memory of violence, of covetousness and mortal hatred, as if it had known no other enjoyment but that of intemperance, of pride and of cruelty.

In the records of all periods misfortune has left more traces than happiness. Great evils form the ground-work of history. We are perhaps inclined to assume without much evidence that, roughly speaking, and notwithstanding all calamities, the sum of happiness can have hardly changed from one period to another. But in the fifteenth century, as in the epoch of romanticism, it was, so to say, bad form to praise the world and life openly. It was fashionable to see only its suffering and misery, to discover everywhere signs of decadence and of the near end—in short, to condemn the times or to despise them.[15]

No other epoch has laid so much stress as the expiring Middle Ages on the thought of death. An everlasting call of *memento mori* resounds through life.[16]

In earlier times, too, religion had insisted on the constant thought of death, but the pious treatises of these ages only reached those who had already turned away from the world. Since the thirteenth century, the popular preaching of the mendicant orders had made the eternal admonition to remember death swell into a sombre chorus ringing throughout the world. Towards the fifteenth century, a new means of inculcating the awful thought into all minds was added to the words of the preacher, namely the popular woodcut. Now these two means of expression, sermons and woodcuts, both addressing themselves to the multitude and limited to crude effects, could only represent death in a simple and striking form.[17]

In the evaluation of the dominant moods of any historical period it is important to hold fast to the fact that there are always islands of self-sufficient order—on farms and in castles, in homes, studies, and cloisters—where sensible people manage to live relatively lusty and decent lives: as moral as they must be, as free as they may be, and as masterly as they can be. If we only knew it, this elusive arrangement *is* happiness. But men, especially in periods of change, are swayed by alternating world moods which seem to be artificially created by the monopolists and manipulators of an era's opinions, and yet could not exist without the highly exploitable mood cycles inherent in man's psychological structure. The two most basic alternating moods are those of carnival and atonement: the first gives license and leeway to sensual enjoyment, to relief and release at all cost; the second surrenders to the negative conscience which constricts, depresses, and enjoins man for what he has left unsolved, uncared for, unatoned. Especially in a seemingly rational and informed period like our own, it is obvious how blithely such moods overshadow universally available sets of information, finding support for luxurious thoughtlessness at one time, for panicky self-criticism at another. Thus we may say that beside and beyond a period's verifiable facts and official doctrines, the world image "breathes." It tends to expand and to contract in its perspectives, and to gain or lose solidity and coherence. In each careless period latent panic only waits for catastrophe—famines, pests and depressions, overpopulation and migration, sudden shifts in technology or in leadership—to cause a shrinkage in the world image, a kind of chill attacking the sense of identity of large masses.

We briefly outlined above the expansion of earthly space in Luther's times. But every expanding opens frontiers, every conquest exposes flanks. Gun powder and the printing press could be used against their users; voyages revealed a world of disquieting cultural relativities; wider social contacts increased the chances of ideological contamination and of further inroads of plague and syphilis. The impact of all these Pyrrhic victories, and of the spiritual decline of the papacy and the fragmentation of the empire, produced both a shrinkage of that official perspective which was oriented toward eventual salvation, and an increase in the crudity and cruelty of the means employed to defend what remained of the Church's power of persuasion. Thus it is probable that in Martin's childhood and youth there lurked in the ideological perspective of his world, perhaps just because the great theologians were so engrossed in scholasticism, a world image of man as inescapably sinful, with a soul incapable of finding any true identity in its perishable body. This world-image implied only one hope: at an uncertain (and maybe immediately impending) moment, an end would come which might guarantee an individual the chance (to be denied to millions of others) of finding pity before the only true Identity, the only true Reality, which was Divine Wrath.

Among the increasing upper urban classes, among the patricians, merchants, and masters who were the town fathers of the ever more important cities, the reaction was developing which eventually became the northern Renaissance. These upper classes no more wanted to be the emperor's then growing economic proletariat than they wished to end on the day of judgment as God's proletariat who (as they could see in the paintings which they commissioned) were to be herded into oblivion by fiery angels, mostly of Italian extraction. This attitude reflected the discrepancy between the era of unlimited initiative then dawning and the era coming to an end which subordinated man's identity on earth to a super-identity in heaven. But these two eras, all too simply set off against each other as the Renaissance and the Middle Ages, corresponded, in fact, to two inner world moods; their very conflictedness corresponded to man's conflicted inner structure.

We are far ahead of ourselves. Yet, we must face the fact that when little Martin left the house of his parents, he was heavily weighed down by an overweening superego, which would give him the leeway of a sense of identity only in the obedient employment of his superior gifts, and only as long as he was more Martin than Luther, more son than man, more follower than leader.

Hans Luder in all his more basic characteristics belonged to the narrow, suspicious, primitive-religious, catastrophe-minded people. He was determined to join the growing class of burghers, masters, and town fathers—but there is always a lag in education. Hans beat into Martin what was characteristic of his own past, even while he meant to prepare him for a future better than his own present. This conflictedness of Martin's early education, which was *in* and *behind* him when he entered the world of school and college, corresponded to the conflicts inherent in the ideological-historical universe which lay *around* and *ahead* of him. The theological problems which he tackled as a young adult of course reflected the peculiarly tenacious problem of the domestic relationship to his own father; but this was true to a large extent because both problems, the domestic and the universal, were part of one ideological crisis: a crisis about the theory and practice, the power and responsibility, of the moral authority invested in fathers: on earth and in heaven; at home, in the market-place, and in politics; in the castles, the capitals, and in Rome. But it undoubtedly took a father and a son of tenacious sincerity and almost criminal egotism to make the most of this crisis, and to initiate a struggle in which were combined elements of the drama of King Oedipus and the passion of Golgotha, with an admixture of cussedness made in Saxony.

2

At about the seventh year, says Aristotle, man can differentiate between good and bad. Conscience, ego, and cognition, we would say, are by then sufficiently developed to make it probable that a child, given half a chance, will be able and eager to concentrate on tasks transcending play. He will watch and join others in the techniques of his society, and develop an eagerness for completing tasks fitted for his own age in some craftsmanlike way. All this, and not less, is implied when we say that a child has reached the "stage of industry."

In his seventh year Martin was sent to a school which would teach him Latin—then the principal tool of the technology of literacy. Obviously only parents with higher aspirations for their children would send them to such a school, the license to conduct which was leased out by the town, in the same way the town mill was leased to the miller and left to him to run. Magister and miller may have differed in their preparatory training, and in the product they processed, but their economic problems were not dissimilar, and their labor policies were both directed at driving hard bargains. Halfway-qualified teachers were available to schools like these only when they could get no other work—while they were still young, or when they were no longer employable. In either case they were apt to express their impatience with life in their treatment of the children, which was very similar to the treatment that the town miller's men gave their donkeys. The teachers rarely relied, and therefore could not rely, on conscience, ego, or cognition; instead they used the old and universal method of *Pauken*, "drumming" facts and habits into the growing minds by relentless mechanical repetition. They also drummed the children themselves *mit Ruten in die Aefftern*, on the behind, other body parts being exempt.

According to the professor, an occasional "lusty caning" did not harm Martin any more than it did the other children: but the professor and his school must present Martin as entirely intact and unweakened by any ordinary or special childhood event, so that the divine event, the catastrophe, which later concluded his academic education so unexpectedly, appears as divine interference. The priest and the psychiatrist, however, make the most of Luther's statement, made in middle age, that the hell of school years can make a child fearful for life. In retrospect, Luther found that the gains in learning were in no way commensurate with the "inner torture." At the most, he felt, such teaching prepared a man to be a priest of low caliber, a *Pfaff;* otherwise he was not taught enough to "either cackle or lay an egg." Medically-minded biographers may go a bit too far in saying that Luther's nervous system was undermined in those days. It is certain, however, that the disciplinary climate of home and school, and the religious climate in community and church, were lumped together in his mind as decidedly more oppressive than inspiring; and that, to him, this seemed a damned and unnecessary shame. He blamed his atmosphere for his special monkishness, his intensity of monastic "scrupulosity," his obsessional preoccupation with the question of how on earth one may do enough to please the various agencies of judgment—teacher, father, superior, and most of all, one's conscience. But remember, he said all this after he had taken his vow and broken it in disgust.

School children, Luther reports, were caned on the behind; it is probable that home discipline was concentrated on the same body area. To those people who believe in corporal punishment, this seems to take the sting out of the matter, and even to make it rather funny. We grant that the buttocks can take a lot of pressure, and lend themselves to bawdy jokes; but we cannot ignore the fact, brought out by the researchers of psychoanalysis, that the anal zone which is guarded and fortified by the buttocks can, under selective and intense treatment of special kinds, become the seat of sensitive and sensual, defiant and stubborn, associations. The devil according to Luther, expresses his scorn by exposing his rear parts; man can beat him to it by employing anal weapons, and by telling him where his kiss is welcome. The importance of these ideas in Luther's imagery and vocabulary has been indicated; we will return to them.

In medieval schools the institution of the company spy or the office informer—today part of our adult life—was systematically developed among the children. One boy (you surely did not think girls learned Latin?) was secretly appointed *lupus* by the teacher. He marked down the names of those who spoke German, swore, or otherwise acted against the rules. At the end of the week the teacher applied one stroke for each point of bad behavior. Luther says he once received fifteen. Note the over-all injunction against verbal freedom: against speaking impulsively, or in German, or in the vernacular; and note also the occurrence of a judgment day at the end of each week when there was hell to pay for sins recorded on a secret ledger, sins committed so far in the past one might not even remember them. This temporal and relentless accumulation of known, half-known, or unrecognized sins was a sore subject in all of Luther's later life. He apparently associated it with another experience with temporal qualities—the experience of learning that nothing was ever good enough for teacher or father, and that any chance to please them seemed always remote, always removed by one more graduation in one more, one better, school.

We should mention in passing what Luther later did not find worth commenting on, namely, that in school he also learned choir singing and read some Latin authors. The students of Latin were required to sing in church and there can be little doubt that despite the clouds of mistrust which Luther preferred to remember so exclusively, there must have been moments and performances which permitted his inner treasure of vocabulary and melody to flower.

At fourteen Martin was sent to Magdeburg; he never cared to specify what school he attended there. Magdeburg must have impressed him: a city of about fifteen thousand inhabitants, bustling with continental commerce; clerical life there flourished quietly, except for occasional festivals and processions of combined patrician and churchly splendor. Martin spent only one year in Magdeburg; then his father sent him to Eisenach, further up the academic ladder and further out into the world of big city burghers.

But before the youngster left Magdeburg he had come in contact with those poorest of clerics, men who lived their religion, the *Nullbrueder*. Their name means Zero Brothers, and symbolizes the rockbottom which they were determined not to forget. These Brothers of the Common Life, as they were also called, did not teach children ordinary subjects. Rather, they had the permission of town and teachers to visit with or be visited by the children for purposes of *conversio*, for lessons in the *devotio moderna*. They seem to have given these children a pretty accurate taste of the kind of exhortation and introspection which characterizes monastic education; for they spoke to them of the tests of pure love, of the proper vigilance against sin, of the real turning away from this world. Most of all, as pietists they underscored the depth and purity of personal religious involvement, using such terms as *Gottinnigkeit* and *Herzgruendlichkeit*, which denote the mystical feeling of an innermost unity with God, down in the "bottom of your heart." These men, who in preceding years had had to struggle for permission to preach in Magdeburg, as if they were missionaries in a foreign land, seemed to know what they were talking about.

And in the middle of Magdeburg's proud Broadstreet, Martin also encountered one of the few thoroughly Catholic phenomena which in later years he spoke of with respect and reverence: "I saw with my own eyes a prince of Anhalt, a brother of the Bishop of Merseburg, walk and beg for bread on Broadstreet, with the skullcap of the order of the Barefeet, carrying like a donkey on his back a sack so heavy it bent him to the ground. He had so castigated himself by going without food and sleep that he looked like the picture of death, nothing but skin and bones. And, indeed, he died soon thereafter. . . . Whoever saw him could not help smacking his lips with reverence (*schmatzt vor Andacht*) and could not help being ashamed of his own worldly condition." [18]

No reason was ever given for Martin's transfer to Eisenach; Margareta Luder had family there, but this circumstance apparently proved quite irrelevant for Martin's social life in that city. But perhaps Martin's interest in the monastic phenomena encountered in Magdeburg was reason enough for his anxious father to send him into a more "healthy" milieu. Certainly Martin found this milieu in Eisenach. He came to know and to live in the home of some modest patricians, a family of Italian extraction named Cotta, and to be well acquainted with the Schalbe family. Legend has it that he found in Ursula Cotta a matronly friend who appreciated his musicality and piety, took pity on his homeless condition (for his relatives had not taken him in), and bestowed on him quite an active motherly interest, and maybe another kind of womanly feeling. To this purpose legend disposes of her husband, who, however, was well and about, and friendly to Martin. It is, at any rate, interesting to note this attempt to provide Martin with a second mother who is supposed to have recognized in the lonely boy the imaginative and musical capacities which he probably had been able to share with his embittered real mother, when he was only a small child. This legend also provides that immortal picture of the young Martin earning his bread by singing in the streets. But singing in the streets was for that era what working in the summer is for students in the United States today. Most do it, although only some really need it, and only a few of these desperately; some think it is a good thing for them to act as if they need it, and some come to like it as a historical ritual, a bow to the days of the pioneers. For others it is the only way out of spending the summer with their families. Whether or not Martin needed it more than others, he sang alongside those who needed it less, and he probably enjoyed it more. "Crumb-seekers," these students were called. As for their allegedly captive audience, a famous account has these "nervous" children disperse in terror at the sudden grunt in the dark of a manly voice; but the man who belonged to the voice was approaching with a gift of sausages.

At any rate, in the house of the Cottas Luther became acquainted with the life led by modest, pious, and musical patricians. In Eisenach, also, he met and became devoted to Vicar Brown, in whose house the cultivation of music joined with the humor and rhetoric of the Humanist tradition. When Martin was ordained as a priest a few years later, he invited Vicar Brown to the ceremony; in his letter (the earliest of his extant correspondence) he judged it too forward of him to invite the Cottas and the Schalbes: yet it is clear that he wished the Vicar would transmit the news. Whether or not any of the Eisenachers came is not known; and at any rate, Hans Luder monopolized the show.

Next we find Martin in college in Erfurt, at the age of seventeen. Needless to say, he had been a good student throughout his school years. What kind of boy was he, by then? This depends on what you intend to make of the sudden "conversion" which abruptly halted his academic career. It depends on how you have learned to simplify the extraordinary.

The Latin-schoolboy had a special status in the world of children. He wore a uniform which marked him as a future magistrate, academician, cleric, or privy-counselor—at any rate, one of the literate class who knows how things hang together in the stars and in the books. In his uniform (and neither schoolboy nor university student was permitted to appear in public in anything but a uniform), he naturally abstained from throwing snowballs; even ice-skating was not for him. It was a good uniform with which to express (and to hide) a precocious conscience. Beyond this, how much Martin was or was not one of those boys with thick hides who can adjust to any system, make the most of whatever status the system provides, and otherwise live by what they can get away with in the present and what they can hope to do to others in the future, is not known. Except for the one measly nut he had stolen earlier, we have no record that he indulged in those small physical, verbal, and moral explosions without which strictly-kept children rot inside. Rather, he was one of the best students all the way through; and there are indications that he did rot in a slow way, often sinking into a kind of sadness. This does not mean, however, that he did not maintain, up to the very gates of the monastery, the role of *guter Geselle*, a "good fellow," with its active good will in social and musical affairs.

With only this information, anybody can sketch his own Martin, and I have already indicated some of the sketches which have been made. Here is my version. I could not conceive of a young great man in the years before he becomes a great young man without assuming that inwardly he harbors a quite inarticulate stubbornness, a secret furious inviolacy, a gathering of impressions for eventual use within some as yet dormant new configuration of thought—that he is tenaciously waiting it out for a day of vengeance when the semideliberate straggler will suddenly be found at the helm, and he who took so much will reveal the whole extent of his potential mastery. The counterpart of this waiting, however, is often a fear of an early death which would keep the vengeance from ripening into leadership; yet the young man often shows signs of precocious aging, of a melancholy wish for an early end, as if the anticipation of prospective deeds tired him. Premonitions of death occur throughout Luther's career, but I think it would be too simple to ascribe them to a mere fear of death. A young genius has an implicit life plan to complete; caught by death before his time, he would be only a pathetic human fragment.

A good fellow tries to live to the full in historical reality, and to accept as his ideology the boisterous and snobbish ways of youth. Martin tried, but he did not succeed. He became burdened with that premature sense of judgment which wishes to receive and to render a total accounting of life before it is lived; one might say that he refused to begin life with an identity of his own before some judgment had been rendered on everything past which might prejudice his coming identity.

Like many an inhibited and deep-down sad youth, Martin utilized his musical gifts, his lute-playing and singing, to remain a welcome good fellow among a circle of friends. But he soon acquired the nickname of Philosophus. The professor thinks this was because Luther was so good in disputation; the psychiatrist, because he was so morbid in it. It is probable that the nickname referred to Martin's uncommon and probably heavy sincerity and his wish to find certainty in formulation—an attitude which was foreign to the elegant and logical scholastic attempts to reconcile Aristotelian physics and the Last Judgment. He was probably too much of a peasant in his intellectual heaviness, and also too much of a poet, for whom meaning and form and feeling must coincide.

I think that Martin was nicknamed Philosophus because the students felt, some with scorn, some with admiration, that here was one who meant it.

Erfurdia Turrita was a walled city of about twenty thousand, Germany's most populous, situated at an important crossing of international tradeways. Except for the patrician solidity of its center, it was undeveloped as far as city-planning goes; but it boasted a university with the largest student body in Germany, and with an academic standing rivaling Prague's. The best of its faculties was the School of Law. Hans Luder's fondest dream was that Martin should graduate from it.

In the university of Erfurt Martin continued to lead a rather regimented life. He made one or two good and life-long friends among his classmates, but otherwise in all probability he remained remote from the young people who led the free life, with its "scent of wine, beer, and wenches," as the psychiatrist puts it. Legend will have it that in Erfurt Luther joined the circle of freethinkers around Mutianus Rufus, the New Humanists; Mutianus is said to have influenced him greatly. However, the professor proves that this famous circle did not yet exist in Luther's student days. He plucks each petal of this alleged circle by showing that each of its future members was elsewhere at the time, and then disposes of the center by quoting a letter in which Mutianus asks a friend, ten years after Martin had left the college in Erfurt, who that fiery preacher in Wittenberg by the name of Luther was, anyway. At best (or at worst), then, Luther in his college days was exposed to unsystematic Humanist influences, especially through his highly gifted friend, Crotus Rubeanus. He may have found support for his musical gifts and for his interest in poetry; he did take Virgil and Plautus with him when he later entered the monastery. But if at this time this group believed in free love, in some unsystematic way, and if the belief happened to touch the student Martin, it could only have bewildered him; an invitation to sexual freedom can only aggravate an already present identity conflict. The New Humanism, then, at best reinforced Martin's avocations. It did not free in him either faith or rebellion; at the most, it contributed to his wish to seek silence.

To attend the university Martin was obliged to live in a "burse"— this means he lived in crowded quarters and under a discipline borrowed from the monastery. The students wore dignified uniforms of a semi-clerical design (albeit with a rapier on the side) and were strictly supervised; up at 4:00 a.m., to bed at 8:00 p.m. Lectures, seminars, and disputations were compulsory, and started at 6:00 a.m. in the summer and 7:00 a.m. in the winter. The food was good (Professor Scheel has found the menus) [19] and there was a light beer.

At the time of matriculation, each burse held a "deposition," a kind of initiation rite, during which the novice was dressed up as the beast that henceforth he was not to be. Pigs' teeth were stuck in the corners of his mouth and a hat with long ears and horns put on his head. This creature was demolished, not without roughness, and with it the novice's moral corruptibility. Dousing completed the "baptism." Then the academic identity was put on. In medieval ceremonialism, every estate had its uniform, which involved a definite status, not only in earthly functions, but in the whole divine system, from the center of which, in fact, emanated the only true identity-giving power. So there was fun in these initiations, and the usual awe-increasing cruelty; but there was also a sense of taking a step up in the divine scale. Here is what Luther himself said when, some years later, it was his turn to make deposition speeches. He made a play on "deposition," which means a turning away from, a renouncing of old ways, and the verb *deponere*, which equals our "taking somebody down": "Humble yourselves and learn patience, for you will be 'taken down' for the rest of your lives (*Ihr werdet Ewer Lebenlang deponiert werden*) by the town dwellers and by the country folk, by the noblemen and by your wives. . . . I started my deposition in Wittenberg [one of Luther's frequent retrospective mistakes] when I was young [*adolescens*]; now that I am heavier [*gravior*] I also suffer heavier depositions [*graviores depositiones*]. Thus, your deposition is only a symbol of human life.[20] . . . Therefore, obey your monitors [*monentibus*] and your praeceptors, honor the magistrates and the female sex, and *non in propatulo minguentes*—and those who do not piss in public." [21]

When Martin applied for the bachelor's degree a year and a half later, he swore to extensive reading in the following fields: grammar, logic, rhetoric, natural philosophy, spheric astronomy, philosophy, physics, and (last and least) psychology. The main authors were Priscian, Petrus Hispanus, and Aristotle and Aristotle and Aristotle: *Parva Logicalia, Priorum, Posteriorum, Elencorum, Physicorum, De Anima, Spera Materialis.*[22]

Two years later, Martin was ready for his Master's, having read, studied, and discussed more specialized works on the heavens (*De Caelo*), on growth and decay (*De Generatione et Corruptione*), on meteorology (*Metheororum*) and smaller works of Aristotle. To complete the seven free arts, Euclid's mathematics was added, as well as arithmetic (*De Muris*), the theory of music (an elective), and planimetry. A Master's sweep of subjects also included moral philosophy, metaphysics, "politics," and economics (*Yconomicorum*). At one time or another, Martin had also become more or less acquainted with Albertus Magnus, Thomas Aquinas, Averroes, Avicenna, Alfragan, and Sacrobosco.

So, young Luther knew a lot; he remained an Aristotelian for life, although as time went on he had fewer and fewer opportunities to refer to natural science. He began his teaching career as a "moral philosopher," and taught Aristotle for a whole year; this may surprise some readers as much as it surprises students of psychoanalysis when they hear of Freud's extensive publications in physiology, written before he turned to psychology. Physics, to Luther, continued to deal with the "motion of things," and philosophy with the laws deduced from *visibilibus et apparentibus*. But it is clear that in the world of Catholic dogma, as well as in Martin's superstitious mind, there was much, indeed, that was neither visible nor in any way apparent. In every seat of learning in Christendom the tenor of academic teaching depended on the kind of connection which the dominant philosophers cared to make, or were forced to make, between the scientific and the theological. Official teaching in Erfurt was pervaded with a particular academic ideology, the so-called Occamist version of Aristotelianism; and if we remember that Aristotle, before he fell into the hands of Occam, had already made the long trek from ancient Greece to and through the Islamic seats of learning, to and through the orbit of the Roman Church, we will not expect that his philosophy could contribute the unified world view, nor the unity of spiritual attitude that Martin sorely needed.

William Occam had been a rebel within the Church. He had dared to contradict the Pope on a matter always embarrassingly vital, which was kept alive by the memory of St. Francis and by the order of the Franciscans, of which Occam had been a member: he had supported the *Fraticelli*, men who claimed that St. Francis, and Christ before him, had denied private property to a Christian. Occam went to jail for his opinion, but found protection with a German prince, to whom he is supposed to have said, "You defend me with your sword and I will defend you with my pen." Thus there is much in Occam, more than would be appropriate to list at this point, that predicts Luther, although Occam never denied that divine truth was instituted in the Roman Church. His personality as well as his teachings have made it easy for Catholic detractors, who consider Occam the low point in medieval philosophy, to call Lutheranism nothing but a degeneration of Occamism. The fact is that a form of Occamism was dominant, not only in the university, but also in the Augustinian monastery of Erfurt.

There is no need at this point to discuss the place of Occamism in the broad development of Catholic theology and philosophy. It is important, however, to understand that it was the first academic-theological ism which engulfed Luther, and that this happened before he had the necessary intellectual equipment to see its relativities and interdependencies in the history of thought. Martin was then, as he remained later, a provincial in a grand style. He was apt to identify completely with a small human circle and with a vital set of local problems. When he later burst into universality, it was not on the basis of an extensive knowledge of the state of universal questions, but rather because he was able to experience what was immediately about him in new ways. By the same token, his immediate surroundings could increase his sadness and his wrath, as if they had been devised for his personal suffering. It is therefore necessary to try to understand the world image which was presented to Luther in Erfurt, and to understand what import this world image had for a young man who, because of his temperament and age, was in desperate need of deriving from what he was taught a meaning superior to the conflicting moods of living. At Erfurt he learned to master logic and rhetoric; he was also presented with certain basic facts of natural science, for some of the Occamists, especially in Paris, had done fundamental work in physics. But as far as an ideological unification between the nature of physical things and the nature of the supernatural was concerned, Martin was faced with the famous Occamist deadlock—the doctrine of the absolute mutual exclusion of knowledge and belief, philosophy and theology.

The universe taught to Martin by his teachers Usingen and Trutvetter in Erfurt, looked like this:

All is motion, for only through alteration by motion do potentialities become realities. The universe moves in ten orbits: the seven planetary orbits, the firmament of stars, the crystalline sky, the sphere of prime motion. Only the home of God, above it all, does not move.

The earth is in the center of this universe; but, alas, it is minute, not more than a point. It thus exists in a paradox as tantalizing as man's: although central, it is negligible; and man, seemingly so frightfully important to God, remains quite expendable.

All bodies are subject to irreversible laws of *Generatio* and *Corruptio*—but not God. He can resurrect what has died, and can, at less than a moment's notice, bring to an end all that lives.

Man, like all bodies, even angels, lives in a prison circumscribed by the laws of space and time. But God has a "repletive presence"; He exists wholly in one place and time, and equally wholly in all others. He can will Christ's total presence in any number of spaces, and at different times; this explains why the body of Christ is present in all hosts.

What can man will, then? Oh, everything—within the physical world. He realizes his *liberum arbitrium* in free decisions and in the vigorous development of his capacities. By making correct choices he acquires an inner *habitus* which disposes him toward good works and even to acts of love, and makes him recognize and like such works and acts. Yet all of this nowhere affects his status in the eyes of God. Through baptism and confession he can become pleasing to God and potentially acceptable; but God retains the *potentia absoluta*, the right to remain arbitrary in bestowing grace, and free *not* to honor the grace which he has already bestowed.

Thus God has created reason, and Aristotle. He even has made reason capable of recognizing its own limits and pitfalls. But reason can never hope to understand God; and Aristotle, while he knew everything, also knew nothing, for he knew not revelation. Whether or not God himself is reasonable, then, and whether he chooses to be lenient, or wishes to be reliable, are matters of belief and of obedience to faith; they will not be known until the end of the world, the moment when one comes to be judged.

In the age-old conflict between realism and nominalism, Occam had formulated a moderate nominalism. He taught that concepts are only symbols of things and exist only in the act of giving meaning, *in significando;* while things exist by themselves. This scepticism, however, was limited by the assurance that the intellect, if it could create things out of itself, would create a world just like the real one: for both ideas and things come from God and there is an exact correspondence between the number of ideas which God put in man's head and the number of things out of which he made the physical universe. Thus Aristotle could have his physical universe, and Plato his ideas, and God could have them both, mirroring each others' works—an ideal solution for the budding scientific mind which wished to experiment with things, but not a convincing solution for young minds who desperately wish to know how things and ideas, specifics and universals, earth and heaven, hang together. In other words, a very reasonable solution, but not an emotionally convincing one, especially for a young person in whom justification had become the core-problem: how to *know* when God justifies—and why.

Rationally speaking, one can well see why many honest minds were rather relieved to find declared as unthinkable that which could not be thought to a conclusion, and to have described as unapproachable a God whom previous philosophers had endowed with a most tortuous logic and a most ignoble willingness to make deals with clever sinners. This kind of candidness Luther later continued to maintain; in this regard he called Occam his master. On the other hand, the jigsaw puzzle of Aristotelian and Augustinian pieces which Luther received in college was incomplete and uncompletable. It permitted the new rationalists to have free reign with things; but it recommended blind faith to those who were seeking emotional and credal certainty. No wonder that one of Erfurt's most prominent teachers, Usingen, later concluded his academic career by entering the Augustinian monastery to which, by then, his pupil Luther had preceded him.

Some of Luther's detractors claim that Occamism is all that he learned in college, and that little else was added in the monastery, Luther was, they say, a pious Occamist in his docile years and not more than an anti-Occamist in his rebellion. But later as we will see, when Luther began to rebel, philosophical and theological concepts were to him only old baskets for new bread, the hot, crisp bread of original experience.

Nevertheless, it is true that the first discipline encountered by a young man is the one he must somehow identify with unless he chooses to remain unidentified in his years of need. The discipline he happens to encounter, however, may turn out to be poor ideological fare; poor in view of what, as an individual, he has not yet derived from his childhood problems, and poor in view of the irreversible decisions which begin to crowd in on him. Occamism was all that Martin had; those who mistrust the divine origin of the subsequent crisis in his life say it was bad for him. On the other hand, one can always say that anything that helped to make a great man was good for him and for the world. But perhaps history has abused this blank check.

3

In February, 1505, Martin had become *Magister Artium*, a Master of Arts; the second best student of seventeen. He later gratefully acknowledged the torchlight ceremonies which marked the occasion: "I still claim that no temporal worldly joy could equal it." Academically speaking, he could now join the faculty, lead disputations, become the master of a burse, and eventually a dean. Most important, he was now free to embark on his father's dream, the study of the law in the best of law schools. His father presented him with a copy of the *Codex Juris Civilis*, and began to address him with the respectful *Ihr* (you) instead of the intimate *Du* (thou). (*Sie* was not as yet in use.) The father also lost no time in looking around for a suitable bride, "honorable" enough, and "of means." From the end of April to the end of May, when the law semester started, Martin had several weeks of waiting on his hands. During this time something happened to him: his sadness reached a degree which called for some kind of decision. Some biographers have explained it by citing the death of a good friend by violence; others have said that the plague killed two of his brothers during this period. But the friend was not a close one, and he died from an illness; and the brothers died later, though at an equally significant time. Once again, however, the legends contain a truth: Martin seems to have brooded over the question of death and the last judgment. It is quite likely that his ruminations were intensified by sexual temptations in this period of lessened pressure of work.

There is nothing to indicate, however, that Martin did not apply himself fully to his studies when the semester started. Yet in the middle of it he asked for the quite unusual permission to take a short leave. He went home. Nobody seems to know what happened there. But it stands to reason that Hans demanded an accounting. Some think that Martin objected to the study of law, and may even have mentioned the monastery as a possible career. Others deny this, because it would negate the assumption that the subsequent decision to enter the monastery came as if from without and suddenly, by way of a divine "catastrophe." Luther, years later, reminded Hans of some remarks, made at an unspecified time, to the effect that the father had declared his son not to be cut out for monastic life.[23] I cannot find a better time when this could have been said than on the occasion of that impulsive visit home, and particularly in connection with the father's plans for the son's early and prosperous marriage. If Martin was already thinking or talking of the monastery, then there would have been an open clash of wills, which would provide a simple explanation for the break which was to occur. On the other hand, Martin must be assumed to have been at the time in the throes of a conflict which (as we will explain in the next chapter) must have made the idea of a marital commitment repugnant to the point of open panic. Again, we do not know whether this feeling was transmitted to the father; but we do know that the son, when he did marry twenty years later, having in the meantime taken the vows of celibacy, broken with the Church, and set fire to the world around him, publicly proclaimed as his first and foremost reason for taking a wife that it would please his father.

At the end of June Martin set out to wander back to college. On July 2nd, only a few hours from Erfurt, near the village of Stotternheim, he was surprised by a severe thunderstorm. A bolt of lightning struck the ground near him, perhaps threw him to the ground, and caused him to be seized by a severe, some say convulsive, state of terror. He felt, as he put it later, *terrore et agonis mortis subitae circumvallatus*:[24] as if completely walled in by the painful fear of a sudden death. Before he knew it, he had called out, "Help me, St. Anne . . . I want to become a monk." On his return to Erfurt, he told his friends that he felt committed to enter a monastery. He did not inform his father.

Nobody, of course, had heard him say the fateful words. He himself had experienced them as imposed on him (*drungen und gezwungen, coactum et necessarium*).[25] In fact, he had felt immediately afterwards that he did not really want to become a monk (*Ich bin nicht gern ein munch Geworden*).[26] Yet he felt bound by what he considered to be a vow and began to think of the experience as a frightful call from heaven: *de caelo terroribus*. As for his automatic response, if indeed it was a vow at all, it was a highly ambivalent one. For he had called on his father's patron saint, with the intent to disobey his father; to the saint who prevents sudden death, with a promise to enter the profession which prepares for death; to the saint who makes one rich, with a wish for lifelong poverty. These and many more ambivalences crowded into this moment. According to his own report it is even questionable that his declaration of intent or wish really amounted to a vow to become a monk; he simply told St. Anne that he wanted to become one, and asked for her help. Was it his idea that she might intercede with the father? In the moment of supreme terror, did he indulge in an appeal to a motherly mediator?

Martin debated the matter with some friends, who were divided in their opinions about the binding quality of his experience. On July 17, 1505, he knocked on the door of the Augustinian Eremites in Erfurt and asked for admission. This was granted, as usual, for a provisional period. Only from behind the walls of the monastery did he write to his father.

Was this thunderstorm necessary? The professor believes that it was God's way of calling Martin away (*abgerufen*) from a glamorous career which the young man had every reason to desire. The psychiatrist assumes that the event was only the climax of an agitated depressive state which gradually had ruined the perspective of that career. The priest, however, sees the experience as a somewhat phony device to muscle into the monastic profession; the Augustinians should have known better than to fall for it.

A student of motivation cannot well ask what motivates God to do something extraordinary; yet he may wonder what, in Martin's world, would at that moment call for an un-Aristotelian thunderstorm. The monastic profession was not an uncommon career; it was even (especially for a man of Luther's academic training) a respectable way of becoming a scholar and of eventually rejoining academic work. There must have been nearly as many priests, monks, and nuns in Erfurt as there were professors and students. The city area included, besides the Augustinians, a Benedictine, a Dominican, a Carthusian, and a Cistercian monastery. To join, Martin had only to walk a block or two from the burse of St. George where he then lived and knock on a garden door. The Augustinian was an order which sought to combine strict monastic observances with geographic closeness to centers of educational and of philanthropic need. Academically, the Augustinian monks were highly regarded; socially, they were representative of the upper and middle classes. God, it would seem, would not have had to use extraordinary means to get a monastic career launched under such conditions.

St. Paul's conversion, to which Luther's was soon to be compared, was a different matter. He was anything but a young and provincial person. Of cosmopolitan origin, he was in public life. He was not a Christian. In fact, as deputy prosecutor for the high priest's office, he was actively engaged (and engaged fully: "breathing out threatenings and slaughter") in the mission of arresting the Damascan followers of Christ. His conversion on the way to Damascus was not only immediately certified as being of apostolic dimension by God's independent message to Ananias; it also immediately became equivalent to a political act, for Paul, the prosecutor, took sides with the defendants whom he was committed to bring to justice. It was a heroic conversion.

The "conversion" of the young man in sober Saxony was anything but heroic. It committed him to being *monos*, a professional monk among many, in an honored and thriving institution. The promises of celibacy and obedience made at that time in his life can be said to have relieved him of burdens which he was not ready to assume. The one act of heroism possible in his life-situation was, in fact, circumvented: he did not go and face his father.

There is one similarity between Luther's experience and St. Paul's which can be formulated only by somewhat stretching a point. The two men, at the time of their conversions, were both engaged in the law, one as an advanced functionary responsible to the high priest, the other as a student owing obedience to the father. Both, through their conversion, received the message that there is a higher obedience than "the law," in either of these connotations, and that this obedience brooks no delay. (This broadened interpretation of the term "law" will make more sense when we discuss the theological connotation of law as against faith in the teachings of both men.)

The dissimilarities of their conversions, however, are more significant. Both men were shaken by an attack involving both body and psyche; they were, in fact, "thrown to the ground" in more or less pathological states. Paul's reported symptoms definitely suggest the syndrome of epilepsy. They both claimed that by a kind of shock therapy, God had "changed their minds." [27] In Paul's attack, which was witnessed by others, Christ himself spoke, implying that, at least unconsciously, Paul had been prepared for a change of mind: "It is hard for thee to kick against the pricks"; in Paul's case it is clear by recorded testimony what the witnesses did and did not see or hear (Acts, 9:7 and 22:9). For Martin, however, the spiritual part of the experience was an intra-psychic one. Not only were there no witnesses; but, most important, Luther himself never claimed to have seen or heard anything supernatural. He only records that *something in him* made him pronounce a vow before the *rest of him* knew what he was saying. His friends' conviction that he was acting under God's guidance was based on nothing but their impressions of the genuineness of his inner life. We must say, therefore, that while Paul's experience must remain in the twilight of biblical psychology, Martin can claim for his conversion only ordinary psychological attributes, except for his professed conviction that it was God who had directed an otherwise ordinary thunderstorm straight toward him. We are not in the least emphasizing the purely psychological character of the matter in order to belittle it: Martin's limited claims, coupled with a conviction which he carried to the bitter end, show him to be an honest member of a different era.

There remains one motive which God and Martin shared at this time: the need for God to match Hans, within Martin, so that Martin would be able to disobey Hans and shift the whole matter of obedience and disavowal to a higher, and historically significant, plane. It was necessary that an experience occur which would con-

vincingly qualify as being both exterior and superior, so that either
Hans would feel compelled to let his son go (and that, remember,
he never could and never would do) or that the son would be able
to forswear the father and fatherhood. For the final vow would
imply both that Martin was another Father's servant, and that he
would never become the father of Hans' grandsons. Ordination
would bestow on the son the ceremonial functions of a spiritual
father, a guardian of souls and a guide to eternity, and relegate the
natural father to a merely physical and legal status. But as we will
see—and this disrespectful phrase is entirely in order here—all hell
broke loose after that ordination.

Hans, of course, sensed all this and refused to be matched. Let
us be blunt and say he was not going to be cheated out of his dearest
investment; for he already represented that capitalistic trend in
Germany which was beginning to doubt that the Church's monopoly on the other world justified her voracity about fertile lands,
rich taxes, and gifted people. He could not foresee that his son
would one day take leadership in these matters and arrange for the
Wittenberg tea party.

The father refused permission even for that one year of probation,
which is all the Augustinian order bargained for at first. He went
almost mad (*wollte toll werden*) and refused all fatherly good will
(*allen Gonst und Veterlichen Willen*). The mother, too, and her
family, obediently swore the son off. This was gruesome enough.
But then, "pestilence came to Martin's help," as the theological
biographers put it. Two of Martin's brothers died. Martin's friends
used this circumstance, with somewhat horrible logic, to convince
Hans that he should give his oldest son to God as well. What the
mother said at that point is not recorded. So Hans consented—
which the professor thinks, "could suffice" for Martin.[28] But Martin
was not one to take half a yes for an answer. He knew well enough
that the father had consented in a state of mourning (with *ein un-
willigen traurigen Willen*) and certainly without that total good will
(that *gantzen Willen*) which was to become such a fateful concept
in Martin's scruples and ruminations, and eventually also in his
theological thought. The father did not mean it; and for better or
for worse, Martin later became the man who gave conscience that
new dimension of credal explicitness, of "meaning it."

But did Martin, at this point, really mean it himself? Some biographers believe Luther to have been theologically sincere in this experience; others believe him to have been sincerely deluded; again, others think, with Hans, that there was an element of insincerity, or, at any rate, of rebellious impulsiveness in it all—for this is what Hans must have had in mind when he later said that that bolt of lightning may have emanated from a "*Gespenst*," a ghost. I would agree a little with each of these formulations, and entirely with none. I think of the young Sioux Indians who went out into the prairie for a vision quest, dreamed in a state of ascetic trance the kind of dream which they knew was required, and after having convinced their tribal experts of the genuineness of the dream lived out with full assurance whatever career the dream had ordered them to follow—even if this career called for severe self-humiliation, or on occasion, suicide. Were they sincere? I think of the old Yurok woman who gave me the account, reported in *Childhood and Society*, of her call at the age of seventeen to the profession of shaman. She had a series of deeply disconcerting and obviously hysterical upsets and frightening dreams, all of a prescribed content, destining her against her wish and conscious will to become an honored and effective tribal doctor. Was she sincere? But what are we to think of the sincerity of the young Chinese men and women of today—heirs of an old ideology of ancestor worship—who must publicly and convincingly denounce their fathers as reactionaries, after a course of indoctrination during which their sincerity is constantly challenged and narrowed down to the proper criteria for really meaning their new devotion to "The People's Will"? [29] Are they sincere?

These and other questions concerning conversions and indoctrinations in young adulthood call for a special, an intermediary chapter in which we can formulate our psychological stand. All these experiences are at least convincing in their total psychological involvement—whether one calls it inspiration or temporarily abnormal behavior—in that they give a decisive inner push to a young person's search for an identity within a given cultural system, which provides a strong ideological pull in the same direction.

We are asking questions for which we are not yet ready. Nevertheless, it is possible to place Luther's experience in a sociological context. A struggle between God and a father for the son's allegiance was to some extent a typical event in Martin's day. Erasmus, Luther's cosmopolitan counterplayer, defied his father. And Calvin (in some ways Luther's Paul) reports his struggle thus: "My father had destined me for theology when I was still a small boy. But when he saw that legal knowledge everywhere enriched those who cultivated it, he was induced by this hope suddenly to change his intentions. Thus it was brought about that I was recalled from the study of philosophy to the learning of law; but although in obedience to my father I tried to give it my faithful attention, God guided my course by the secret bridle of his providence in another direction." [30]

For the present, let us conclude with the summary account which Luther, years later, gave of his conversion: "When I was a young magister in Erfurt, verily, I used to go around in sadness, oppressed by the *tentatio tristitiae*. But God acted in a miraculous way and drove me on, innocent as I was; and He alone, then, can be said to have come a long way [in bringing it about] that there can be no dealing between the Pope and me." [31] Here all the elements of the experience are condensed in two sentences: a special mental state bordering on the pathological; the juxtaposition of God's deliberate interference and Martin's innocent passivity; and the whole extent of God's plan which, theologically and teleologically speaking, made the thunderstorm necessary, that is, the rift between Luther and the Pope. The conversion was necessary so that Martin could give all his power of obedience to God, and turn all his venom of defiance against the Pope. For this purpose, then, a moratorium was also necessary to provide time and a seemingly wrong direction, so that Martin (as Luther put it later) could really learn to know his true historical enemy, and learn to hate him effectively.

We must concede entirely that Luther, when he entered the monastery, had no inkling of the particular role which he was to play in religious history. On the one hand, he was in search of a highest good. As Nietzsche put it: "Luther wanted to speak to God directly, speak as himself, and without embarrassment." [32] But in theology he also found that great and shiny evil which was powerful enough (as only the white whale was shiny and powerful enough for Captain Ahab) to draw upon itself the wrath that was in this mutilated soul. That evil was the Roman papacy.

CHAPTER

IV

Allness or Nothingness

MARTIN at this point was not yet a professional religionist. He was still an ordinary, if educated, young man. Even his educated status he was about to forfeit in principle; for in entering the hostel between the outer and the inner wall of the monastery, he renounced the educational distinction which he had earned on the outside. And were he to be admitted to the inside, he could have no assurance that he would be able to continue his career as an intellectual. The guardians of the order would be obliged first to disabuse him of any idea he might have that worldly distinction could penetrate the threshold of the cloister. It can be assumed that the Erfurt Augustinians, belonging to the stricter congregation of the observant orders of Saxony, were somewhat more determined to make this clear than many other orders which had become repositories for the supernumerary sons of the German nobility, or retreats for scholasticists. On the other hand, these guardians were in all probability quite unimpressed with the story of the thunderstorm, although later, when they knew Martin better, some of them were obliged to recognize the sincerity of a call in him, or, at any rate, the eeriness of an uncommon motivation. Now, however, there was no rushing, but rather a cautious playing for time and for a search for clues to the applicant's spiritual and mental state.

So, he was less than somebody in any category; he was more nobody than at any other time. And in the anonymous period immediately ahead of him he found decided happiness—for a while. This may seem rather understandable to those who see Luther either as a bland young man and gifted good fellow under God's orders to proceed as told, or as a very sick young man in search of a spiritual hospital for lack of a mental one. Our own sense of the inner economy of a man, however, insists that in this interim, this quiet before the real storm, we must account as well as we can for some of the psychological problems inherent in the historical fact that this same young man, only a decade later, emerged as his time's greatest orator, publicist, showman, and spiritual dictator. We can only account for this fact by assuming a fierce, if as yet quite dumb, struggle in him between destructive and constructive forces, and between regressive and progressive alternatives—all in balance at this time.

Before we leave his childhood behind, therefore, I will discuss here, in an intermediary chapter, the dimensions of identity diffusion. This will lead us to a few common denominators and in fact, the lowest ones, present in this young great man and in other young men in history and in case histories. The base line to which we hold at the beginning of this chapter may at times seem all too base, especially to readers who are not familiar with the developments to be reported in the second half of this book: the deep personal regression which accompanied Martin's progress into manhood and into theology; and the forces of wrath which he unleashed even as he freed new voices of faith. The story of the fit in the choir has prepared us for the pathological dimension in the spiritual struggle to come. We shall enlarge on this dimension in the direction of *desperate patienthood* and then in that of *fanatic leadership;* and finally, discuss a theme which these two conditions have in common: *childhood lost.*

It is probable that in all historical periods some—and by no means the least gifted—young people do not survive their moratorium; they seek death or oblivion, or die in spirit. Martin must have seen such death of mind and spirit in some of his brethren, and came to feel close to it more than once. Those who face the abyss only to disappear we will, of course, never know; and once in a while we should shed a tear for those who took some unborn protest, some unformed idea, and sometimes just one lonely soul, with them. They chose to face nothingness rather than to submit to a faith that, to them, had become a cant of pious words; a collective will, that cloaked only collective impotence; a conscience which expended itself in a stickling for empty forms; a reason that was a chatter of commonplaces; and a kind of work that was meaningless busy-work. I am speaking of those "outsiders" who go their lone way, not those who come back to poison the world further with a mystical literature which exhorts man to shun reality and stay outside, like Onan.

Some today seek psychiatric help—strange young creatures of pride and despair, of sick minds and good values, of good minds and fractured perspectives. Often, of course, therapists can only note that their pride in not having wanted to adjust is a cover up for not having been able to do so from way back. But not always, by any means. Sometimes a fierce pride of long standing can be detected which makes it very hard to decide whether the inability to adjust to a given available environment, with the means demanded by that environment, had not also meant an unwillingness to forgo the nourishment of latent needs deeply felt to be essential to the true development of an identity. The therapeutic problem in such cases transcends the questions of what environment a young person should have adjusted to and why he was not able to do so, and rather concerns a delineation of those means of adaptation which the patient can afford to employ without losing an inner coherence. Once he knows his cure and his goal, he must become well enough to make the "environment" adapt to him—an intrinsic part of human adaptation which has been lost sight of in popularized versions of Darwinian and Freudian imagery.

The fact that psychiatric treatment today has become a sanctioned form of moratorium in some countries and classes does not mean, of course, that the diagnoses which go with the treatment exhaust the problem at hand. On the contrary; the diagnoses merely serve to circumscribe the existing dangers of malignancy and to point up warning signals not to be taken lightly under any circumstances. But we are concerned in this book with a general delineation of a life crisis, a delineation which is indispensable to the search for avenues of therapy, and for an understanding of the ego's task at the height of youth.

That extreme form of identity diffusion which leads to significant arrest and regression is characterized most of all by a mistrustful difficulty with mere living in time. Time is made to stand still by the device of ignoring the usual alternation of day and night, of more active and less active periods, of periods given more to work and talk with other people, and of those given over to isolation, rumination, and musical receivership. There also may be a general slowing up that can verge on catatonic states. It is as if the young person were waiting for some event, or some person, to sweep him out of this state by promising him, instead of the reassuring routine and practice of most men's time, a vast utopian view that would make the very disposition of time worthwhile. Unless recruited outright, however, by an ideological movement in need of needy youths, such an individual cannot sustain any one utopian view for long. Martin was recruited into a system rigidly regimenting time; we will see what he did with this utopia.

There is, of course, also a tortuous self-consciousness, characterized at one time by shame over what one is already sure one is, and at another time by doubt as to what one may become. A person with this self-consciousness often cannot work, not because he is not gifted and adept, but because his standards preclude any approach that does not lead to being outstanding; while at the same time these standards do not permit him to compete, to defeat others. He thus is excluded from apprenticeships and discipleships which define duties, sanction competition and, as it were, provide a status of moratorium. For these reasons Martin had not been able to continue his studies, although his later capacity for work was, most of the time, phenomenal.

Most of all, this kind of person must shy away from intimacy. Any physical closeness, with either sex, arouses at the same time both an impulse to merge with the other person and a fear of losing autonomy and individuation. In fact, there is a sense of bisexual diffusion which makes such a young person unsure about how to touch another person sexually or affectionately. The contrast between the exalted sexual fusion of his autoerotic dreams and the complete sense of isolation in the presence of the other sex is catastrophic. Here again, whatever sexual moratorium the society's mores offer most young people in a given setting cannot be shared by the patient, whether it is determined abstinence, sexual play without genital encounter, or genital engagement without affection or responsibility.

We know nothing about Martin's relations to girls before he entered the monastery, but we do have hints of autoerotic scruples.

which returned later much intensified. We know also that his father wanted him to marry early; and it is quite probable that it was this double commitment to career and marriage which Martin had to escape at all cost. Music, at such times, can be a very important means of socializing and yet of communing with one's emotions: and Martin was a master in using music as a bridge to others, and also as a means of creating distance.

Finally, the use of sharp repudiation, so eagerly indulged in by intolerant youth in an effort to bolster its collective identity with a harsh denunciation of some other "kind," be it on a religious, racial, or social basis, is blunted in such a person. He alternates between extreme self-repudiation and a snobbish disdain for all groups—except perhaps, for memberships whose true roots and obligations are completely outside his reach. One thinks of the "classical" yearnings of young Europeans or of the appeal which foreign totalitarian parties have for some young Americans, as do the lofty teachings of Eastern mystics. Here the need to search for total and final values can often be met only under the condition that these values be foreign to everything one has been taught; we have already indicated that Martin's very participation in a most traditional monasticism ran counter to his father's secular aspirations. We will call all self-images, even those of a highly idealistic nature, which are diametrically opposed to the dominant values of an individual's upbringing, parts of a *negative identity*—meaning an identity which he has been warned *not* to become, which he can become only with a divided heart, but which he nevertheless finds himself compelled to become, protesting his wholeheartedness. Obviously such rebellion can serve high adventure, and when joined to a great collective trend of rebellion (as happened with Martin) can rejuvenate as it repudiates. In malignant cases, however, the search for a negative identity soon exhausts social resources; in fact, no rebellious movement, not even a self-respecting delinquent gang, would consider taking such an individual as a member. For he rebels and surrenders on the spur of the moment, and cannot be relied on to be honestly asocial unto death.

When such young people become patients, they illustrate the depth of regression which can ensue from an identity-crisis, either because the identity-elements they were offered as children were not coherent—so that one may speak of a defect in this connection

—or because they face a perplexing set of present circumstances which amounts to an acute state of ideological undernourishment. The most dramatic characteristic of work with such patients is their tendency to make intense and yet contradictory demands of the psychotherapist. In this they truly regress; for either openly or covertly they expect from the therapist the kind of omniscience an infant attributes to his mother when he seems to assume that she should have prevented the table from hitting him, or at any rate from being hard and sharp; or that she should be able to hold him firmly and to let him go freely at the same time, that is, at a time when he himself does not know which he wants. But even the paradoxical form which the patient's demands, to his own chagrin, can take concerns his very essence as an individual. He wants to have the right to act like nobody, and yet to be treated as quite a somebody; he wants to fuse with the therapist in order to derive from him everything the parents were or are not; yet he is afraid to be devoured by an identification with the therapist. The outstanding quality of these patients is *totalism*, a to be or not to be which makes every matter of differences a matter of mutually exclusive essences; every question mark a matter of forfeited existence; every error or oversight, eternal treason. All of this narrows down to something like Jacob's struggle with the angel, a wrestling for a benediction which is to lead to the patient's conviction that he is an alive person, and, as such, has a life before him, and a right to it. For less, such patients will not settle. I have called this the "rock-bottom" attitude, and explained it as the sign of a perverted and precocious integrity, an attempt to find that immutable bedrock on which the struggle for a new existence can safely begin and be assured of a future. The patient desperately demands that the psychotherapist become for him as immediate and as close, as exclusive and as circumspect, as generous and as self-denying, a counterplayer as only a mother of an infant child can be. It is clear that these patients want to be reborn in identity and to have another chance at becoming once-born, but this time on their own terms. Needless to say, we can offer the patient nothing but our willingness to jointly face the odds that are the lot of all of us.

Where so-called schizophrenic processes take over, the rock-bottom attitude is expressed in a strange evolutionary imagery. Total feeling becomes dehumanized, and eventually even de-mammalized. These patients can feel like a crab or a shellfish or a mollusk, or even abandon what life and movement there is on the lowest animal level and become a lonely twisted tree on the ledge of a stormy rock, or the rock, or just the ledge out in nowhere. I must leave the psychiatric discussion of this to another publication; here it suffices to say, that at no other time in life can severe regression to a play with nothingness appear in such systematized form, and yet be, as it were, experimental, an adventure in reaching inner rock bottom to find something firm to stand on. Here the therapist cannot be optimistic enough about the possibility of making contact with the patient's untapped inner resources; on the other hand, it is also true that he cannot be pessimistic enough in the sustained apprehension that a mishap might cause the patient to remain at the rock bottom, and deplete the energy available for his re-emergence.

Other patients cling to a make-believe order of compulsive scrupulosity and of obsessive rumination. They insist on what seems like almost mock order for the world of man, a caricature of logic and consistency; Martin is a classical example of this. The eyes of such young people are often lifeless and out of contact; then they suddenly scan your face for its sincerity or even its mere presence; these patients, who according to popular judgment could be said to be "not quite there" most of the time, are all too suddenly and flamingly there. They can appear as remote, as lifeless, as impenetrable, as they say they feel; and yet, there are those moments of mutual recognition when they do seem to trust themselves and you, and when their smile can be as totally present and rewarding as only an infant's first smiles of seeming recognition. But at this point the struggle just begins—as, indeed, does the infant's.

In this brief and impressionistic picture I have, for the sake of their common symptoms, lumped together men of different times and of different type, not hesitating to prejudice the case for the great young man to whom this book is devoted. But I wonder whether many readers will have read this account without having a sense of recognition. Either they themselves have felt and acted like this at one time, or they have been such a person's counter-player: his parent or teacher, his friend or young spouse. Perhaps this recognition will help us to know Martin better and marvel the more at his self-transcendance.

2

Centuries later, there appeared in Germany another young man who radically underbid Martin in his choice of temporary Nothingness; a young man who likewise re-emerged from his moratorium as a leader of the German nation, matching Luther little in constructiveness, and outdoing him totally in systematic political destructiveness. This man, of course, was Adolf Hitler. Of his childhood we know little beyond that which he offered the world as part of his propagandistic autobiography. Let us now see what kind of a young man he was.

Young Adolf, so the only friend of his youth, August Kubizek, reports [1] was also subject to an occasional "good hiding" by his father, who combined the petty authoritarianism of a small official with a general shiftlessness and an inclination toward adultery, alcohol, and brutality—that is, at home, where he could afford it. This father, himself the illegitimate son of a poor servant girl, was determined to make a civil servant out of the son, obviously with the implication that he should climb to the top in this narrow hierarchy. But Adolf would have none of it, as he repeats with the stubborn monotony of a propaganda drum in *Mein Kampf*. His friend says he never spoke disrespectfully of this father; but he went his own way, which was at least negatively defined by the conviction that no school or occupation within the system could contain him. On the positive side, there was a strange preoccupation:

When Adolf and I strolled through the familiar streets of the good, old town [Linz, Austria]—all peace, quiet and harmony—my friend would sometimes be taken by a certain mood and begin to change everything he saw. That house there was in a wrong position; it would have to be demolished. There was an empty plot which could be built up instead. That street needed a correction in order to give a more compact impression. Away with this horrible, completely bungled tenement block! Let's have a free vista to the Castle. Thus he was always rebuilding the town. . . . [2] He gave his whole self to his imaginary building and was completely carried away by it. Once he had conceived an idea he was like one possessed. Nothing else existed for him—he was oblivious to time, sleep and hunger. . . . He could never walk through the streets without being provoked by what he saw. Usually he carried around in his head, at the same time, half a dozen different building projects, and sometimes I could not help feeling that all the buildings of the town were lined up in his brain like a giant panorama. . . . He felt responsible for everything that was being built. I often got confused and could not distinguish whether he was talking about a building that existed or one that was to be created. But to him it did not make any difference; the actual construction was only a matter of secondary importance. . . . The old theatre was inadequate in every respect, and some art lovers in Linz had founded a Society to promote the construction of a modern theatre. Adolf immediately joined this society and took part in a competition for ideas. He worked for months on his plans and drafts and was seriously convinced that his suggestions would be accepted. His anger was beyond measure when the Society smashed all his hopes by giving up the idea of a new building and, instead, had the old one renovated.[3]

Outwardly, this seeking for a new path showed itself in dangerous fits of depression. I knew only too well those moods of his, which were in sharp contrast to his ecstatic dedication and activity, and realized that I couldn't help him. At such times he was inaccessible, uncommunicative and distant. It might happen that we didn't meet at all for a day or two. If I tried to see him at home, his mother would receive me with great surprise. "Adolf has gone out," she would say, "he must be looking for you." Actually, Adolf would wander around aimlessly and alone for days and nights in the fields and forests surrounding the town. When I met him at last, he was obviously glad to have me with him. But when I asked him what was wrong, his only answer would be, "Leave me alone," or a brusque, "I don't know myself." [4]

The two friends later moved to Vienna, where Adolf failed to be accepted either in art school or in the school of architecture. But he soon began to "rebuild the Hofburg," the castle of the Austrian emperors, and conceived large-scale plans for workers' houses, meanwhile exhorting his friend, his "one audience" (as Freud called Fliess) first with Wagnerian, then with socialist, and finally with anti-Semitic, harangues.

But suddenly, *he disappeared*. His last letter to Kubizek makes violent fun of the opera-house commission of Linz. He was then nineteen. In his abject poverty, he must have lived in the lowliest hostels for migrants and bums. At any rate, he shunned his family and Kubizek.

About his emergence, decades later, as an ex-corporal and ex-war-neurotic of the German Army, a revolutionary and avenger, and eventually a dictator, Kubizek has only this to say:

What the fifteen-year-old planned, the fifty-year-old carried out, often, as for instance in the case of the new bridge over the Danube, as faithfully as though only a few weeks, instead of decades, lay between planning and execution. The plan existed; then came influence and power and the plan became reality. This happened with uncanny regularity as though the fifteen-year-old had taken it for granted that one day he would possess the necessary power and means. Indeed, the plans which that unknown boy had drawn up for the rebuilding of his home town, Linz, are identical to the last detail with the Town Planning Scheme which was inaugurated after 1938.[5]

Kubizek's memoirs concerned the young Hitler. The aging one, according to H. R. Trevor-Roper,[6] having laid waste to half of Europe,

dreamed of an elegant retirement in Linz. While Germany was crumbling in ruins, he occupied himself with ever more elaborate architectural plans. He was not (as his enemies said) redesigning Buckingham Palace for his own use; he was envisaging a new opera-house and a new picture gallery for Linz.

But when the end was close and certain, the builder turned into a fanatic destroyer. As his most beloved and most gifted protégé, Speer (himself an architect and then in charge of German war industry) put it:

He was deliberately attempting to let the people perish with himself. He no longer knew any moral boundaries; a man to whom the end of his own life meant the end of everything.[7]

Speer quickly sabotaged Hitler's orders for the destruction of German industry, a piece of high treason for which Hitler forgave him with a tear a few days before he killed himself. Speer concludes:

I suspect that he was not happy with his "mission"; that he would rather have been an architect than a politician. He often clearly expressed his aversion from politics, and even more from military matters. He disclosed his intention of withdrawing after the war from state affairs, to build himself a large house in Linz, and there to end his days. . . . He would then be soon forgotten and left to himself. . . . Apart from Fräulein Braun he would take no one with him. . . . Such were Hitler's day dreams in 1939.[8]

And Trevor-Roper reports that in 1945, when he visited Hitler's Berlin bunker, the last headquarters of the Third Reich and the scene of Hitler's suicide, he found one room still full of illustrated books on opera-house architecture.[9]

This account illustrates the eerie balance between destructiveness and constructiveness, between suicidal Nothingness and dictatorial Allness, in a young man who at fifteen "felt responsible for everything that was being built," that is, was dominated by an overweening conscience and a kind of premature integrity such as characterizes all ideological leaders; he had selected, with deadly obsessiveness, *his* medium of salvation: architecture. Maybe, maybe, if he had been permitted to build, he would not have destroyed. Many a delinquency, on a smaller scale, begins by society's denial of the one gift on which a destructive individual's precarious identity depends —for instance, Prew's bugle in *From Here to Eternity*. But in the end, Linz and history had to be rebuilt together; and indeed, shortly after World War II had broken out, Hitler ordered the rebuilding of Linz to begin. Now and again, history does seem to permit a man the joint fulfillment of national hopes and of his own provincial and personal strivings.

I will not go into the symbolism of Hitler's urge to build except to say that his shiftless and brutal father had consistently denied the mother a steady residence; one must read how Adolf took care of his mother when she wasted away from breast cancer to get an inkling of this young man's desperate urge to cure. But it would take a very extensive analysis, indeed, to indicate in what way a single boy can daydream his way into history and emerge a sinister genius, and how a whole nation becomes ready to accept the emotive power of that genius as a hope of fulfillment for its national aspirations and as a warrant for national criminality.

Demolishing and rebuilding real houses and cities was the original obsession of this man, outlasting the most systematic destruction of men and values. One would like to believe that great men of other, more "abstract" aspirations—in science or theology, say—are totally removed from any comparison with men of political and of destructive military action. While we learn to mistrust power seekers, we glorify men of science, determined to consider their role in making machines of destruction possible as a historical accident which they surely did not desire when they directed their genius to the mastery of physical forces. However, if one scans the whole period of nationalism and invention which Luther helped to herald and which Hitler helped to bring to its global crisis, one may well want to reconsider the relationship between the will to master totally, in any form, and the will to destroy. Leonardo, the creator of the immortal da Vincian smile, was also an inveterate tinkerer with war machines; on occasion he caught himself, and relegated a design to the bottom of a deep drawer. Today, however, only large-scale reconsideration of conscious aims and unconscious motives can help us.

The memoirs of young Hitler's friend indicate an almost pitiful fear on the part of the future dictator that he might be nothing. He had to challenge this possibility by being deliberately and totally anonymous; and only out of this self-chosen nothingness could he become everything. Allness or nothingness, then, is the motto of such men; but what specific gifts and what extraordinary opportunities permit them to impose this alternative on whole nations and periods—of this we know little.

Hitler was a totalitarian leader. In his middle thirties Luther became the leader of a rebellion, too; and we will later point out trends in him which may have prepared his nation for the acceptance of a leader like Hitler. In the meantime, however, his moratorium was one of shared anonymity: he became Father Martinus in a brotherhood which cultivated collective self-denial in the face of eternity. For him, the struggle between destruction and construction would be fought out on theological grounds. *Existential justification* was his chosen text, and he applied it to the hometown level of his father, as well as to the cosmic level of his church.

Politics is the most inclusive means of creating a world order in this world; theology is the most systematic attempt to deal with man's existential nothingness by establishing a metaphysical Allness. The monastery, in its original conception, is a systematic training for the complete acceptance of earthly nothingness in the hope of partaking of that allness. The aim of monasticism is to decrease the wish and the will to master and to destroy to an absolute minimum. "I was holy," Luther said, "I killed nobody but myself." [10] To this end, the monastery offers methods of making a meditative descent into the inner shafts of mental existence, from which the aspirant emerges with the gold of faith or with gems of wisdom. These shafts, however, are psychological as well as meditative; they lead not only into the depths of adult inner experience, but also downward into our more primitive layers, and backward into our infantile beginnings. We must try to make this clear before we encounter the imagery of Martin's theological struggles, so that we can build a bridge between the historical condition of greatness and its precondition in individual childhood. Ideological leaders, so it seems, are subject to excessive fears which they can master only by re-shaping the thoughts of their contemporaries; while those contemporaries are always glad to have their thoughts shaped by those who so desperately care to do so. Born leaders seem to fear only more consciously what in some form everybody fears in the depths of his inner life; and they convincingly claim to have an answer.

3

In his *Shaping of the Modern Mind*, the historian Crane Brinton reports a psychological observation. He introduces it with the kind of virginal apology observers often use to divorce themselves from the professional psychology they so heartily distrust: "To be provocative I shall say all normal people are metaphysicians; all have some desire to locate themselves in a 'system,' a 'universe,' a 'process' transcending at least the immediate give-and-take between the individual and his environment; for all normal people the conscious lack or frustration of some such understanding will result in a kind of metaphysical anxiety." [11] Then he tells this story:

I recall a conversation among adults with a five-year-old boy present, listening, but not quite actively in the talk. Something came up which gave the boy the coveted chance to wedge his way into the adults' world. The father let the boy have his say, and then remarked offhand, "This was seven years ago, before you were born, before you were even conceived." The boy's face went suddenly empty, and in a moment he burst into tears. It is hazardous to try to reconstruct what went on in his mind, but there is no doubt that something in those words shocked him deeply. "Before you were born" he almost certainly could, like all children of his age, take in his stride; but though like most progressive parents his had probably already tried to present him with the facts of life, the "before you were even conceived" must have thrown him quite off his stride, left him confronted not merely with a puzzle, with a problem like the hundreds he had to tackle daily, but with a fundamental mystery. For the moment, he was alone in the universe—indeed, without a universe; his was a grave metaphysical anxiety.

Let us look at this episode of psychopathology of everyday child life, and at its interpretation. I shall say first that this little boy's particular reaction must have been overdetermined. His age suggests that he may have been doubtful as well as sensitive about the way in which he was created; and his father may have seemed to him to be bragging just a bit too much in company, and reacting to his son's intrusion into the conversation by using the word "conceived," which emphasized his own role in the child's emergence from nothingness. The little boy, then, was up against a number of "fundamental mysteries." Let us not forget that his father, probably too civilized to be harsh in an ordinary way, played God rather impolitely and at the same time emphasized his prerogatives in regard to the mother by referring to the boy's conception. But it must be admitted (and this is the reason why I found this little story arresting) that there may well be something in the boy's anxiety which is not quite explained either by a sudden impairment of his self-esteem, by anger with the overweening father, or by discomfort over the biological riddle of the act of conception. If this something is to be called "metaphysical," it can only mean that the boy's mind may suddenly have comprehended the limitations of physical existence. We can always counter any doubts about our biological origin with ordinary defenses and typical phantasies; but we are helpless against the recurrent discovery of the icy fact that at one time we did not exist at all—particularly helpless when as children we are acutely deprived of parental sponsorship. It is even probable that much of the preoccupation with mysterious origins which occurs in infantile phantasies and in the myths of peoples is an attempt to cover up, with questions of whence and how, the "metaphysical" riddle of existence as such.

What Brinton, extending to the boy an intellectual courtesy, calls "metaphysical anxiety," is like an ego-chill, a shudder which comes from the sudden awareness that our nonexistence—and thus our utter dependence on a creator who may choose to be impolite—is entirely possible. Ordinarily we feel this shudder only in moments when a shock forces us to step back from ourselves, and we do not have the necessary time or equipment to recover instantaneously a position from which to view ourselves again as persistent units subject to our own logical operations. Where man cannot establish himself as the thinking one (who therefore is), he may experience a sense of panic; which is at the bottom of our myth-making, our metaphysical speculation, and our artificial creation of "ideal" realities in which we become and remain the central reality.

The sense of identity, which is not wanting in most adults, prevents such feelings of panic. To be adult means among other things to see one's own life in continuous perspective, both in retrospect and in prospect. By accepting some definition as to who he is, usually on the basis of a function in an economy, a place in the sequence of generations, and a status in the structure of society, the adult is able to selectively reconstruct his past in such a way that, step for step, it seems to have planned him, or better, he seems to have planned *it*. In this sense, psychologically we *do* choose our parents, our family history, and the history of our kings, heroes, and gods. By making them our own, we maneuver ourselves into the inner position of proprietors, of creators. If we are able to weather the repeated crises throughout childhood and youth, and become ourselves the begetters and protectors of children, then most of us become too busy for metaphysical questions. Yet, unconsciously, we are by no means sure, not just that we are the begetters of a particular child, which we mostly can convince ourselves of reasonably well, but that in any respect we can be a *first* cause, a *causa causans*. This doubt helps to make us overevaluate those jealousies and rivalries, those racial and personal myths, those ethnocentricities and egocentricities, that make us feel that if we *are* more caused than causing, at least we are a link in a chain which we can proudly affirm and thus, somehow will.

We are able to feel like a *causa causans* if we accept the inevitable in such a way that it becomes ornamented with some special pride— pride in our power to resign ourselves, or pride in the inevitable as something so patently good that we surely would have chosen it if it had not chosen us. If adult man, then, ever comes close to an ego-chill, he has available automatic recourse to a context in which he is needed, or in which others will him so that he may will them, or in which he has mastered some technique which brings visible returns. He forgets the sacrifices which he has to make to achieve this functional relatedness to other occupants of his cultural universe. He forgets that he achieved the capacity for *faith* by learning to overcome feelings of utter abandonment and mistrust; the sense of free *will* by resigning himself to a mutual limitation of wills; relative peace of *conscience* by submitting to, and even incorporating into himself, some harsh self-judgments; the enjoyment of *reason* by forgetting how many things he wanted to solve and could not; and the satisfaction of *duty* by accepting a limited position and its obligations in his technology. In all these areas he learns to develop a sense of individual mastery from his ability to adapt himself to a social system which has managed to orchestrate religion, law, morals, and technic; he derives from the accrual of his sacrifices a coherent measure of historical identity. He can further enhance this feeling of identity by partaking of the arts and sciences with all their grandiose displays of magic omnipotence. Deep down he believes that a Toscanini writes the works he conducts, nay, creates them out of the orchestra while he is conducting; and that an Einstein creates the cosmic laws which he predicts.

The child is not yet in possession of such a seemingly self-sustaining universe; and he often is not willing, before he is forced to, to suffer all the adult sacrifices. He may therefore develop deep anxieties; and these, especially when they are interwoven with psychosexual phantasies, belong to the best documented phenomena in psychoanalytic literature. Psychoanalysis has emphasized and systematized the sexual search of childhood and youth, elaborating on the way sexual and aggressive drives and contents are repressed and disguised, to reappear subsequently in impulsive acts and in compulsive self-restraints. But psychoanalysis has not charted the extent to which these drives and contents owe their intensity and exclusivity to sudden depreciations of the ego and of material available as buildingstones for a future identity. The child does have his parents, however; if they are halfway worth the name, their presence will define for him both the creative extent and the secure limitations of his life tasks.

The one most exposed to the problem of his existential identity is the late adolescent. Shakespeare's Hamlet, a very late adolescent with a premature, royal integrity, and still deeply involved with his oedipal conflicts, poses the question of "to be or not to be" as a sublime *choice*. The introspective late adolescent, trying to free himself from parents who made and partially determined him, and trying also to face membership in wider institutions, which he has not as yet made his own, often has a hard time convincing himself that he has *chosen* his past and is the choser of his future. Moved by his ravenous sexuality, his commanding aggressive power, and his encompassing intellect, he is tempted to make premature choices, or to drift passively. When he is able to make few choices, they have a greater finality because they decide his estate: peasant, miner, or leaseholder in Hans' inventory, lawyer or monk in Martin's. When he must make many choices, as he does in our society, they may provoke a false sense of freedom, of indefinite time in which to experiment, and thus lead to moments in which it becomes suddenly clear to him that even in playing around he has been typed, and in trying things out, become committed to them.

Whether or not all this comes upon the young person suddenly and traumatically depends on his society. Some cultures prepare him in childhood and youth by symbolic ceremonials which convincingly anticipate all these ego-dangers; some cultures limit and retard his awareness, and so fortify him against all suddenness; others offer magic rites and confirmations which make him a member of a group with a strongly predefined identity; while others teach him social and technological methods of mastering dangerous forces which take the forms of enemies, animals, and machines. In each case the young person finds himself part of a universal framework which reaches back into an established tradition, and promises a definable future. But in a time of rapid change, be it the disintegration of the old or the advancement of the new, the meaning of confirmation changes. Some ceremonies and graduations, while ancient and profound, no longer speak to young people; others, while sensible and modern, are somehow not magic enough to provide that superlative shudder which alone touches on the mystery of experience. Many young people, eager for an image of the future, find the confirmations and ceremonies offered by their parents' churches, clubs, or orders designed more for their parents' spiritual uplift than for their own. Others go along with the make-believe identities proffered in many occupational and professional schools, but find that streamlined adaptiveness proves brittle in the face of new crises. What academic institutions teach and preach often has little to do with the immediate inner needs and outer prospects of young people.

Today this problem faces us most painfully on that frontier where leaderless and unguided youth attempts to confirm itself in sporadic riots and other excesses which offer to those who have temporarily lost, or never had, meaningful confirmation in the approved ways of their fathers, an identity based on a defiant testing of what is most marginal to the adult world. The mocking grandiosity of their gang names ("Black Barons," "Junior Bishops," "Navahoes," "Saints"), their insignia, sometimes even tattooed into the skin, and their defiant behavior clearly indicate an attempt to emulate that which gives other people the background of a group identity: a real family, nobility, a proud history—and religion.

4

Nietzsche's fitting diagnosis that Luther wanted to speak to God directly and without a trace of embarrassment describes Martin's more personal and more impatient version of St. Paul's "For now we see through a glass, darkly, but then face to face: now I know in part, but then shall I know even as also I am known." [12] But Martin's search, as his whole treatment of the thunderstorm shows, was also younger and sadder: "He who sees God as angry does not see Him rightly but looks upon a curtain, as if a dark cloud had been drawn across His face." [13]

It would be much too easy (although some stalwart opponents of all interpretation would consider even this easiest and most obvious explanation far-fetched) that Hans' son was seeking in religion what he could not find in Hans.

The search for mutual recognition, the *meeting face to face,* is an aspect in his and in all religion which we must consider if we are to understand the deepest nostalgia of lonely youth. True lovers know this, and they often postpone the self-loss feared in the sexual fusion in order that each may gain more identity in the other's glance. What it means *not* to be able to behold a face in mutual affirmation can be learned from young patients, who, unable to love, see, in their more regressed states, the face of the therapist disintegrate before their horrified eyes, and feel themselves fall apart into fragments of oblivion. One young man patient drew and painted dozens of women's faces, cracked like broken vases, faded like worn flowers, with hard and ungiving eyes, or with eyes like stars, steely and blinking, far away; only when he had painted a whole and healthy face did he know that he could be cured, and that he was a painter. As one studies such symptoms and works them through in therapeutic encounters,[14] one can only become convinced of the astonishing fact that these patients have partially regressed to a stage in the second part of the first year and that they are trying to recover what was then achieved by the concordance of cognitive and emotional maturation—namely, the recognition of the facial features of familiar persons, the joy of feeling recognized when they come, and the sorrow of feeling disapproved of when they frown; and, then the gradual mastery of the horror of the strange face.[15]

It is remarkable to behold how in the infant's development into a human being with the capacity for a firm "object-relationship"—the ability to love in an individualized sense—growing cognitive ability and maturing emotional response early converge on the face. An infant of two to three months will smile even at half a face; he will even smile at half a painted dummy face, if that half is the upper half of the face, is fully represented, and has at least two clearly defined points or circles for eyes; more the infant does not need, but he will not smile for less. Gradually, however, other conditions are added, such as the outline of a (not necessarily smiling) mouth; and only toward the eighth month does the child energetically indicate that certainly no dummy and not even a smiling face as such can make him respond with maximum recognition; from then on he will only respond to familiar people who act as he has learned to expect—and act friendly. But with this recognition of familiarity and friendliness also comes the awareness of strangeness and anger; not because the child, as many parents feel, has suddenly become fearful, but because he now "knows," he has an investment in those who are committed to his care, and he fears the loss of that investment and the forfeiture of that commitment. The activity which begins with something akin to a small animal's inborn response to minimum cues develops, through the gradual recognition of the human face and its expression, to that degree of social discrimination and sensitivity which marks the human being. And once he has made the investment in humanity and its learning processes, the human child knows fears and anxieties quite unthinkable in the small animal which, if it survives at all, has its environment cut out for it as a field of relatively simple and repetitive signs and techniques.

Mothers, of course, and people with motherly responses, like to think that when even a small baby smiles, he is recognizing them individually as the only possible maternal person, as *the* mother. This, up to a point, is good. For the timespan of man's dependence on the personal and cultural style of the person or persons who first take care of him is very long: and the firmness of his early ego-development depends on the inner consistency of the style of that person. Therefore, the establishment of a mutual "fixation"—of a

binding need for mutual recognition between mother and child—
is essential. In fact, the infant's instinctive smile seems to have exactly that purpose which is its crowning effect, namely, that the
adult feels recognized, and in return expresses recognition in the form
of loving and providing. In the beginning are the generous breast
and the eyes that care. Could this be one of the countenances which
religion promises us we shall see again, at the end and in another
world? Is there an ethology of religion?

Those who fail in their once-bornness, we said, want to have another chance at being born. It often seems as though they want to
be made over by the same mothers who give physical birth to them;
but this, as we can now see, would be too literal an assumption. For
that "first birth," to which all of their symptoms are related, is the
emergence of their consciousness as individuals, a consciousness born
from the interplay of recognitions. Whoever is the maternal attend-
ant to that early phase is man's first "environment," and whatever
environment is then first experienced as such remains associated with
"mother." On the security of that first polarisation of a self and a
maternal matrix are built all subsequent securities. "Mother" is the
person (or the persons) who knows how to convincingly offer
provision and screening: the provisions of food, warmth, stimulation in answer to the infant's searching mouth, skin, and senses; and
the screening of the quality and quantity of his intake so as to avoid
both over- and under-stimulation. The new human being, therefore,
experiences his appetites and aversions together with the personal
care (and care means provision *and* caution) he gets. They form his
first world; but so do those moments when he feels uncared for,
alone with his discomfort and his rage. For these, however, he has
at his disposal signals with an immediate appeal to the mother, which
sooner or later bring more or less response from her: the regularity
and predictability of her responses are the infant's first world order,
the original paradise of provision. During the first year of life, the
reality of the provider thus gradually emerges from the original
matrix as a coherent experience, a verified fact, a sound investment
of love and trust—and the infant has matured enough to experience
coherently, verify reasonably, and invest courageously.

This bipolarity of recognition is the basis of all social experience.
Let nobody say that it is only the beginning, it passes, and it is,
after all, childish. Man is not organized like an archaeological mound,

in layers; as he grows he makes the past part of all future, and every environment, as he once experienced it, part of the present environment. Dreams and dreamlike moments, when analysed, always reveal the myriad past experiences which are waiting outside the gates of consciousness to mingle with present impressions. Man at all times wants to be sure that the original bipolarity is intact, especially when he feels tired, doubtful, unsure, alone—a fact which has been utilized by both theology and psychoanalysis.

In that first relationship man learns something which most individuals who survive and remain sane can take for granted most of the time. Only psychiatrists, priests, and born philosophers know how sorely that something can be missed. I have called this early treasure "basic trust"; it is the first psychosocial trait and the fundament of all others. Basic trust in mutuality is that original "optimism," that assumption that "somebody is there," without which we cannot live. In situations in which such basic trust cannot develop in early infancy because of a defect in the child or in the maternal environment, children die mentally. They do not respond nor learn; they do not assimilate their food and fail to defend themselves against infection, and often they die physically as well as mentally.[16]

One may well claim for that earliest meeting of a perceiving subject with a perceived object (which, in turn seems to "recognize" the subject) the beginning of all sense of identity; this meeting thus becomes the anchor-point for all the developments which culminate, at the end of adolescence, in the establishment of psychosocial identity. At that point, an ideological formula, intelligible both in terms of individual development and of significant tradition, must do for the young person what the mother did for the infant: provide nutriment for the soul as well as for the stomach, and screen the environment so that vigorous growth may meet what it can manage.

Of all the ideological systems, however, only religion restores the earliest sense of appeal to a Provider, a Providence. In the Judaeo-Christian tradition, no prayer indicates this more clearly than "The Lord make His Face to shine upon you and be gracious unto you. The Lord lift up His countenance upon you and give you peace"; and no prayerful attitude better than the uplifted face, hopeful of being recognized. The Lord's countenance is apt to loom too sternly, and His son's on the cross to show the enigmatic quality of total abandonment in sacrifice; but painters and sculptors fashion a faintly smiling face for the Madonna, graciously inclined toward the infant, who responds with peace and gaiety until, in the Renaissance, he stands up and, fully confident, motions away from her. We can see the search for the same smile of peace in the work of Eastern painters and sculptors, although their Buddhas seem closer to being the over-all parent *and* the child, all in one. It is art, the work of the visually gifted and the visually driven, in conjunction with religion, which puts such emphasis on the face; thought expresses the original symbiotic unity as a state of being firmly and yet flexibly held, imbedded in a *Way*.

One must work with children who cannot learn to say *I*, although they are otherwise healthy, and beautiful, and even soulful, to know what a triumph that common gift of "I" is, and how much it depends on the capacity to feel affirmed by maternal recognition. One basic task of all religions is to reaffirm that first relationship, for we have in us deep down a lifelong mistrustful remembrance of that truly *meta*-physical anxiety; *meta*—"behind," "beyond"—here means "before," "way back," "at the beginning." One basic form of heroic asceticism, therefore, one way of liberating man from his existential delimitations, is to retrace the steps of the development of the I, to forego even object relations in the most primitive sense, to step down and back to the borderline where the I emerged from its matrix. Much of Western monasticism concentrates on prayer and atonement, but the Eastern form cultivates the art of deliberate self-loss: Zen-Buddhism is probably its most systematic form.

"I did not know the Christchild any more," (*non novi puellum*) Luther said later,[17] in characterizing the sadness of his youth: he had lost his childhood. In a moment of terror he appealed, not to the Madonna, but to his father's occupational saint, St. Anne. But he always objected to the Madonna's mediation in the then popular scheme of religion. He wanted *God's* recognition. A long way stretched ahead of him before he was able to experience, through Christ rather than through Mary, the relevance of the theme of mother and child in addition to that of father and son. Then he could say that Christ was defined by two images: one of an infant lying in a manger, "hanging on a virgin's tits," (*hanget an einer Jungfrau Zitzen*); *and* one of a man sitting at his Father's right hand.[18]

5

But what destroyed in our infantile past, and what destroys in the depth of our adult present, that original unity which provides the imagery of our supreme hopes?

All religions and most philosophers agree that it is *will*—the mere will to live, thoughtless and cruel self-will. In one of the few passionate passages of his *Varieties of Religious Experience*, William James describes specifically one of the manifestations of the will to live:

The normal process of life contains moments as bad as any of those which insane melancholy is filled with, moments in which radical evil gets its innings and takes its solid turn. The lunatic's visions of horror are all drawn from the material of daily fact. Our civilization is founded on the shambles, and every individual existence goes out in a lonely spasm of helpless agony. If you protest, my friend, wait till you arrive there yourself! To believe in the carnivorous reptiles of geologic times is hard for our imagination—they seem too much like mere museum specimens. Yet there is no tooth in any one of those museum-skulls that did not daily through long years of the foretime hold fast to the body struggling in despair of some fated living victim. Forms of horror just as dreadful to their victims, if on a smaller spatial scale, fill the world about us to-day. Here on our very hearths and in our gardens the infernal cat plays with the panting mouse, or holds the hot bird fluttering in her jaws. Crocodiles and rattlesnakes and pythons are at this moment vessels of life as real as we are; their loathsome existence fills every minute of every day that drags its length along; and whenever they or other wild beasts clutch their living prey, the deadly horror which an agitated melancholiac feels is literally right reaction on the situation.

It may indeed be that no religious reconciliation with the absolute totality of things is possible. Some evils, indeed, are ministerial to higher forms of good; but it may be that there are forms of evil so extreme as to enter into no good system whatsoever, and that, in respect of such evil, dumb submission or neglect to notice is the only practical resource.[19]

The tenor of this mood is immediately convincing. It is the mood of severe melancholy, intensified tristitia, one would almost say tristitia with teeth in it. James, at this point, takes recourse to the "geologic times" far behind us, and to the reptiles way below us— creatures who devour one another without sin and are not condemned for it by any religion. He also quotes the playfully cruel domestic cat, who shares with man an ecology of intermediary human institutions. The cat does not feed itself in direct inter-dependence with a sector of nature, but receives food, as man does, as a result of a social division of tool-labor. The cat's relation to the mouse has thus lost the innocence of ecological interdependence, and the cat's needs are refined, like ours.

James is clinically and genetically correct, when he connects the horror of the *devouring* will to live with the content and the dis-position of melancholia. For in melancholia, it is the human being's horror of his own avaricious and sadistic orality which he tires of, withdraws from, wishes often to end even by putting an end to himself. This is not the orality of the first, the toothless and depend-ent, stage; it is the orality of the tooth-stage and all that develops within it, especially the prestages of what later becomes "biting" human conscience. There is, it would seem, no intrinsic reason for man's feeling more guilty or more evil because he employs, enjoys, and learns to adapt his gradually maturing organs, were it not for the basic division of good and bad which, in some dark way, estab-lishes itself very early. The image of a paradise of innocence is part of the individual's past as much as the race's. Paradise was lost when man, not satisfied with an arrangement in which he could pluck from the trees all he needed for upkeep, wanted more, wanted to have and to know the forbidden—and bit into it. Thus he came to know good and evil. It is said that after that he worked in the sweat of his brow. But it must be added that he also began to invent tools in order to wrest from nature what it would not just give. He "knew" at the price of losing innocence; he became autonomous at the price of shame and gained independent initiative at the price of guilt. Next to primary peace, then, secondary appeasement is a great infantile source of religious affect and imagery.

In a strange counterpart to the quotation from James, Luther later pictured God himself as a devourer, as if the wilful sinner could expect to find in God's demeanor a mirror of his own avarice, just as the uplifted face of the believer finds a countenance inclined and full of grace: "He gorges us, with great eagerness and wrath . . . he is an avaricious, a gluttonous (*fressige*) fire." [20] Thus, in the set of god-images in which the countenance of the godhood mirrors the human face, God's face takes on the toothy and fiery expression of the devil, or the expressions of countless ceremonial masks. All these wrathful countenances mirror man's own rapacious orality which destroys the innocent trust of that first symbiotic orality when mouth and breast, glance and face, are one.

There is a bizarre counterpart to this imagery of one face mirroring another. We have already indicated that in Luther's more popular imagery, the behind is the devil's magic face. He imprints it on a location as his official signature, he exposes it to man's view to provoke him; and he himself cannot stand to have man's defiant behind (and the odors emanating therefrom) brought into the vicinity of his face. To show the behind, then, is the utmost of defiance, as any number of colloquialisms in Luther's expanding rhetoric suggest.

This set of images, too, has an infantile model, in what Freud called the "anal" stage of psychosexual development, a stage originating in the child's sensual experiences in that fascinating part of his body which faces away from him, and which excretes what he learns to consider dirty, smelly, and poisonous. In supplementing Freud's scheme of infantile psychosexual stages I have suggested a psychosocial scheme in which the stage characterized by Freud's *anality* also serves to establish psychosocial *autonomy* which can and does mean independence, but does and can also mean defiance, stubbornness, self-insistence. What in the oral stage is basic mistrust, in the anal becomes *shame*, the loss of social innocence, the blushing awareness that one can "lose face," have "too much cheek," and suffer the wish to be invisible, to sink into the ground. Defiance, obviously, is shame's opposite; and it makes sense that the wilful exposure of the behind came to mean a defiant gesture of shamelessness; to face the devil in this position means to offer him the other set of cheeks. No doubt when Martin learned to speak up, much that he had to say to the devil was fueled by a highly-compressed store of defiance consisting of what he had been unable to say to his father and to his teachers; in due time he said it all, with a vengeance, to the Pope.

The Luder family, while traditional in structure, offered an extreme degree of moralistic paternalism, and, quite probably, a minimum degree of that compensatory free-for-all of small and highly satisfying delinquencies which barnyard, street, or park can provide for lucky children. The father's prohibitory presence, and the anticipation of his punishment seem to have pervaded the family milieu, which thus became an ideal breeding ground for the most pervasive form of the Oedipus complex—the ambivalent interplay of rivalry with the father, admiration for him, and fear of him which puts such a heavy burden of guilt and inferiority on all spontaneous initiative and on all phantasy. Where rebellion and deviousness are thus successfully undercut, and where, on the other hand, the father's alcoholic, sexual, and cruel self-indulgence obviously break through his moralistic mask, a child can only develop a precocious conscience, a precocious self-steering, and eventually an obsessive mixture of obedience and rebelliousness. Hans Luder was a "jealous God," one who probably interfered early with the mother's attempt to teach her children how to be before he taught them how to strive. It was probably his father's challenging injunction against the little boy's bond with his mother which made it impossible for Martin to accept the intercession of the holy Mary. But when a father usurps motherhood, he puts an additional and unbearable burden on that second of man's great nostalgias, which cannot be described better than it was by Thomas Wolfe:

From the beginning . . . the idea, the central legend that I wished my book to express—had not changed. And this central idea was this: the deepest search in life, it seemed to me, the thing that in one way or another was central to all living was man's search to find a father, not merely the father of his flesh, not merely the lost father of his youth, but the image of a strength and wisdom external to his need and superior to his hunger, to which the belief and power of his own life could be united.[21]

At first, of course, fathers are non-mothers, the other kind of person. They may be part of the maternal environment, but their specificity is experienced only later—when, exactly, I cannot say. Freud's oedipal father has clarified much, but, as sudden clarifications do, he has also obscured much. True, fathers are impressive as the mothers' powerful counterplayers in contexts not quite knowable, and yet deeply desirable and awe-provoking. But they are also importantly involved in the awakening of the child's identity. Fathers, it appears, were there before we were, they were strong when we were weak, they saw us before we saw them; not being mothers—that is, beings who make the care of babies their business —they love us differently, more dangerously. Here, I think, is the origin of an idea attested to by myths, dreams, and symptoms, namely, that the fathers (as some animal fathers do) could have annihilated us before we became strong enough to appear as their rivals. Much of the thanks we bring to potentially wrathful gods (who, we think, know our thoughts) is really thanks for their generosity in suffering us to live at all. Thus, we owe our fathers two lives; one by way of conception (which even the most enlightened children can visualize only very late in childhood); the other by way of a voluntary sponsorship, of a *paternal* love.

In anxiety and confusion, children often seem to take refuge from their fathers by turning back to their mothers. But this occurs only if the fathers are not there enough, or not there in the right way. For children become aware of the attributes of maleness, and learn to love men's physical touch and guiding voice, at about the time when they have the first courage for an autonomous existence—autonomous from the maternal matrix in which they only *seem* to want to remain forever. Fathers, if they know how to hold and guide a child, function somewhat like guardians of the child's autonomous existence. Something passes from the man's bodily presence into the child's budding self—and I believe that the idea of *communion*, that is, of partaking of a man's body, would not be such a simple and reassuring matter for so many were it not for that early experience. Who never felt thus generated, "grown," as an individual by his father or fathers, always feels half annihilated, and may perhaps be forced to seek a father in the mother—a role for which the mother, if she assumes it, is blamed afterwards. For there is something which only a father can do, which is, I think, to balance the threatening and forbidding aspects of his appearance and impression with the guardianship of the guiding voice. Next to the recognition bestowed by the gracious face, the affirmation of the guiding voice is a prime element of man's sense of identity. Here the question is not so much whether in the judgment of others the father is a good model or a bad one, but whether or not he is tangible and affirmative. Intangibly good fathers are the worst.

As we grow beyond our early childhood, more and more classes of men become the "fathers" of our newly-acquired insights and techniques: grandfathers, uncles, neighbors, and fatherly teachers. If we call such fathers "father-surrogates," we empty an important function of its true significance in an effort to understand its potential perversion; this may lead us, as therapists, to cut off our own noses in order to present impersonal enough faces for our patients' father-transferences. We should study what, if not fathers, we really are; for men who wash their hands of their function in the life of youth are as evil, even if by default, as the "bad" fathers whom they despise. In their youth children need, in addition to fathers who will guard the beginnings of their identities, guarantors of their established identity; in this only the luckiest personal father can participate. If he insists on a monopoly in this regard, as Hans did, he asks for rebellion, smouldering or flaming.

We will meet all of these fathers in Martin's life, some on earth and some in heaven, some in Hans' return performances, and some in strikingly new thoughts. In the meantime, we may recognize another basic arrangement of the human and the divine face in the combination of the sinner who feels so totally guilty that he wants to *hide his face*, to be totally nobody, and his counterpart, the God who *turns his back*, who looks away into the eternal darkness—the terrible, the hidden God.

Just because Martin's case makes the interpretive step from the punishing father to the avenging God so easy, it was necessary, in this interim chapter, to remind ourselves what other nostalgias and mortal fears may have been enveloped in his sadness.

First Mass and Dead Ends

Martin became "simple monk"; in fact, "beggar monk." This image has entrenched itself as the proper propagandistic baseline from which to chart his miraculous rise to theological prominence. Miraculous it would have been from any baseline. But the Augustinian Hermits were far from being beggars, economically speaking; nor were they hermits, monastically speaking. They were a thriving corporation of relatively wealthy monasteries; at one time, there were thirty thousand members, with a central office in Rome. In Erfurt the Augustinians occupied a campus of 7500 square meters, and owned real estate, rich fields, and vineyards. The highly educated *patres*, in whose ranks Martin was soon to be received, had, to serve them in manual labor, a lesser class of *fratres*, lay-brothers who, although pledged for life, were kept illiterate and unordained. When Martin shouldered his sack and went begging with a companion, therefore, he stepped down only symbolically to the level of the begging monks, many of whom were members of the Church's proletariat and had brought monkhood into disrepute.

The history of monkhood displays a number of variables which may help to describe Martin's order. Originally, of course, monks *were* hermits, deliberately seeking a state of radical readiness for that lonesome valley which must be crossed alone, sooner or later. Eventually they organized into groups of parallel aloneness; later, they joined in permanent convents and developed definite styles of ritual observance. By some law of opposites, which seems to govern the development of extreme positions, monkhood started with a social arrangement of total isolation and ended with one of total regimentation. The dimension of monkhood defined by the form of domicile is *eremitical-conventual;* the Augustinians belonged to the most progressive convents, with permanent mother-houses and regional congregations organized as in a small state.

Eremitical seclusion is, of course, the most basic asceticism. It sacrifices the ameliorating presence of the others, as well as comparison and sharing with others, and thus invites temptation in that crudest, most insane form to which painters of St. Anthony's torment have tried to give recognizable features. Nor does eremitic existence permit that break in introspective concentration which joint ritual observances afford. One cannot ponder on the dimensions of monasticism without visualizing St. Francis in the various roles which he taught himself. He experienced all the variations, including that of founding an order; and then returned to the purity of eremitical asceticism on that wooded mesa on top of Mount Alverno.

Not far from there, in the delicious woods of Vallombrosa, monastic life reached one of its heights in the perfection of *contemplation,* a variable which finds its opposite extreme in hard *manual labor,* such as the Trappists perform in their communal life. Our clerical Augustinians observed certain hours of contemplation and did a minimum of manual work, mostly in taking care of their own premises. But they had their monastic handymen, and managed farms and vineyards rather than worked them. On the other hand, they were highly industrious in their singing and in their studies, and maintained a close association with universities.

Another variable of monkhood concerns the techniques chosen for perfecting the soul. These may range from methods of extreme *self-abnegation,* which reduce the body to its own shadow, to extremes of self-denying *service* to sick or needy human beings. The Augustinians were relatively moderate in prescribed abnegations (although Martin soon insisted on making out his own prescriptions), but highly-disciplined in observances, and well-trained for the spiritual care and the educational advancement of others.

This all clearly places them on one side of the remaining variable: *mysticism* versus *intellectuality.* Martin, as we know, had met the Brothers of Common Life in Erfurt and had heard them inveigh against intellectualism in faith. In the Augustinian monastery he studied and discussed mysticism; but he adhered to the scholastic tradition until his own original religiosity made him break out of it. The advanced course of general studies in his monastery was famous, and was said to be far superior to those of the Dominicans and Franciscans.

All in all, then, the Augustinian Hermits, while belonging to a congregation of monasteries pledged to strict observances, and generally respected for it, attempted to combine the best and the most reasonable in monastic tradition; and it is obvious at once that although Martin may have disobeyed his father by becoming a monk, quite in his father's spirit, he chose the best school within his horizon.

He also chose something akin to a clerical upper-middle-class. All the world was Catholic; and to become a monk merely meant to find an entrance, on a defined professional level, to the Catholic empire's hierarchy of clerical employees, which included in its duties diplomacy; the administration of social welfare in countries, counties, cities, and towns; spiritual ministration; and the more or less ascetic cultivation of personal salvation. The fact that Luther took upon himself the latent sadness of his age and the spiritual problems of its theology marks him as a member of an ideological, maybe even somewhat neurotic, minority. Among the Augustinians of his time, he was a strange, a noteworthy, and sometimes a questionable, monk.

The vast majority of the representatives of an empire are not concerned with ideology. They mouth the current line of official doctrine, and rarely know what hits them when they suddenly find themselves on the losing side of an ideological issue because they bet on the wrong protectors. Then, as now, one could live without ever making a decision of faith, if one was only cautious enough to stick to the right levels: the captains of the bishoprics and their entourage; the chief bureaucrats who kept government going while the fanatics burned; or the mindless employees who served in the manner most recently ordered from above. On the lowest level, also, the ideology of faith hardly mattered; the increasing clerical proletariat was miserably poor and totally subservient and unprincipled. Not even the scholastic intelligentsia (which always produces the most current intellectual adjustments to dogma, and therefore feels ahead of its time) was really concerned with matters of the spirit, not to speak of personal faith. Within any of these groups there was no need for embarrassing sincerity, nor for an incautious insistence on the enforcement of the dogma. As in all monopolistic enterprises, the law interfered with convenience only if some fanatic, or fool, dragged an issue into the open. Thus many bishops and priests lived in concubinage, their female companions being respectfully greeted, *wie sich das gehoert*, by their titles of "Mrs. Vicar," or whatever it was. But marriage was against the law.

Only in the middle did the patrician-and-public-servant, burgher-and-scholar kind of cleric exist, who shared with the emerging middle class the search for a new sincerity, a new identity: economic, cultural, and spiritual. When Martin joined the Augustinian order he became part of that clerical middle class which corresponded to, and overlapped with, the class in which his father wanted him to find a foothold. He chose one of the best organized, most sincere, and least corrupted parts of the Church—and joined an organization, furthermore, which offered a flexible career. On the sociological surface of it, it is not entirely clear why Martin's choice of a basic training in monasticism should have been such a scandal to his father, or such a dramatic decision on the part of the son. Only if we remember that his father wanted him to be politically ambitious in a new, a secular sense, rather than spiritually good, can we understand that Martin was choosing a negative identity when he decided to become a monk; and he soon indulged in further contrariness by trying to be a better monk than the monks.

Martin first lived in the *domus hospitum*, the hostelry where the guests were housed: within the walls of the compound, but not within the cloister. Here he received by letter his father's permission, such as it was. Having found favor with the prior's admissions committee, he was offered a reception for one probationary year. The reception began with a general confession to the prior himself, and a haircut—not yet a tonsure. Then, at an appointed hour, he was led into the *Kapitelsaal* where the prior was seated in front of the altar. "What is your wish?" he asked. Martin, on his knees: "God's grace and your indulgence (*Barmherzigkeit*)." The prior motioned him to rise and proceeded to ascertain a few routine facts: the prospective novice was not married; he was not a slave or otherwise economically committed; and he did not suffer from any secret disease. Then the prior warns him: only a tough course could teach him to renounce his will. Food will be scarce, and clothing rough; there will be vigils in the night, and daily work. Strength will be sapped by fasting, pride by begging, spirit by isolation. The young man persists and is "received." The convent sings *Great Father Augustin* and the novice is invested with the black and white Augustinian habit, the large cowl and the scapular which, falling to the feet in front and in back, encloses the monk by day and by night, and in his grave. "May God invest you with a new man," the prior prays, postponing, as yet, the blessing of the habit. A general recitation follows and a procession of all to the choir, two by two, novice and prior last. As the final hymn is intoned, the novice lies before the altar, his arms spread away from him, like Christ's on the cross. "Not he who began, but he who persists will be saved," concludes the prior, and offers him the kiss of peace.[1]

Martin was then ready to be introduced into the microcosm of the monastery which, whatever his future in the clerical hierarchy, was to enclose him tightly and securely for a period of indoctrination. That indoctrination was not only a matter of learning new contents of thought, but a process of completely reconditioning his sensory and social responses to a minutely arranged environment. This process is familiar to us also from the modern phenomenon of thought reform, which makes cold psychological and political science out of the intuitive wisdom embodied in such an ancient procedure as the Augustinian monastery's. For a young man of Martin's passionate sincerity, in danger as he may have been of a malignant regression (and Luther later clearly admitted such a potential) or at any rate of most upsetting *tentaziones*, the immersion into a planned environment which took over from minute to minute decisions about what was good for the common cause and goal and what was bad, may have felt like a repetition on a grand style of the earliest maternal guidance. And, indeed, Luther later said, "In the first year in the monastery the devil is very quiet."[2]

Here are some details of the regime, and their psychological rationale. The novice is assigned a cell a little more than three meters long, three wide. The door cannot be locked and has a large opening for inspection at any time. There is one window, too high to allow one to see the ground. There is a table, a chair, a lamp; a cot with straw and a woolen blanket. The room cannot be heated. No ornamentation of any kind, no individual touch, is permitted. Thus begins that fasting of the senses, that vacuum of impressions, that dearth of ever-changing social cues, which is the necessary milieu for indoctrination: it opens the individual wide to the contradictory voices within him, and therefore makes him grasp more avidly whatever avenue toward a new identity is offered. Not only the input, but the output must also be regulated: the future orator must, first of all, learn silence. Within his own four walls not a word must escape him, not even in prayer. The master of novices, the only human being who may enter his cell, communicates with him only by signs. Outside his cell, the whole monastery is a checkerboard of times and places where silence is or is not mandatory. Special permission is required for private conversation, and must be overheard by a superior so that it does not become an escape valve for boast or banter, flattery or gossip. Above all, laughter is to be avoided. During meals, when it is easiest to relax and fraternize (provided that the food has been apportioned fairly), the monks must listen and not talk, a *lectio* is fed into their ears while the food enters their mouths. Thus, not only are the customary ways of letting oneself be diverted and guided by the changing spectacle of community life carefully restricted, but the customary ways of seeking verbal contact. The achievement of giving perspective to the present by small talk about things that have happened or things that will happen—be it only the weather—is denied. All verbal and vocal energy, and all postural and gestural expression, are channelled into a very few highly emotional outlets: prayer, confession, and above all, psalmody.

Seven times in twenty-four hours (*septies in die laudem dixi Tibi*) the monks pray in the choir in the liturgic fashion: two choirs challenging and responding to each other in antiphonic psalmody, or a solo voice asking for a joint refrain in responsorial psalmody. This activity follows the decree in Ephesians 5:19 that better than drunkenness by wine "is making melody in your heart to the Lord" in the spirit of the psalms. The Augustinians were proud of and famous for their psalmody; and it was certainly not a coincidence that Martin, for whom song had assumed such exclusive importance, chose the order which combined the cultivation of the voice with strict observance and intellectual sincerity. Later, when he became a professor, he gave his first lectures on the psalms. This may have been a coincidence of the academic schedule; but what he did with it was not.

"Have you ever heard more profound, intimate, or enduring poetry than that of the Psalms? And the Psalms were meant to be sung when one is alone. I know they are chanted by crowds gathered under a single roof for religious services; but those who intone them are no longer members of a multitude. When one sings them, he withdraws into himself; the voices of the others resound in his ears only as an accompaniment and reinforcement of his own voice— I notice this difference between a crowd gathered to recite the Psalms and one brought together to see a play or hear a speaker: the first is a true society, a company of living souls, wherein each exists and subsists separately; the second is a shapeless mass, and each member of it only a fragment of the human swarm." [3] Thus writes de Unamuno, the Spanish philosopher and freelance Protestant.

For the first of the liturgies, the monks are awakened by a bell at about 2 a.m.—except in high summer, when this liturgy is sung at the end of the long day. The liturgy begins (as the last one ends) with prayers to Mary, *sanctae dei genetrici*, the mother of God, who will intercede with her sternly judging son: "For you are the sinner's only hope."

Food is not taken until noon, and on fast days not until early afternoon—that is, not before four liturgies have been completed; between them, there is domestic work, study, and instruction from the master of novices.

During the first year, the task of adjusting to the new cycle of wakefulness and rest superimposed on the usual alternation of day and night, and the matter of absorbing the detailed rules and observances with their traditional rationale, took enough time and attention to create a moratorium, during which individual ruminations and scruples were forgotten. This moratorium was reinforced by the community practice of cornering and labelling, and thus jointly mastering, the common devil by methodical confession. There is a vast difference between being the lonely self-repudiated victim of a personalized evil (as Martin had been, and soon would be again),

and joining others in the militant repudiation of a powerful yet
well-defined common enemy.

The practice and method of confession is well known. Of special
interest to a clinician is the weekly *Schuld capitel*, the joint confession. Having jointly prostrated themselves, the monks, one after
another, the oldest leading, confessed to transgressions against the
rules. But they also denounced their brothers by calling on them
in the third person ("may Brother X remember") to confess certain transgressions which had been observed by others. The principles of group therapy evolved in our day explain why such mutual
confessions and denunciations had a salutory effect on the group:
they were all governed by complete equality and the subject matter was limited to themes of communal concern; consequently, the
possible kinds of confession, and their relative appropriateness, became clearly delineated. More personal material belonged to regular
confession, or to additional confession especially requested; "deadly
sins were entirely and exclusively reserved for the prior," according
to one biographer.

This was the routine to which the novice was committed. Those
who could not adjust to it were free to leave at any time without
recrimination, to try other orders, or to rejoin public life. But it
makes sense that a young man like Martin would, during the first
phase of this experience, find in this whole arrangement a self-
chosen prison of salutary silence; a welcome system of naming and
communicating evil worries; and a devotional discipline for his singing voice (his "conflict-free" sphere of expression), all of which
permitted him to postpone, as a moratorium should, decisions of
utmost explosiveness. It must also be affirmed that in the cloister individuals of less explosive inner potentials could find lasting inner
peace, together with a character adjustment compatible with the
final limitations and the possible evasions of the monastic scheme;
and unquestionably a few found true spiritual and characterological
fulfillment. There is undoubted psychological wisdom in such
schools of indoctrination as those of Catholic monasticism. These
schools continue to this day and on occasion are clearly described
in the literature; a comparison with similar methods of indoctrination
used for entirely different ideologies during different periods of
history reveals a common psychological rationale which is relatively

independent of the beliefs to be taught. Students of the modern system of Chinese thought reform discuss the necessary elements for its success: removal from family and community and isolation from the outer-world; restriction of sensory intake and immense magnification of the power of the word; lack of privacy and radical accent on the brotherhood; and, of course, joint devotion to the leaders who created and represent the brotherhood.[4]

Indoctrination is charged with the task of separating the individual from the world long enough so that his former values become thoroughly disengaged from his intentions and aspirations; the process must create in him new convictions deep enough to replace much of what he has learned in childhood and practiced in his youth. Obviously, then, the training must be a kind of shock treatment, for it is expected to replace in a short time what has grown over many formative years; therefore, indoctrination must be incisive in its deprivations, and exact in its generous supply of encouragement. It must separate the individual from the world he knows and aggravate his introspective and self-critical powers to the point of identity-diffusion, but short of psychotic dissociation. At the same time it must endeavor to send the individual back into the world with his new convictions so strongly anchored in his unconscious that he almost hallucinates them as being the will of a godhead or the course of all history: something, that is, which was not imposed on him, but was in him all along, waiting to be freed.

It stands to reason that late adolescence is the most favorable period, and late adolescent personalities of any age group the best subjects, for indoctrination; because in adolescence an ideological realignment is by necessity in process and a number of ideological possibilities are waiting to be hierarchically ordered by opportunity, leadership, and friendship. Any leadership, however, must have the power to encase the individual in a spatial arrangement and in a temporal routine which at the same time narrow down the sensory supply from the world and block his sexual and aggressive drives, so that a new needfulness will eagerly attach itself to a new world-image. At no other time as much as in adolescence does the individual feel so exposed to anarchic manifestations of his drives; at no other time does he so need oversystematized thoughts and overvalued words to give a semblance of order to his inner world. He therefore is willing to accept ascetic restrictions which go counter to what he would do if he were alone—faced with himself, his body, his musings—or in the company of old friends; he will accept the *sine qua non* of indoctrination, lack of privacy. (The Church could never have become an ideological institution on the basis of hermitism.) Needless to say, good and evil must be clearly defined as forces existing from all beginning and perseverating into all future; therefore all memory of the past must be starved or minutely guided, and all intention focused on the common utopia. No idle talk can be permitted. Talk must always count, count for or against one's readiness to embrace the new ideology totally—to the point of meaning it. In fact, the right talk, the vigorous song, and the radical confession in public must be cultivated.

Our bottomless incredulity in the face of Russian trials or Chinese reforms has shown us that an appreciation of the sincerity in an ideological system other than our own is extremely difficult. This is partially because our own ideology, as it must, forbids us ever to question and analyze the structure of what we hold to be true, since only thus can we maintain the fiction that we chose to believe what in fact we had no choice but to believe, short of ostracism or insanity; while we are more than eager to find the logical flaws, and particularly the insincerity and captivity, in one who operates in another system. We may therefore fail to understand that the indoctrinated individual of another era or country may feel quite at peace and quite free and productive in his ideological captivity, while we, being stimulus-slaves, ensnared at all times by a million freely chosen impressions and opportunities, may somehow feel unfree. As Luther said, a man without spirituality becomes his own exterior. On the other hand, a man deprived of opportunity to orient himself in the world can become the hallucinatory slave of inner convictions which he wants to maintain at any price because he must accept them at all cost.[5]

These are some of the psychological laws underlying the monastic system just described as well as newer systems of ideological conversion; all the systems are experiments in first aggravating and then curing the identity diffusion of youth.

The rationale of the rigid monastic system must be affirmed in principle, therefore, even though the clinician cannot help wondering what substitute expressions of tension, attraction, and repulsion develop, like an underground chorus competing with the pious discipline of the choir. Against the austere background of uniformity, the peculiarities of the single monk must have stood out strongly indeed. James Joyce—that literary Protestant—described how, when all the larger issues seemed to have been solved by confession and Mass, the young artist was plagued by "childish and unworthy imperfections [such as] anger at hearing his mother sneeze. . . . Images of the outbursts of trivial anger which he had often noted among his [Jesuit] masters, their twitching mouths, close-shut lips and flushed cheeks, recurred to his memory, discouraging him, for all his practice of humility." [6] We will soon see that even in these first years, minor and major irritations built up in Martin—irritations which later swelled to propagandistic proportions after he had broken his vow. He may well be believed, however, when later he described the very first year in the monastery as "fine, tranquil, and godly," particularly since he also had a good, if frank, word for his master of novices: "doubtless a good Christian under his damned cowl." [7] During basic training the best comes out in many instructors and the worst in others. This seems contradictory only if one does not know how close the best and the worst are to each other in any situation in which the human conscience is called upon to combine power with righteousness. In contact with new recruits, even some of the most hard-bitten veterans want to convince themselves that the metier to which they have given a devoted and obedient life is an honorable, an inspired, one.

A year after his reception, Luther was admitted to the "profession." Again he was led to the prior before the altar. "Now you must choose one or the other: to leave us or to renounce the world . . . but I must add, once you have committed yourself, you are not free, for whatever reason, to throw off the yoke of obedience. For you will have accepted it voluntarily while still free to discard it."

Again, a new garb is brought in; this time it is officially blessed by the prior: "Him whom it was your will to dress in the garb of the order, oh Lord, invest him also with eternal life." Now the prior undresses the novice: "The Lord divest you of the former man and of all his works"; and "The Lord invest you with the new man." Psalmody. "I, brother Martin, profess and promise to obey the Almighty God and the Holy Virgin, and you, brother Winand, prior of this monastery, in the name of the vicar-general of this order . . . and to live without property and in chastity according to the rule of St. Augustin. . . . unto death." [8]

In conclusion, the prior promised Martin, at the price of obedience, eternal life: *Si ista servas, promitto tibi vitam aeternam.*

Soon after his profession, Martin was told that he was destined for the priesthood. This was to be expected in the case of an M.A. of such caliber, as was also his later selection for a lectureship. In neither case could he, personally, have chosen his course, nor could he have decided against it. This was the first step beyond being a simple monk, and thus beyond his original vow. Obedience had once again brought him face to face with an authority's ambitious scheme for a new graduation for him, with other graduations in store.

He was at this point as free from temptations as he would ever be, and at the same time, unquestionably a part of a minutely scheduled life. It makes psychiatric sense that under such conditions a young man with Martin's smouldering problems, but also with an honest wish to avoid rebellion against an environment which took care of so many of his needs, would subdue his rebellious nature by gradually developing compulsive-obsessive states characterized by high ambivalence. His self-doubt thus would take the form of intensified self-observation in exaggerated obedience to the demands of the order; his doubt of authority would take the form of an intellectualized scrutiny of the authoritative books. This activity would, for a while longer, keep the devil in his place. However, neither Martin nor Hans could leave well enough alone for long.

The preparation for priesthood included the study of works on the basic concepts of Catholicism. Outstanding among these was Gabriel Biel's interpretation of the Canon of the Mass, a book by which Martin was deeply moved and soon deeply troubled: reading it made "his heart bleed." He immersed himself in the dogma; but the Canon of the Mass was disquieting to him because it became obvious to what an extent he would have to assume the supreme worthiness of the priest who transfers to others the very presence of Christ, and the very essence of His blood sacrifice. Martin's tendency toward obsessive rumination seized on the fact that the priest's supreme worthiness depended on the inner status with which he approached the ceremony and on his attentiveness to the procedure itself. Interestingly enough, slips of the tongue or involuntary repetitions of words or phrases were considered to mar the effectiveness of the prescribed words. Biel makes it very clear, however, that only a reasonable suspicion of an unconfessed deadly sin could prevent the priest, on any given day, from approaching the Mass; only conscious contempt of its rules should keep him from conducting it. Once he has started celebrating it, however, not even the sudden thought of a not-previously-remembered deadly sin should interfere with its completion. This liberal interpretation was quite in keeping with the general tone of the other authority on clerical procedure, Jean Gerson of the University of Paris, an Occamist like Biel. However, to Martin, all rules had gradually become torment. Monastic rules in themselves were a ritual elaboration of the scrupulousness which belongs to the equipment of our conscience; and for this reason, a monastic priest, protected as he was from many of the world's evils, and equipped as he was with special avenues of grace by confession, was expected to master them, not to be obsessed by them. Special vestments to be worn during Mass had to be complete and correct; thoughts could not stray; important phrases had to be completed without halting, and, above all, without repeating—all of these simple rules became potential stumbling blocks for Martin's apprehensions.

A priest's first Mass was a graduation of unique import. Therefore a celebration was planned, and his family, according to custom, was invited to attend. "There," Luther later said in a strange table-talk, "the bridegroom was invested in the light of torches with *horas canonicas;* there the young man had to have the first dance with his mother if she was alive, even as Christ danced with his mother; and everybody cried." [9]

The books do not say whether or not Luther's mother was invited; it may well be that only male relatives were expected to attend. Martin did invite his father, who wrote back that he would come if the monastery would suit his schedule. It did. Hans arrived on the appointed day, leading a proud calvacade of twenty Mansfeld citizens, and bringing twenty *Gulden* as a contribution to the monastery's kitchen. "You must have a good friend there," one of the marveling onlookers is said to have remarked.

There are a number of versions of the two decisive events of that day: Martin's anxiety attack during the Mass, and Hans' attack of loud anger during the following banquet. In regard to both instances the more dramatic versions claim public commotions: they say that Martin was about to flee the ceremony, but was restrained by a superior, and that during the banquet the father denounced the assembled staff of the monastery. Luther himself later often contributed to the embellishment of the events, reporting things which had taken place only in conversation or entirely in his own mind. This is owing partially to the folksy exaggeration of his table-talk vocabulary, partially to the literalism of his listeners, and partially to his distinct tendency to retrospective dramatization, which I will call *historification* in order to avoid calling one more process "projection." I mean by this that Luther may honestly have remembered as a detailed event in time and space what actually occurred only in his thoughts and emotions. It is clear that his upbringing in the miner's world, with its reifications and rumors, facilitated this tendency, which came to full bloom when Luther had to accept his final identity as a historical personality.

First, then, the Mass. Luther may or may not have meant it literally when he said later that he had felt like fleeing the world as a Judas, and had actually made a motion to run away when he read the words, *Te igitur clementissime Pater*, which appeal "to the most merciful Father"; he suddenly felt that he was about to speak to God directly, without any mediator.[10] The professor finds this incredible, because Luther must have known that these words are followed by the phrase, *Per Jhesum Christum filium tuum Dominum nostrum supplices rogamus et petiamus*, which refers to God's Son as the transmitter of our supplications to His Father. But however it came to pass that Luther ignored this phrase, we must accept his assurance that he "almost died" from anxiety because he felt no faith (*weil kein Glaube da war*).[11] No witness, however, reports that he really made a move to leave the altar.

As is so often the case with Luther, exaggerations and conjectures can neither enhance nor destroy the simple dramatic constellations which characterized his moments of fate. In this moment he had the presence of the Eucharist in front of him—and the presence of the father behind him. He had not yet learned to speak with God "without embarrassment," and he had not seen his father since the visit home before the thunderstorm. At this moment, then, when he was to mediate between the father and The Father, he still felt torn in his obedience to both. I would not be willing to give exclusive precedence to the theological conflict (as the professor does) or to the personal-neurotic one (as the psychiatrist does) in this condensed, intensive experience. Martin, at this moment, faced the Great Divide of his life, as every young man must sooner or later— the divide which separates, once and for all, the contributaries to the future from the regressive rivulets seeking the past. In front of him was the Eucharist's uncertain grace; behind him his father's potential wrath. His faith at that moment lacked the secure formulation of the nature of mediatorship which later emerged in the lectures on the Psalms. He had no living concept of Christ; he was, in fact, mortally afraid of the whole riddle of mediatorship. Because of all this, he may well have been morbidly sensitive to some theological problems which only much later did he have the courage to face and challenge as true moral problems.

The Eucharist's long history had served to confuse its meaning more than to clarify it. It had started in Paulinian times as a highly devotional meal to commemorate that Passover which had turned out to be the last supper. As a ritual meal, it is a supremely sublimated version of a long series of blood sacrifices and rituals culminating in the devouring of flesh, first human, then animal, for the sake of magic and spiritual replenishment. In the original *Eucharistia* the community "gave thanks": they ate bread from the same loaf and drank wine from the same cup, thus remembering, as Christ had asked them to do, his sacrificial death. This is a sublimated act because Christ had not only made the supreme sacrifice, self-chosen and human ("I am the lamb"); he had also made each man's responsibility inescapably personal: "Let a man examine himself, and so let him eat of that bread, and drink of that cup . . . for if we would judge ourselves, we should not be judged." [12] True, Paul had berated those earliest communities for not being quite able to keep competitive voraciousness out of this rite; but, alas, they were simple folk.

What those not-so-simple folk, the theoreticians and the politicians of the church, subsequently did with this rite made it as different from its original form as all totalitarian reality is different from a revolutionary idea. This difference is not accidental; it is in the psychological nature of things. What is driven out by young rebellion is always reinstated by the dogmatism of middle age.

Dogma, given total power, reinstates what once was to be warded off, and brings back ancient barbaric ambiguities as cold and over-defined legalisms so unconvincing that, where once faith reigned, the law must take over and be enforced by spiritual and political terror. And when conscience and dogma once enter into an alliance with terror, man sinks below anything in nature or in his own primitive history; he creates a hell on earth, such as no god could invent elsewhere.

When those early Christian folk heard it said: "For we being many are one bread, and one body: for we are all partakers of that one bread," [13] and when they heard it said: "Take, eat; this is my body, which is broken for you: this do in remembrance of me," [14] they participated in magic formulations of the kind which can only be created by a merger of the imagery of the unconscious with the poetry of the people.

Our unconscious preserves the images of our early, preverbal childhood. Before we knew the separateness of things and the differences that are in names, we experienced certain basic modes of existence. We once felt at one with a maternal matrix from which we received the substances of life—not merely food, but everything we could then experience as positive, as an affirmation of our existence: personal warmth, and the nourishment of our senses and of our anticipations. However, we also experienced incidents in which bad substances, even including substances that first felt good, seemed to choke our trusting organs of acceptance, or poison us from within our own bowels. At these times, only care, the original *caritas*, could save us with a new infusion of good substances. In a way, deep down, we never know better than this. This earliest stratum of experience remains effective throughout life. In primitive milieus it leads to superstitious ideas and acts of acquiring beneficial substances through the consumption of flesh and blood from significant bodies; and to ideas and acts in which evil is identified with curses inflicted by and on substances and bodies, and dealt with through sorcery.

In *Childhood and Society*, I reported a daily ritual of a California Indian tribe of salmon fishermen which indicates how the sanctity of intake was impressed on the children of a singularly avaricious and bitterly capitalistic tribe: "During meals a strict order of placement is maintained and the children are taught to eat in prescribed ways; for example, to put only a little food on the spoons. to take the spoons up to their mouths slowly, to put the spoon down while chewing the food—and, above all, to think of becoming rich during the process. Nobody speaks during meals so that everybody can keep his own thoughts on money and salmon, . . . attitudes which, to the Yurok mind, will in the end assure the salmon's favor. The Yurok during meals makes himself see money hanging from trees and salmon swimming in the river." [15]

More rational beings often cannot deal with these matters openly; they express them in more or less malignant personal quirks, or they work them out in their dreams, those gifts of nature which permit us to commune with our unconscious and emerge clear-eyed. In these unconscious ideas lies much power for personal recovery and creative activity, which cultural institutions can augment with the healing factor of artistic or ritual form. But in these ideas also lies our greatest vulnerability and exploitability, because no matter how rational we are, our unconscious seeks ways in which it can manifest itself. If we do not live in a time and a place which permit it creative manifestation, we are easy prey to the experts and the leaders who somehow know how to exploit our unconscious without understanding the magic reasons for their success; and consequently their success contributes to their being corrupted by leadership. Dogmatic leaders are the worst, for they combine a mortal scrupulosity with a deadly unscrupulousness, a mixture which permits them to take command of our conscience. They know how to dull our perception so that they can involve us in mythical realities which we can neither manage to believe completely, nor afford to quite disbelieve.

The questions of whether Christ meant it when he said, "This is my body," and whether the version, "This cup is the new testament in my blood" [16] comes closer to his meaning than "This is my blood of the new testament" [17] became over the centuries questions of mortal scrupulosity. They eventually led to ritual murder as the theologians fortified their position by suppressing old and new forms of creative thought, and as the masses, sensitized by spiritual terror and by horror of the plague, stampeded for the well-guarded gates to heaven.

Symbolically enough, the name of that early and primitive communion changed from *Eucharistia*, which means thanksgiving, to *Missa*, which means (or was thought to mean) the dismissal of the unworthy. The original selection of the worthy was an introspective responsibility, fulfilled almost by "tasting" one's inner condition: "For he that eateth and drinketh unworthily, eateth and drinketh damnation to himself, not discerning the Lord's body. For this cause many are weak and sickly among you, and many sleep." [18] It then developed into a matter of worthiness by mere works, by participation in more and more meaningless and idolatrous observances. True, Paul had found that more people were sickly and asleep than were capable of some introspective discipline; so that one may well argue that from a mass-psychological point of view, early Christianity demanded too much of too many. It is obvious also that our neo-Paulinian, Martin Luther, can be said to have demanded too much of his day and even of himself; and in the end, the Lutheran state-church was the best that could be had under the given historical and personal circumstances. But the greatest advances in human consciousness are made by people who demand too much, and thus invite a situation in which their overstrained followers inevitably end up either compromisers or dogmatists. It is therefore necessary constantly to reformulate those advances in human consciousness and to ask how it happens, again and again, that the best become the worst enemies of the good. A council of the best finally decreed that Christ's body and blood are truly and substantially contained in the bread and in the wine; this decree made into a law, subject to thought control and terror, that which had begun as a moral force and might have continued so if allowed to remain an intrinsic part of perpetual communal revival.

All these ideas seem to have been far from Martin's conscious mind and theological thought at the time of his first Mass. But his later works and acts testify that in some rudimentary form the ideas were already in his mind at that point. Most biographers claim that doubt in the Mass itself could not have contributed to Martin's anxiety attack, for was he not, years later, still morbidly obsessed with the idea of celebrating Mass before certain altars in Rome? And so much so, that he almost wished his parents dead so that he could make the special contribution to their salvation offered by the papal chamber of commerce? To the clinical mind, however, the very obsessional, and by then utterly hopeless, preoccupation with the Mass only demonstrates that long before Luther could face the issue squarely, the Eucharist had been eroded by scruples and ambivalences of long standing.

We have quoted Luther's statement that as he celebrated his first Mass he was overcome by the feeling that he had to face God directly without a mediator. We must now discuss his other impending encounter: the one with his earthly father. Is it not astonishing that the biographers who have tried to account for Luther's anxiety have not considered it worth emphasizing that he had not seen his father since his impulsive visit home; and that he had not, as yet, faced him to see —yes, in his face—the result of that extracted permission? Could not Martin foresee that his father would be essentially unreconstructed and ready to remind Martin of the obedience due him, knowing, in turn, quite well that the son had never wholly relinquished his filial obedience—and that he never would, never could? In Martin's first Mass the paradox of paternal obediences was fully propounded. Martin, who had sought the identity of a monk, had been ordered to become a priest, a dispenser as well as a partaker of the Eucharist. There is no use saying he should have been glad: like other great young men, Martin never felt worthy of the next step in his career. Later he thought and said he would surely die when he was ordered to become a professor; and still later, after his unexpectedly triumphant entrance into Worms, when it was clear that he could not escape being the people's reformer, he stood most meekly before the emperor and was hardly audible. As always, he first had to grow into the role which he had usurped without meaning to. And this first and anxious anchorage of his future identity as a responsible churchman had to be witnessed by the father, who cursed it (and said so presently) as his son's final escape from the identity of being most of all Hans' son. The attempt of the biographers to separate the mystic presence of the Eucharist and the oppressive presence of the father is invalid in view of what happened later that day, and forever after.

It cannot be denied that Martin asked for it—he could not let his father go any more than the father could let him go. Martin knew that he had not won his father's *gantzen Willen*, his whole will. But during the meeting which they had after the ceremony, "as we sat at the table, I started to talk with him with a childish good comportment, wanting to put him in the wrong and myself in the right, by saying: 'Dear father, why did you resist so hard and become so angry because you did not want to let me be a monk, and maybe even now you do not like too much to see me here, although it is a sweet and godly life, full of peace?' But there [the father] carried on, in front of all the doctors, magisters and other gentlemen: 'You scholars, have you not read in the scriptures that one should honor father and mother?' " [19] And as others started to argue with him, Hans Luder said what was as good as a curse: "God give that it wasn't a devil's spook" [20] (*Satanae praestigium, Teuffel's Gespenst*)— referring, of course, to the thunderstorm on the road to Erfurt, Martin's "road to Damascus." As Luther wrote to his father publicly when he had become a great man: "You again hit me so cleverly and fittingly that in my whole life I have hardly heard a word that resounded in me more forcefully and stuck in me more firmly. But," he added—putting the father in his place more than a decade after the event—"but I, secure in my justice, listened to you as to a human being and felt deep contempt for you; yet belittle your word in my soul, I could not." [21]

What would not some of us give if, in certain decisive moments, we could have felt clearly and said calmly to a parent what the great man could write only after many years: "I listened to you as to a human being" (*Te velut hominem audivi et fortiter contempsi*)? But at the time, Martin, too, fell silent. As he confessed later, he heard God's voice in his father's words, which helped to make the fusion of presences fatefully permanent. His father, he felt, had not given his benediction "as to a betrothal," and God had denied him the experience of the Eucharist. But for less, Martin (Hans' son) could not settle and remain whole; he would yet find the right word "to speak to God directly."

He was alone now; alone against his temperament, which his father had predicted would refuse submission to celibacy; and alone against his wrath, which his father had shown was indomitable in the Luders. Incredible as it seems, at this late date Martin was thrown back into the infantile struggle, not only over his obedience toward, but also over his identification with, his father. This regression and this personalization of his conflicts cost him that belief in the monastic way and in his superiors which during the first year had been of such "godly" support. He was alone in the monastery, too, and soon showed it in a behavior that became increasingly un-understandable even to those who believed in him. *To be justified* became his stumbling block as a believer, his obsession as a neurotic sufferer, and his preoccupation as a theologian.

2

Luther's complaint that his father refused to "give him away," as it were, in his new marriage is meaningful in many ways. It shows how much he had tried to believe that he, Hans' son, would be able to settle for the passivity of professional penitence—he in whom was stored (one is tempted to say coiled) the striking power of one of the most powerful minds of his age. His childlike appeal during the festive dinner betrays the same attempt at self-deception. No wonder his father smelled a rat; and no wonder Martin heard God's voice in the father's angry retort: it was, at the same time, the voice of their temperamental affinity and of their joint proud conviction that *their* devil was too peppery for refined theology, and *their* temperament too strong for reformed monkishness.

This spiritually unsuccessful ordination ended Martin's honeymoon with monasticism and doomed their marriage to an eventual divorce which confused all the retrospective information about Luther's next phase. While he was still in the cloister nothing much was found worth recording about this excitable and yet impressive monk. Only after his dramatic separation from monasticism did he and the other monks begin to appraise his years of monkhood in bitter earnest. Whatever ends in divorce, however, loses all retrospective clarity because a divorce breaks the *Gestalt* of one love into the *Gestalten* of two hates. After divorce the vow "until death us do part" must be explained as a commitment made on wrong premises. Every item which once spelled love must now be pronounced hate. It is impossible to say how good or how bad either partner really was; one can only say that they were bad for each other. And then the lawyers take over and railroad the whole matter into controversies neither of the partners had ever thought of.

Later, when Luther had become his own best and worst lawyer, he wrote some magnificent treatises in which breathed a new spirit, a new marriage. As polemics, they pushed aside the old facts and theories rather than taking considered account of them. But Luther also, and especially in private, historified (in the sense above defined) into the old conditions whatever they had subjectively become for him, and in his historifications shows all the flippancy, plaintiveness, and vulgarity of an undisciplined divorcee. Among his statements is his assertion that his superiors had encouraged his self-torment by suggesting continuous waking, praying, and reading, so that his health had been systematically undermined. Yet he reported himself that in 1510 he was able to walk from Erfurt to Rome, which was exceptionally rainy that year, and back over the wintry Alps, without any sign of weakness worse than a fleeting cold. He also complained that the monastery's official policy was to consider the omission of a little word like *enim* during Mass a sin almost as big as adultery and murder. But much of the blame for the importance which was attached to these statements—and to such grotesque historifications as that he had to fight for the right and opportunity to study the Bible which, in fact, had been put into his hands when he entered the monastery as the only personal book to remain in his possession—falls to his followers, who could not see that his justification needed no such exaggerations, and who simply did not want to see what a naively irresponsible talker their religious leader could be during his later years.

It is equally impossible to take at face value what his erstwhile colleagues said of him after his separation from the Church to which they remained true. Before he left, there seems to have been a certain willingness on their part to consider his peculiarities ("I must have been a very strange brother," [22] he said himself afterward) as what today we would dismiss as "tension." Some were even willing to interpret his impulsivities, as long as they seemed to serve the Church, as being of the traditional Paulinian kind. After he had begun to appear to some like a *new* St. Paul, however, all of his activity was reevaluated by others as demonic possession and mere personal orneriness. To utilize these opinions to diagnose periodical insanity, as Luther's medical critics have done, does not seem to be permissible even if Erasmus the All-Adjustable, in the heat of their dispute, later called Luther a raving maniac and a drunkard.

At any rate, the older Luther is not under discussion here. What attacks and hallucinations are reported of Martin seem to have been hysterical. Martin, lying in bed, might phantasy himself dwelling among angels; and then, in a rapid turn of mood, and with a reawakened identification with the miners' suspicion of things that glitter too brazenly, would think that the angels were really devils. But we cannot recognize any of the characteristics of a true hallucination in such a phantasy. Rather, it represents, as do many of Luther's accounts of his often very outer inner life, an obvious, obsessive self-testing of the credulity which his father had challenged. The same thing is true of such unreconstructed Mansfeldianisms as his report that one night the devil made such a big noise that Martin took his books and went to bed in pursuance of his formula that nothing checks the devil better than open contempt. Students of today might be glad if they had such a hallucinatory excuse to retire. But it seems certain, and is fully documented by his friends, that Luther in those years suffered from acute anxiety, and would wake up in a cold sweat ("the devil's bath," as he called it); that he developed a phobia of the devil which in the way of typical obsessive ambivalence gradually included the fear that the very highest good, such as the shining image of Christ, might only be a devil's temptation; that he came to fear and even hate Christ, in spite of his superiors' patient arguments, as one who came only to punish; and that he had strange fits of unconsciousness which, in one case, the fit in the choir, are suspected of having been accompanied by convulsions. Today we would feel that such an attack might be the internal result of stored rage in a young man who is trying to hold on to his obedient, pious self-restraint, and has not yet found a legitimate outer object to attack or a legitimate weapon with which to hit out about him.

It seems entirely probable that Martin's life at times approached what today we might call a borderline psychotic state in a young man with prolonged adolescence and reawaked infantile conflicts. But the caricatures later created by both sides of the divorce, which were publicized with all the abandon of the then new yellow press, fail to explain the historical fact that Martin was promoted step by step with never a delay up the ladder of responsible positions in priesthood, administration, and teaching. By the time he became the reformer, he was by no means a simple monk but a prior, a district-vicar for eleven monasteries, and a professor of theology in the chair previously held by the provincial vicar himself. For more than a decade, then, the marriage cannot have gone so badly.

At the same time, however, that he was becoming increasingly busy, the monastic realities apparently gradually came to take second place to a fanatic preoccupation with himself. It bespeaks Luther's general sturdiness and intellectual soundness that he could fulfill the duties required of him even while the gulf between their official meaning and his fanatic inner struggles seemed more and more omi-

nous to him, and probably also to some of his superiors and colleagues. At the same time, a theological system of increasing self-
assertiveness was founded on fragments of mood swings and of intuitive thoughts which later found their climax, as well as their con-
ceptual unification, in the "revelation in the tower." Such a painful
and prolonged incubation is by no means rare in young great men
who can give birth to a living creation only when they are ready
to take care of it, which is only possible when they have found the
main executive of their identity (in Martin, the Word), and have
seen the potential of intimacy in the kind of friendship which Martin found only in Wittenberg, around Staupitz, and among the humanists. In the cloister all three factors—his sense of identity, his potential for intimacy, and the discovery of his generative powers—
were stubbornly engaged in the life-or-death struggle for that sense
of total justification which both the father and The Father had
denied him, and without which a *homo religiosus* has no identity at
all.

It would be hard, indeed, to describe the Martin of the middle
monastery years as a great young man, although Protestant biographers have given their all to this impossible task. It would be easier
to describe him as a sick young man who later became great—and
greatly destructive; and this, too, has been done with relish. Although I am indebted to both of these schools, I will, within the
limits of the task which I have set for myself, try to outline in what
ways Martin was a young great man, sickness and all. Whether or
not mankind can afford its great men, sickness and all, is another
question. Before we can even approach it we must first learn to recognize the afflictions of our favorite heroes, as well as the madness
in those great men whom we could do without. For, short as our
lives are, the influence of the men we elect, support, or tolerate as
great can indeed be a curse felt far beyond the third and fourth
generation.

In the case of great young men (and in the cases of many vital
young ones of whom we should not demand that they reveal at all
costs the stigmata of greatness in order to justify confusion and
conflict), rods which measure consistency, inner balance, or pro-
ficiency simply do not fit the relevant dimensions. On the contrary,
a case could be made for the necessity for extraordinary conflicts,
at times both felt and judged to be desperate. For if some youths

did not feel estranged from the compromise patterns into which their societies have settled down, if some did not force themselves almost against their own wills to insist, at the price of isolation, on finding an original way of meeting our existential problems, societies would lose an essential avenue to rejuvenation and to that rebellious expansion of human consciousness which alone can keep pace with the technological and social change. To retrace, as we are doing here, such a step of expansion involves taking account of the near downfall of the man who took it, partially in order to understand better the origin of greatness, and partially in order to acknowledge the fact that the trauma of near defeat follows a great man through life. I have already quoted Kierkegaard's statement that Luther lived and acted always as if lightning were about to strike directly behind him. Furthermore, a great man carries the trauma of his near downfall and his mortal grudge against the near assassins of his identity into the years of his creativity and beyond, into his decline; he builds his hates and his grudges into his system as bulwarks—bulwarks which eventually make the system first rigid and finally, brittle.

3

Monastic penitence for the sake of his own afterlife and for all mankind's was Martin's profession. To many of us, this seems a strange thing to be professional about, full time. Yet, in his most personal search for justification, Martin used the methods of his profession which were designed to solve spiritual problems in a particular way: the "seared, the cauterized conscience," Luther later called that solution. At any rate, the vicissitudes of his most personal search cannot be accounted for outside of the system, which came more than half-way to meet him. No course of training invented specifically to intensify neurotic strain in a young man like Martin could have been more effective than the monastic training of his day. Luther later reported that he saw others go insane, and that he felt that he might also. But there is no reason to assume that a greater number of individuals went insane in this setting than would be slated for failure in other kinds of indoctrinations. Any indoctrination worth its ideological salt also harbors dangers, which bring about the unmaking of some and the supreme transcendence of others.

In this connection I am led to think of my own profession: let me make the most of a strange parallel. Young (and often not so young) psychoanalysts in training must undergo a training procedure which demands a total and central personal involvement, and which takes greater chances with the individual's relation to himself and to those who up to then have shared his life, than any other professional training except monkhood. Because the reward for psychoanalytic training, at least in some countries, is a good income; because, for decades, the psychoanalyst seemed primarily preoccupied with the study of sexuality; and because psychoanalytic power under certain historical conditions can corrupt as much as any other power, an aura of licentiousness is often assumed to characterize this training.

The future psychoanalyst, however, must undergo a personal psychoanalysis. This is a "treatment" which shares fully with the treatment of patients a certain systematic interpersonal austerity. Over the decades, psychoanalysts have accepted the formal setting of the almost daily appointment as the natural arrangement for eliciting the analysand's free associations. However, this natural setting for a spontaneous production is both an exercise in a new kind of asceticism, and a long-range experiment determining in large measure the free verbal material which it provokes.

There is, first of all, what I would like to call the asceticism of the "expendable face." The analysand reclines on a couch at the head of which the analyst sits; both of them put, as it were, their faces aside, and give the most minute attention to the patient's verbal productions which are interrupted by the analyst only when his technical sense demands that an interpretation be given. He, of course, can see, not the analysand's face, but his gestures and postural changes; while the analysand sees the ceiling, maybe the top of a bookcase, or one and the same picture for hundreds of hours. (I wish to acknowledge a small fragment of an original Greek sculpture in faintly glowing marble.) The restriction of the visual field, the injunction on muscular or locomotor movement, the supine position, the absence of facial communication, the deliberate exposure to emerging thought and imagery—all these tend not only to facilitate ordinary memory and meditation; they produce (as they are supposed to do) a "transference neurosis," that is a transfer to the analyst and the analytic situation of the irrational and often unconscious thought contents and affects which characterize the analysand's symptoms or blindspots.

The analyst patiently continues to explain the patterns of unconscious thought, whether the material strikes him as boring or lurid, appealing or nauseating, thought-provoking or infuriating. It stands to reason, however, that when a devotional denial of the face, and a systematic mistrust of all surface are used as tools in a man's worklife, they can lead to an almost obsessional preoccupation with "the unconscious," a dogmatic emphasis on inner processes as the only true essence of things human, and an overestimation of verbal meanings in human life. The risks and the chances inherent in this method are analogous to those in Martin's scruples. Into the ears of a master whose face is averted, and who refuses in any personal sense either to condemn or to justify, temptations are revealed which one never dreamt of, or never knew one dreamt of until one began to understand dreams and to recognize the maneuvers of self-deception. Impulses are communicated, some before and some after they have achieved a bit of delinquent expression; for a while, these impulses can play havoc with a candidate's previous adjustment, including his adjustments to the individuals close to him, who cannot for the life of them see why a person has to get sick in order to learn how to cure others. Nonetheless, all that counts once the process is in motion is the candidate's increasing ability to converse with his own unconscious well enough to recognize the unconscious motivations of others and his preparation to tolerate without flinching his patients' transference neuroses: for they will make a good parent out of him and a bad one, and they will deify him and vilify him in language so spontaneous that not even a priest would dare to evoke or to tolerate it. His own transference neurosis, it is hoped, will be cured before he is exposed to those of his patients.

Before he sees patients, however, the subjective phase of the training, the personal analysis, must overlap with years of practical and theoretical training in the new science. Often this means training in the particular awareness and habitual conceptualization cultivated by a particular training institute, usually founded by or around the person or the ideas of a particular leader, often come from far; although unified standards are now being organized on a national scale. It is obvious, however, that no organizational rules can entirely contain, nor any existing experience invariably predict, the destructive and creative spirits which will be freed by such a combination of the personal, the professional, and the organizational. Thus psychoanalysis also has its monkhood, its monkishness, and its monkery.

My point is this: the fact that psychoanalysis was fully exposing sexuality for the first time in human history, in all its variations and transformations and its irrelations to logic and ethics, obscured the fact that a new kind of asceticism had been invented, a heroic abnegation of the kind which produces new steps in moral awareness. What man has always been most proud of—the rationalization of the irrational with esthetic, moral and logical preoccupations—became no more than a surface ripple on a body of infinitely deep water.

As a radical method of cure one can only say that psychoanalysis helps those who are well enough to tolerate it, and intelligent enough to gain by it over and above the cure of symptoms. As an intellectual experience, however, it is like other ascetic methods in specifically arousing and giving access to certain recesses of the mind otherwise completely removed from conscious mastery.

This brief reflection helps to clarify what the more thoughtful monks faced in their procedures, and what the teaching monks were up against with Martin.

Take, for example, the problem of Martin's *tristitia*. A certain kind and degree of *tristitia* was a requirement of monkhood; some individuals were more inclined to *tristitia*, some less, and for that very reason it was necessary to make it a disciplined and shared matter. Discipline meant not only that a monk had to be on guard against forgetting that man is mortal and constitutionally imperfect; it also meant that he could not let a constant awareness of these facts turn into melancholic rumination which would serve only itself. He therefore had to develop a methodical self-observation through systematic meditation and professional confession. For most mortals it was enough to avoid temptations or to confess them; the monk had to go toward and challenge them since they were the constant tests of true, inner firmness. He had to cultivate a systematic suspiciousness of motives, which at the same time he could not allow to become either scrupulosity or a masochistic seeking after self-condemnation.

Comparable difficulties occur in psychoanalysis in our particular method of uncovering by free association our hidden thoughts and our sleeping temptations, scanning our consciousness in order to follow freely and verbalize honestly any trend of thought without being in any way selective. This is, of course, something one can only try to approximate; anybody brash enough to say he can do it is surely not gifted for it. But not everybody could or should even try. In some, conscious control is too rigid; they may be slated for excellent performances in other fields of endeavor in which such control is paramount. In others, the impulses rushing to be realized in consciousness are too strong, and might be more productively applied were they to remain unverbalized. Furthermore, the method may make some people sicker than they ever were. The decision about whether the results to be expected will justify taking this risk is difficult; but well-trained people are usually able to make it with some confidence.

When such a responsible invention for the disciplined increase of inner freedom becomes widely used as a therapy and as a method of professional training, it is bound to become standardized so that many will be able to benefit from it who of their own accord would never have thought of such strenuous self-inspection, and who are not especially endowed for it. A standardized procedure calls for uniform application, an application which would have been much too uniform for those who initiated the method. Here training analysts are—on rare occasions, to be sure—aware of the other side of the coin: the predicament of Martin's superiors when they found they had a young great man on their hands. If such a man, possessing the potentialities of truly original self-inspection and the fierce pride that is attached to originality—if such a man should apply to us for training, would we recognize him? Would we accept him? Could we keep him? Could he fit his budding originality into our established methods? And could we do justice to him, within a training system increasingly standardized and supervised? But these questions are directed too much to ourselves. Such a man will take care of himself, whatever our methods. Let us see how Martin managed.

In his original search for aloneness and anonymity, Martin felt that silence, discipline, worship, and confession were godly. Somehow he must have hoped to escape into a life of obedience to God which would eventually come to count also as obedience to a reconciled father. Not without provocation, the father had called whatever unconscious bluff existed in this plan; and after that the rebellion was on, albeit in the ambivalent form of overobedience. Or so I interpret the period that followed Martin's first Mass, with all its strenuous attempts to make monkhood absurd by trying to obey its rules too scrupulously. Some extraordinary young people, who have trapped themselves in an ordinary niche of social life, as Martin had in the monastery, and barricaded themselves in with massive compulsive compensations, can escape their fortified prison only by making themselves seemingly very small, and actually very slippery. A severe abnegation may develop with a mixed neurosis—put together of fragments of a number of neuroses—which at times borders on the psychotic. This syndrome has been discussed as an acute identity diffusion; under all the wretched confusedness, one can usually recognize a certain zest in the production of problems, a rebellious mocking in dramatic helplessness, and a curious honesty (and honest curiosity) in the insistence on getting to the point, the fatal point, the true point.

And thus Martin set out to torment his preceptors. It is quite possible that this happened as they, in turn, set out to fit him for his new role of priest and his future role of scholar and teacher—all roles which at first he disavowed, although he continued to invite them with his very obedience and extraordinary talent. However, his training seems to have entered a particular austere, introspective, and studious period which he wàs less able to tolerate. His scruples began to eat like moths into the fabric of monkhood which before had felt like a well-woven protection against his impulses. He thus became susceptible to that alliance of erotic irritability and hypersensitivity of conscience which brings identity diffusion to a head. He attempted to counter this alliance with redoubled use of monastic methods, and consequently found himself at times estranged from all three: his upset drives (his "concupiscence"); his confused conscience; and the monastic means and ends.

In confession, for example, he was so meticulous in the attempt to be truthful that he spelled out every intention as well as every deed; he splintered relatively acceptable purities into smaller and smaller impurities; he reported temptations in historical sequence, starting back in childhood; and after having confessed for hours, would ask for special appointments in order to correct previous statements. In doing this he was obviously both exceedingly compulsive and, at least unconsciously, rebellious. And, indeed, his preceptor threatened to punish him for obstruction of confession. It must be remembered that the method of confession was traditional, and was designed to meeet ordinary requirements without upsetting monastic efficiency. Supportive methods existed to help the confessing monk keep to a system: for instance, confessing transgressions in the order of the five senses, then of the seven deadly sins, then of the ten commandments. One can see that even a sincere man, given such a formidable array of possible transgressions, would have relatively little to say, and would be able to feel relieved. But Martin, on the contrary, was inclined to make the formidable most of small things; at one time his superior Staupitz mocked him in a letter in which he said that Christ was not interested in such trifles and that Martin had better see to it that he have some juicy adultery or murder to confess—perhaps the murder of his parents.[23] But nothing could drive Martin deeper into despair than his superiors' refusal to take him seriously: at such moments he became "a dead corpse," he said.

All this is classically compulsive; this kind of concentration on the means to an end, and such ceaseless thinking about these means, separates the seeker more than ever from his aim, which is to *feel* something: in Martin's case, to feel justified in the eyes of God, and to feel there was a possibility of propitiating God. As he became more and more alienated from this aim, he remained bitterly honest about it: in his later lectures on the Psalms, when he came to discuss the effect of penitence, he directed his audience to St. Augustine's confession for a good example, adding: *"Quia extra compunctionem sum et loquor de compunctione"* [24] (Here I talk of penitence and cannot feel it). Instead, he felt most intensely what he wanted most desperately to discard, namely, the unworthy sexual temptations, petty rages, and debasing blasphemies—all of which, it must be remembered, confirmed his father's suspicions, and thus constituted one of the secret weapons of his compulsion: the transformation of the open disobedience to the father (being a monk at all) into a secret obedience to the father's prediction (being a bad monk) under the guise of being obedient to God (being a more than reasonably good monk).

At this point we must note a characteristic of young great rebels:

their inner split between the temptation to surrender and the need to dominate. A great young rebel is torn between on the one hand tendencies to give in and phantasies of defeat (Luther used to resign himself to an early death at times of impending success), and the absolute need, on the other hand, to take the lead, not only over himself but over all the forces and people who impinge on him. In men of ideas, the second, the dictatorial trend, may manifest itself paradoxically at first in a seeming surrender to passivity which, in the long run, proves to have been an active attempt at liquidating passivity by becoming fully acquainted with it. Even at the time of his near downfall, he struggles for a position in which he can regain a sense of initiative by finding some rock bottom to stand on, after which he can proceed with a total re-evaluation of the premises on which his society is founded. In the lectures on the Psalms we can see that wholeness arise which became Luther's theology; first, however, we must note examples of his early total restatements; statements which, during his ongoing crisis, were indistinguishable both from neurotic exaggerations and from delinquent deviations.

As to confession, then, which he later came to call a *laboriosa illa et inutilis ars* [25] he violated it with his superior honesty. He found it impossible to decide whether the reassurance gained from it was really a godly feeling or not; or whether anybody could really differentiate penitential attrition—the mere fear of punishment—from contrition, that complete penitence which culminated in a true love for God the judge, and for mankind. We can easily see the personal and neurotic reference to his own failure as a son in his indecision; indeed, one may say that by radically transferring the desperation of his filial position into the human condition vis-à-vis God, and by insisting, as it were, on a cosmic test case, he forced himself either to find a new avenue toward faith or to fail. Theologically, this later became part of his most radical re-evaluation of all works— that is, of all attempts to win a righteous God's favor by special efforts and graduations. On the other hand, faced with a compromise advanced by Gerson, namely, that God demanded only that one do what is in one's power (*quod in se est*), he rejected this less rigid requirement as an excuse for claiming weakness and an invitation to make deals with God. He called such liberalism a "Jewish, Turkish, and Pelagian" trick—his era's equivalent of a "British, Papist, and Bolshevik danger." The graduated differentiation between deadly and venial sins seemed particularly impossible to him. For if a deadly sin, according to its definition, is one which undermines the life principle of love, how can one who has so sinned find the way back to faith? *Fides non stat cum peccato mortali:* faith does not linger where there is deadly sin. He ended up with apparently total pessimism, denying man's ability to gain God's grace by the fulfillment of any earthly law or observance. He characterized as spiritual prostitution (*fornicatio spiritus*) brazen attempts to gain eternal life with "acts of love." He thus approached an impasse which called for a resolution so total that its full implication was revealed to him only much later, in the "revelation in the tower"—namely, that faith must be there *before* the deed, and that all enforced or prescribed works, if they are begun with indifference or hate and lack faith, love, joy, and will (*Glaub, Lieb, Lust, und Willen*) are doomed to spiritual failure.

In connection with Martin's confessional scruples, we first hear of the problem of "concupiscence"—that is, man's natural endowment of drives which lead him into sin—and of the particular problem of "*libido*," which, next to "*ira*" and "*impatientia*," led Martin into temptation. From everything we have recorded so far, and from what we must anticipate on the basis of historical information, we can well imagine that Martin's much suppressed, and as it were untrained, anger and hate would finally break through in a most disturbing way. It cannot surprise us that he noticed that often it was the very celebration of the Mass which put him in a state of unholy anger. On the other hand, there can be no doubt that in this excitable young man sexual tension accompanied other kinds; and that in this hyperconscientious young man, sexual tension was equated with sexual sin. Neurotic sexual tension, however, cannot be attributed to the mere pressure of natural drives. No doubt it is the more manly and less neurotic man who can endure abstinence at one time, and yet be able to function with undiminished potency at another. In Martin's case, his father's prediction that he would not be able to stand celibacy, and his superiors' assumption that he could, gave the matter a connotation beyond any biological question. Furthermore, it is necessary to differentiate between temptations in the world outside—that is, occasions for sinning which can be avoided with luck and low drive—and those *tentationes* which beset the monk like furious beasts just because his method of training arouses them in order to see whether it can tame them. Psychoanalysts also know a distinction like this: the same systematic introspection which, at the end, is to give the individual intelligent mastery over his drives can first evoke a frenzy never encountered before. *Et tandem furor fiat*, as Luther put it, adding that the mere thought of libidinal matters for the sake of honest appraisal makes them intrude on your honesty. (*Quando magis alignis cogitat de libidine deponenda, tanto magis incidit in cogitatione, ut altera alteram trudet.*) [26]

Luther later, at times naively, at times shrewdly, was frank about his sex-life, revealing different aspects of the matter out of mere impulsivity or his peculiar sense of publicity. He thus provided a neat set of quotations for almost any school of interpretation. Protestant writers, in trying to depict him as a saint made in Germany, present him as a colorless young man, and restrict his masculinity so exclusively to a spiritual bass voice that the psychiatrist is right in saying that these writers make Luther appear "psychoinfantile." Others have described him, also in his own words, as an oversexed monk with secret sins, unfit from the start for celibacy.

Most unlikely, so all authorities agree, are any irregularities with women. Luther denied them disarmingly, claiming that in all his clerical practice he had received confession from three women only; he did not even look at them, he said, although he does seem to have remembered the occasions. The conditions of his life do not make it probable that he could have strayed in this direction. His references to autoerotic experiences, on the other hand, cannot be merely personal confessions characterizing his own sexual idiosyncrasies; they are, rather, meant to throw light on the condition of celibacy and are often only dragged to the surface by theological disputes. Mostly Luther speaks of a state of sexual urge which was aggravated by the very attempts to appraise and to curb it. He mentions release through nocturnal emissions at first as a matter of natural necessity (*ex necessitate corporali*) [27]; but he indicates that in his case this permissable and seemingly biological outlet was drawn into his psychological conflict and paradoxically became aggravated by fasting (*Si quando ego maxime eiunabam. . . . sequebatur pol-*

lutio).[28] Nocturnal emissions in general were felt to be on the border-line between sinful intention and involuntariness; this is obvious from his assertion that monks frequently abstained from celebrating Mass the morning after emissions.

In one of his early lectures Luther goes into considerable detail about the voluntary methods by which "solitary emissions" can be effected, and about the involuntariness of emissions which happen in sleep and even, without one's inner consent (*preter consensum*), in the waking state and in the daytime, adding "as happens to many" [29] (*ut multis contingit*). His discussion in this lecture seems to the psychiatrist a bit too detailed to be clerical routine; but there is a possibility that involuntary releases in the waking state, which are known to occur in young men in tension states associated, for example, with examinations, or with being late, may be more typical in a situation like the monastic one, where a state of morbid watchfulness is heightened to spiritual terror. At any rate, if any specific form of sexual transgression is to be sought in Luther's conflicting references, it would seem clinically most likely that Martin's general state of tension on occasion resulted in a sudden spontaneous ejaculation—an event which would leave a sensitive young man feeling guilty for what he had not intended and relieved by what he could not afford to enjoy. Most of all, however, it left him with the suspicion, or even half-knowledge, that there was more unconscious intention in it—more pleasure, and, most of all, more rebellion—than routine confession would force him to admit. I think that spontaneous ejaculation, rather than masturbation (as the psychiatrist suspects), is what Luther was talking about; although it must be granted that the young man's whole overscrupulous make-up suggests to the clinician guilt feelings probably originating in childhood masturbation. Facts and statistics, however, matter little here; a young man like Martin will make a life of sin out of a very few occurrences and will remain preoccupied primarily with matters of principle: when and how one knows that one "willed" something which "happens" to one, even in a state of only relative consciousness.

James Joyce, in his account of the young artist's temptations after he had renounced, under the impact of a retreat, the habit of visiting prostitutes, described the predicament which basically characterizes

all these temptations, sexual and otherwise—that is, the question of
active intention and passive drivenness:

This idea of surrender had a perilous attraction for his mind now that
he felt his soul beset once again by the insistent voices of the flesh which
began to murmur to him again during his prayers and meditations. It
gave him an intense sense of power to know that he could by a single act
of consent, in a moment of thought, undo all that he had done. He seemed
to feel a flood slowly advancing towards his naked feet and to be waiting
for the first faint timid noiseless wavelet to touch his fevered skin. Then,
almost at the instant of that touch, almost at the verge of sinful consent,
he found himself standing far away from the flood upon a dry shore,
saved by a sudden act of the will or a sudden ejaculation: and . . . a
new thrill of power and satisfaction shook his soul to know that he had
not yielded nor undone all.[30]

Where such events became habitual it can well be, of course, that
the peculiar condition of consciousness required for them would
aggravate the nervous tension to which they testify in the first place.

All in all, then, sexuality became an acute problem to Martin in
connection with the delineation of the possibilities of finding justification by doing and thinking the right things, by omitting the wrong
ones, and by fulfilling the sacrament of penance by confession. All
these possibilities turned into impossibilities in the shadow of what
to him was the most intense *tristitia* of *me habere deum non propi-
tiam*—of having a God whom he cannot propitiate. Only later,
after he had been kidnapped to the lonely Wartburg, where, in a
life of relative comfort and in the absence of monastic routine, he
had to establish his own pattern of work—which, in spite of his
complaints, he did magnificently—did Luther the man face fully
the problem of his temperamental unfitness for what he came to call
the "suicide of celibacy." He then concluded that God made us
men and women as an essential part of our sanity: *ut etiam negando
insanias*. He has endowed us with flesh, blood, and semen so that
we should marry and escape being consumed by perversion: *aloque
horrendis sodomis omnia complebuntur*.[31] As an aging man, Luther
did not hesitate to tell the children and the students around his dinner table that after his marriage he used to touch specified parts of
his wife's body when he was tempted by the devil,[32] and that the
devil lost his greatest battles "right in bed, next to Katie." [33]

In the monastery, however, it was not a question of how one should live—that was clearly defined; but how one should conceptualize things. In this area Martin, being a young great man, observed as he suffered and formulated as he met defeat. Some biographers wish to suggest that by the terms concupiscence and libido Luther for the most part referred to something as housebroken as a "general life-force"; others prefer to think that he always meant straight sex, and primarily his own. Actually, however, Martin clearly anticipated Freud in coming to the conclusion that "libido" pervades the human being at all times. He declined to accept the successful suppression of sexual acts as an evidence of the victory over libido as such. Chastity, he felt, was quite possible, although it was a rare gift, and true only if carried through gaily: "if the whole person loves chastity" (*totus homo est qui chastitatem amat*),[34] as one might well say of St. Francis. He continued to consider this the most desirable state, but he felt that nothing was served by trying to force it, for, he continues, it is also the total person who is affected by sexual excitement (*totus homo illecebris libidinis titillatur*).[35] "By the time it is noticed," he observed, "it is too late. Once it burns. . . . the eye is blind."[36] He also realized that libido, if incited and left unsatisfied, poisons the whole person to such an extent "that it would be better to be dead."[37]

It has been pointed out derisively by churchmen that in all of this rethinking Luther anticipates the pessimism of Schopenhauer's will and the pansexualism of Freud's libido. And it is true that, like them, he gradually came to consider it mandatory that one acknowledge the total power of drives. One can call this attitude defeatism, and Martin's initial insight certainly is based on what he experienced as personal defeat; but one may also view it as his refusal to make his honesty in such things a matter of optimistic denial, or of small victories which serve nothing but self-deception.

Martin's radical reformulation of the power of sexuality is only one aspect of the new baseline which he eventually formulated for the whole spiritual and psychological front; its assumed ethical pessimism and philosophical paradox is, in fact, a psychological verity: we can often actively assert our mastery over a major aspect of life only after we have fully realized our complete dependence on it. Here he becomes ruthlessly psychological: "Since, without our flesh, we would not exist, and could not operate, neither could we exist without the forces of the flesh (*sine vitiis carnis*), nor operate without them." [38] He thus shifts the whole question of free will from the strictly theological formulations of Pelagius and Augustinius to a formulation which anticipates our biological-psychological views.

In some of these quotations I have used the older Luther's words to indicate salient points in Martin's total rethinking; but as early as the *Randnoten zu Lombardus* (1508/09), he states that concupiscence, *i.e.*, our drive endowment, is a leftover of original sin. In this statement, Martin, without seeming to be aware of it, begins to run counter to, and even to misquote, the official doctrine that, because of Christ's sacrifice, we are born with a clean slate and our drives only set in motion a tendency to deadly sin which can be controlled by the sacrament of penance.

In anticipating some of the reformulations which very gradually appeared in Martin's lectures I am trying to illustrate those aspects of his theological scruples which have been, I think rightly, considered part of his personal conflicts. Much of his gradual and radical rethinking achieved an inner coherence only later—when he was forced to state it explicitly in his teaching, and when he was called upon to defend it. Until the time when he listened to his own words and concluded that they sounded good, and when he observed a similar judgment in the eyes of his listeners—until that time his rethinking often seemed to him to be what it partially was when it existed only in fragments, namely, a delinquent denial of the acknowledged avenues to inner peace. At the same time that he insisted on finding his very own way to salvation, he came to formulate as his own most mortal sin (*heisse* Ich *peccatum mortalem*) [39] a state of conscious and outright hatefulness, invidiousness, and contrariness toward God Himself. He was able to learn and preach the official gradations of the quantities and qualities (the *quid* and the *quantum*) of sin and the conditions necessary for the recapturing of grace; but they had no effective intelligibility for him. As Biel specified, there was, in all Occamist liberalism, a condition which could not be waived: one must continue to want God and love His creatures with all one's heart and only for His sake. All of these formulations, so obviously designed to make the life of not too scrupulous professionals bearable and useful, were for Martin so many invitations to search in himself for wholehearted love; to despair of finding it; and then to swing to the other extreme and with totalistic abandon confess that he, on the contrary, hated God. "They teach us to doubt," [40] he said later; and indeed, it would be hard to think of a system more designed to aggravate doubting—in a doubter.

Martin also pursued his lifelong unhappy love, mysticism. All the primitive superstition and German simplicity in him should have found refuge in the mystic's unification with God which needed no formula of justification and which, in fact, left all "thinking" aside. He did yearn for the birth of God's "uncreated word" in his soul; he desired to be physically pervaded with the kind of assurance "that really gets under your skin" [41] (*senkt sich ins Fleisch*). The mystic proclaims as attainable exactly that total piety which Martin desired (*tota corde* and *tota mente; omni affectu* and *toto intellectu*). Bonaventura "drove him nearly mad" [42] with his advice that it is better to turn to grace than to dogma; to nostalgia than to intellect; and to prayer than to study. But, alas, Martin had to admit that he never "tasted" the fruits of such endeavor (*ullum unquam gustum . . . sensi*),[43] sincerely as he had tried. He could not *feel* his way to God.

The fact is that this potentially so passionate man found he could not feel at all, which is the final predicament of the compulsive character. That is, he could not *have* the feelings which he so desperately wanted to feel, while on occasion (as in the fit in the choir) feelings *had him* in the form of phobic terrors and ugly rage.

All of which led to his final totalism, the establishment of God in the role of the dreaded and untrustworthy father. With this the circle closes and the repressed returns in full force; for here God's position corresponds closely to the one occupied by Martin's father at the time when Martin attempted to escape to theology by way of the thunderstorm. Meaningfully enough, when he heard Christ's name or when he suddenly perceived the countenance of the Savior on the cross, he felt as if lightning had struck him. During his first Mass, he had only felt empty and void of all mediation; now he began to hate the sacrificial efforts of God's son. This is what clinicians call a confession compulsion, an acknowledgment that something had been wrong with that first bolt of lightning just as his father had suspected. And so, as Martin put it, the praising ended and the blaspheming began. In the face of such contempt and wilful mistrust, God could only appear in horrible and accusatory wrath, with man prostrate in His sight (*projectus a facie oculorum tuorum*). Martin was further away than ever from meeting God face to face, from recognizing Him as He would be recognized, and from learning to speak to Him directly.

This point was the rock bottom on which Martin either would find the oblivion of fragmentation or on which he would build a new wholeness, fusing his own true identity and that of his time. With the luck and the cunning of a young great man, he found (or maybe we should say, he appointed) a fatherly sponsor for his identity—Dr. Staupitz, who understood his needs, refused to argue with him, and put him to work.

About a year and a half after his ordination, in the winter of 1508 (he was twenty-five years old), Martin was transferred to the Augustinian sister monastery in Wittenberg. There a new university was in the making, under the personal and highly competitive patronage of the Elector of Saxony, who wanted to outdo Leipzig, the ancient university in the other, the ducal, Saxony. It is not quite clear whether Wittenberg should be considered a Siberian desert or an important academic outpost. At any rate, the future cradle of the Reformation was, when Martin first saw it, hardly a town: its population was two thousand, of whom less than one-fifth had income enough to be taxable. The chief industry was brewing, and there was no significant trade. The castle, the chapter-house of All Saints, the lecture hall of the university, and the parish church of St. Mary's were the main buildings, lording it over a miserable town, the marketplace of which was "a dung heap."

In Wittenberg Martin met humanists who became his lifelong friends; he came to be regarded as a valued investment by his future princely protector, Frederic the Wise; and most important for his immediate future, he became intimately acquainted with Dr. Staupitz, the vicar-general of the province and the man who was the fatherly sponsor of Martin's late twenties. Staupitz wanted Martin to preach and to lecture. It surely underestimates his intentions to assume, as the psychiatrist does, that Staupitz merely wanted to give Luther "something to do," although this is exactly the way Staupitz put it in his offhand manner. For old-fashioned occupational therapy, one uses hobbies. Actually, Staupitz groomed Martin for his own chair, one of two which the Augustinians had provided for the University of Wittenberg, a chair Staupitz was neglecting because of his many administrative and diplomatic duties. Thus he acted as a true educational therapist in uniting in one plan of action the special needs of an outstanding and yet endangered member of his flock, and the special demands of a challenging communal reality. The fact that Staupitz recognized Martin's destination as a great orator and interpreter of the Word, and overrode his almost violent objections marks him as a man of therapeutic courage as well as of administrative shrewdness. His answer to Martin's remark made "under the pear tree," which must have been a favorite spot for their sessions, that Staupitz was "killing him" with his demand that he prepare himself for a professorship is justly famous. "That's all right," he said, "God needs men like you in heaven, too." [44] He often seems to have made this kind of disarming answer to Martin's squirming scrupulosities. With these humorous remarks, of a directness and an erudite worldliness which only a man in his dominant position could afford, Staupitz taught Martin a new art; for example, "by saying such things as that he had given up trying to be especially pious, he had lied to God long enough, and without success." [45] Staupitz was an administrator and statesman more than a priest or a teacher; well-groomed and and widely-traveled, he most resembles a shrewd and kindly university president who is not very deep or erudite, but who has the rare ability of making a younger man feel that he is understood. He knew that he could trust Martin. And, indeed, Luther did occupy his chair faithfully for thirty turbulent years. The fact that in the end he also wrecked Staupitz's whole monastic province is another matter which one may or may not choose to consider a sign of Staupitz's shortsightedness. This comfortable man of artistic origin may also have had a certain appreciation of the unhewn and genuinely virginal in young Martin; at any rate, he did not hesitate to assure him that his particular *tentationes* pointed to a more than ordinary destiny. Nor did he, the confessor, hesitate to confess to Martin his own early *tentationes*, and his own fears about preaching and lecturing. These counterconfessions were surprising as well as therapeutic, for Staupitz, by then, felt thoroughly at home in the pulpit. He avoided the use of notes; once, getting stuck in the middle of a long list of biblical names, he said to the congregation, "Thus is pride punished." [46]

Staupitz, of course, did not even vaguely anticipate the extent of the holocaust he was helping to kindle; and it is fascinating to speculate why this older man was so specifically reassuring to a younger one whom he did not *really* understand. It is my impression that Staupitz, like many an all too comfortable German patrician, felt a nostalgia for a creativity which he may have thought he possessed in his own late adolescence, and for potentialities, now bemoaned, which had been sacrificed to the role of church politician and statesman. He may thus have enjoyed fathering something truly religious in Luther; while Luther, in turn, responded with a complete and tenacious father transference of a positive kind, often overestimating the depth of his superior's wit, and opening himself wide to his words so that they might counteract the evil testament of his real father's words. What Staupitz said to him over the years never soured in Luther the way the pronouncements of every other authoritative figure did; on the contrary, Luther later on acknowledged theological debts to him which Staupitz almost certainly disavowed: "father in the evangelium," Luther called him.

When the Reformation came, Staupitz quietly remained in the Church, transferred to another order, and died in a comfortable job in the Austrian Tyrol, while Luther was continuing to credit him not only with having saved him when he was about to drown (*ersoffen*) in his temptations, but also with having provided him with some specific fundamental insights on which the future wholeness of this new theology was to be based. Staupitz, he claimed, once said to him that one is not truly penitent because one anticipates God's love, but because one already possesses it—a simple configuration of a totally reversed time perspective which Luther later thought to be strikingly confirmed in the scriptures. Staupitz may have said this—surely others have; the statement had so much prophetic meaning to Martin only because the right man happened in the right moment to support the total counterswing and the radical reversals inherent in Martin's budding thoughts. At a time when all the traditional methods seemed to confirm only an increasingly desperate sense of isolation, Staupitz evoked enough trust so that Martin was able to experiment with ideas like those he was soon to find deep in himself. This is therapeutic leverage: the therapist knows how to say that particular right thing which, given favorable circumstances and the condition of the patient's needy openness, strikes a deep note—in Martin's case, undoubtedly, the long lost note of infant trust which preceded the emergence of his morbid conscience. The therapist as good father gives retroactive sanction to the efficacy of maternal trust, and thus to the good which was there from the beginning. But reality must provide the supreme ratification of the therapist's pronouncement; and Martin's further study of the scriptures did prove to him that the divine Word had apparently waited for a millennium to give voice to *his* words: "I have faith, and therefore am I justified"—words to which all the world resounded.

Staupitz made other statements equally routine, but in the context of this relationship, equally memorable. We have already quoted his denial that it could have been Christ who terrorized Martin so that he nearly fainted during the procession in which he walked behind Staupitz, who was holding high the holiest of holies. This incident may have been a neurotic symptom, a breakthrough of the infantile fear of the phallic father. Staupitz's earlier admonition is more important and more positive: "to take a good look at the man who bears the name Christus" [47] (*den Mann anzusehen, der da heisst Christus*)—nothing terribly original to say, as theologians have reiterated, pointing to Staupitz's on the whole mediocre stature. But he happened to say it at the right time and in the right place, perhaps under that pear tree in whose shade he gave Martin his first feeling in a long, long time of a benevolent parental presence. This remark meant to Martin that he should stop doubting and start looking, use his senses and his judgment, grasp Christ as a male person like himself, and identify with the man in God's son instead of being terrorized by a name, an image, a halo. Perhaps Staupitz never even said some of these things; maybe he was merely that right person of whom one likes to believe or to remember that he said the right thing.

That anxiety attack during the procession indicates that Martin felt in relation to Staupitz what clinicians call an ambivalent father transference: having learned to trust him, he could not help also weaving him into the punishing-and-revenging complex in which he had earlier involved the image of Christ. Against this complex no trust and no faith ever really quite prevailed, and in one form or another, it remained with Luther to the end. His ambivalence toward Staupitz may also have been expressed in his involvement in a political struggle within his Augustinian province in which he opposed Staupitz. Luther later was able to pass an objective judgment on Staupitz, whom he called *frigidulus*, somewhat cold, and *parum vehemens*, lacking in intensity. But Luther always and ever referred to him as the "father" of these two ideas: that faith comes first; and that we can face God's son and look at him as a man. It should not be forgotten also that Staupitz, in his role as Martin's superior, could afford to make Martin laugh; and humor marks the moment when our ego regains some territory from oppressive conscience. Above all, Staupitz let Martin talk, and made him preach and lecture. Luther was one of those addicts and servants of the Word who never know what they are thinking until they hear themselves say it, and who never know how strongly they believe what they say until somebody objects.

But what guided Staupitz, beside an educator's astuteness? On his deathbed he is supposed to have said that he loved Martin with an affection "surpassing that of woman."

Martin held the chair of Moral Philosophy for about one year (1508/09); then he was called back to Erfurt to be sent on an official errand to Rome. When he returned from Rome, he was immediately sent back to Wittenberg where, in 1512, he became a doctor of theology. But before we reach the end of Martin's moratorium and let him become Luther, the preacher and lecturer, we must take note of that strange interlude, the future reformer's meeting, as deadly as the quiet before the storm, with the center of Latin Christendom.

The Meaning of "Meaning It"

IN GOETHE's day it became fashionable for German and Nordic men of the arts and sciences to divide their lives into the periods "before" and "after" their first trip to Italy—as if a thinking and feeling man's humanist awareness was fully ripe only after Nordic discipline and thought had been combined with the style and sensuality of the Mediterranean.

Luther, too, went to Rome. What we know of this visit and of his reactions, however, indicates not only a monastic self-restriction, but also a decidedly provincial unawareness of the nature and the culture of the South, and a strange anonymity, considering the fact that ten years later he became the Pope's effective antagonist. In the autumn of 1510 he set out for Rome on foot, one of two monks who were to present in the Vicar General's office in Rome an urgent appeal from a number of Augustinian monasteries of the Saxon congregation. These monasteries were opposed to plans already decreed by a papal bull, on recommendation of the General of the Order, Mariano de Genazzano, to give Staupitz, just appointed provincial general of all of Saxony, sweeping power to reorganize the twenty-nine monasteries of his congregation. Twenty-two of the monasteries had approved the plans; but seven objected, among them Nuremberg and Erfurt, the two largest and most influential. Over Staupitz's head they decided to send two representatives to Rome. The official spokesman was probably an older monk from Nuremberg; his mandatory *socius itinerarius* (for an Augustinian never traveled alone) was Father Luther from Erfurt. Exactly what mixture of political principle, inescapable obedience, local loyalty, or personal ambivalence was responsible for Martin's selection for this errand is impossible to know.

By its very absence of any overt sensation, Martin's journey was an event strange to behold. The future reformer, acting as chaperon to an older monk on a regional routine errand to the capital, crosses Southern Germany and Northern Italy, climbs over the Alps and the Apennines, all on foot, and mostly in abominable weather, finally "comes upon the Italian Renaissance," and notices nothing; just as nobody notices anything unusual about him.

He passed through Florence, where, as yet a public novelty of a few years, Michelangelo's gigantic David stood on the porch of the Signoria, a sculptured declaration of the emancipation of youth from dark giants. Little more than a decade before, Savonarola had been burned in Florence: a man of fiery sincerity; a man who, like Martin, had tried academic life, and had found it ideologically wanting; who also had left home to become a monk, and, at the age of twenty-nine, after a long latency as an orator, had burst out preaching against the papal Antichrist. He also became the leader not only of a local political movement, but of an international movement of rebellious northerners. Luther later called him a saint; but there is every reason to believe that at the time of this journey both the visual splendor and the passionate heroism of the Renaissance were to him primarily Italian, and foreign; the social leadership of Savonarola, with its Christian utopianism, must have seemed far removed from whatever Protestant yearning Martin may have felt. What he did notice in Florence was the devoted and quiet *Riformazione* which went along with the noisy and resplendent *Risorgimento:* he admired the personal service rendered to the poor by anonymous aristocrats; he noted the hygienic and democratic administration of hospitals and orphanages.

He and his companion completed their extramural duties in as short a time as possible (as monks should) and took advantage of their trip (as was then routine) to make a general confession at the very center of Christendom. He first beheld The City, as many travelers and pilgrims before and after him, from a certain spot on the ancient Via Cassia; he reached his order's host monastery immediately after having entered through the Porta del Popolo. Once established, Martin seems to have gone about his errand like a representative of some firm or union who accompanies an official to the federal capital to see the secretary of a department about an issue already decided against them. He spent much time commuting from his hotel to the department, and more time there in waiting rooms; never saw the secretary himself, and left without knowing the disposition of their appeal. In the meantime, he saw the sights which one must see and attempted to be properly impressed; also he heard a lot of gossip which, when he returned home, he undoubtedly distributed as inside information. All in all, however, the inner workings of the capital have remained mysterious to him.

In one respect, however, Martin differed from most travelers. Although he accepted most of the trip with sober thought, he approached certain of the routine sights with the fervor of a most desperate pilgrim. His attempt to devote himself, in his spare time, to some highly promoted observances in Rome seems to indicate a last endeavor on his part to settle his inner unrest with ceremonial fervor, by the accomplishment of works.

Those who visualize the beggar-monk awed by the splendor of ancient Rome and seething with vociferous indignation about papal luxury will be disappointed to hear first of all that the city of Rome, at that time, was primarily a wasteland of rubble which Martin had to cross on his daily walks from the Augustinian monastery near the Chiesa Santa Maria del Popolo to the center of town. The ancient city had not been restored since the Normans had burned it in 1084. The only architectural signs of life were monasteries, hunting lodges, and the summer houses of the aristocracy; and the only human signs of life were hordes of brigands. A medieval city, with only twice as many people as Erfurt, and with very little of Erfurt's sedate merchant spirit functioned in the flatlands of the Tiber. Papal Rome itself had the character of an administrative capital with ministries, legations, financial houses, hotels, and inns; it was, at the time, deserted by all important functionaries, who had followed the Pope to a warfront. Every monastic order had a central office in Rome, as well as a mother monastery; but a monk on business would not get any closer to the Vatican than the office of his order's procurator. Martin was able to meet only some bureaucrats, lobbyists, the shyster lawyers, and the political agents attached to the various office-holders; and the prostitutes of both sexes who beset them all.

As for Renaissance splendor, the city architecture did not reflect much of it as yet. Imposing avenues had been planned and partially laid out; and a few grandiose palaces, with rather stern and simple exteriors, had been erected to house the Renaissance which was on the move to Rome. But whatever existed of uniform styles of life and of art was confined mostly to the exclusive interiors of these palaces; the streets were still medieval in character. Michelangelo was at work on the ceilings of the Sistine Chapel, and Raphael was adorning the walls of the Pope's chambers; but these projects were private, and excluded, if not the *popolo* of aristocrats, certainly the populace at large, and all undistinguished foreigners. St. Peter's was in the process of being rebuilt, many of the old buildings having been torn down to make space for that imperial edifice which would not be completed for another century. What in style was a renaissance of Caesarian antiquity, no doubt seemed primarily Italian to the busy German monk; he was interested in works of art only for the sake of some curious historical circumstance, or gigantic proportions, or some surprising realism of technique which always impresses those who have not specifically learned to enthuse about a new style.

In his provincial eagerness to absorb the spiritual possibilities of Rome, Martin visited the seven churches, fasting all the way, in order to be ready for communion in St. Peter's, the last and most important. He had no thought of disengaging himself from the flourishing relic business, and he went eagerly to see the arms of his beloved St. Anne, which were displayed in a church separately from the rest of her bones. He saw with awe the halves of the bodies of St. Peter and of St. Paul, which had been weighed to prevent injustice to the church harboring the other halves. The churches were proud of these saintly slices: some later saints, immediately after their souls' departures, had been carefully boiled to prepare their bones for immediate shipment to worthy bidders. With these and other relics, the various churches maintained a kind of permanent fair where one could see, for a fee, Jesus's footprint in a piece of marble, or one of Judas's silver coins. One sight of this coin could save the viewer fourteen hundred years in purgatory; the wanderer along the holy road from the Lateran Church to St. Peter's had done his afterlife as much good as by a pilgrimage to the holy sepulchre in Jerusalem. And so much cheaper.

It is easy to say that the relics were just for the people and that the Church's intellectuals worked hard to reconcile faith and reason. Luther was, and always remained, one of the people; and like highly intelligent men of any age who do not challenge the propaganda of their government or the advertisements of the dominant economic system, Martin had become accustomed to the worst kind of commercialism. Back in Wittenberg Frederic was displaying such relics as a branch of the Burning Bush of Moses, thorns from the Crown of Thorns, and some of the straw of the Manger. The display even included a hair and a drop of milk from the Virgin herself. Later, of course, Luther raged against both the commercialism and the inanity of such "stinking" practices; in Rome, he still so much wanted to be of the people that he did not really rouse from his medieval twilight world. Only his obsessional symptoms stirred. He ran like a "mad saint" through all the churches in vain, finally advancing up the twenty-eight steps of the Lateran Church on his knees, saying a paternoster on each step in the conviction that each paternoster would free a soul from purgatory (without that soul being consulted, as he dared to comment only years later). Arriving on the top, all he could think was: "Who knows whether it is true?" But then, on the way up he had entertained the classical obsessional thought that he "almost" wished his parents dead so that he could use this golden opportunity to save them more surely.

Also typically, he was bothered most by affronts against the very observance which caused the greatest scruples in himself, namely, the Mass. He was horrorstricken when he heard German courtesans laugh and say that the Roman priests, under their breath, were murmuring "*Panis es, panis manebis, vinum es, vinum manebis*"— Bread and wine thou art, and shall always be. And, indeed, the priests' driving hurry was more than obvious to him, the slow pious German, who had come determined to celebrate the Mass faultlessly at the traditional altars, and get the most value out of the occasion. He did not like to be told, "*Passa, passa*—Hurry up, get on." In Sebastian's Basilica, he saw seven priests celebrate Mass at one altar in just one hour. Worst of all, they did not know Latin, and their careless, furtive, undisciplined gestures seemed a mockery. He had desired above all to say Mass on a Saturday in front of the entrance to the chapel *Sancta Sanctorum;* for this act would contribute materially to his mother's salvation. But alas, the rush was too great;

some mothers, Martin's included, never had a chance. So he went and ate a salted herring. All these hindrances and nuisances, however, were to Martin at the time expressions of the Italian national character, not of the Church's decline. He felt at home in only one church in Rome: Santa Maria dell' Anima, the German church, whose sacristan he remembered long and well.

Luther later mentioned (as far as the records show) only a few impressions of the seventy days of traveling, and they are all utilitarian. He admired the grandiose aqueducts in Rome, and he gave the Florentine aristocrats high praise for their well-run orphanages and hospitals, ignoring whatever other merits they may have prided themselves on. He judged the old St. Peter's acoustics to be as bad as those of the dome in Cologne and the cathedral in Ulm. He liked the fertile valley of the Po; but Switzerland was a "country full of sterile mountains."

Luther ignored the Renaissance and never referred to the esthetic quality of a single one of its statues or pictures, painters, or writers; this is a historical as well as a personal footnote. It takes time, especially for deeply preoccupied people, to comprehend the unity of the beginnings of an era which later will be so neatly classified in history books. Even today, when history has reached the height of journalistic self-consciousness, important trends and events can remain invisible before our eyes. If Luther did not notice the Renaissance, that does not in itself mean that he was not a man of the Renaissance. Erasmus, who had been in Rome a year earlier, and had had access to the papal chambers, never mentioned Michelangelo or Raphael. And Martin was, most of all, a religious egotist who had not learned to speak to either man or God, nor to speak glamorously and in a revitalized vernacular as the Renaissance demanded. He was a provincial Saxon who had studied Latin, Greek, and Hebrew, and who had still to create, out of his own explosive needs, the German language with which to speak to his own people.

The traveler of today, however, will find in the Uffizi in Florence, among the grandiose works of Renaissance painting, Cranach's small, exquisite, and sober portrait of Martin Luther.

2

At this point one could easily fall into the mistake of St. Thomas' colleagues, and be too impressed with what the dumb (and in this case, even German) ox did *not* say. Some have wondered how, in the space of a few years, such a man could grow into a great reformer. Others have suspected that as he was retracing his steps over the wintry Alps, he was seething with well-formulated indignation. Above all, however, his behavior on this trip, and his later utterances concerning it, have been used to bolster the image of Luther as a medieval man, utterly untouched by the Renaissance, to which he seemed blind.

Visually unreceptive he was, to an extraordinary degree. I propose this consideration, however: Luther simply had not reached the end of his creative latency. An original thinker often waits a long time not only for impressions, but also for his own reactions. (Freud was unreceptive to "musical noise," Darwin nauseated by higher literature. Freud did not become a psychoanalyst, nor Darwin an evolutionist, until they had reached the end of their twenties.) In the meantime he lives, as it were, in his preconscious, storing up in other than verbal images what impressions he receives, and keeping his affects from premature conclusions. One could say that Luther was compulsively retentive, or even that he was mentally and spiritually "constipated"—as he was apt to be physically all his life. But this retentive tendency (soon to alternate with an explosive one) was part of his equipment; and just as we assume that psychosexual energies can be sublimated, we must grant that a man can (and must) learn to derive out of the modes of his psychobiological and psychosexual make-up the prime modality of his creative adaptation. The image of Martin inhibited and reined in by a tight retentiveness must be supplemented by one which shows him taming his affects and restraining his speech until he would be able to say in one and the same explosive breath what he had come to really *mean*, what he really had thought through. In order to know himself what he thinks, such a "total" man is dependent on his need to combine intellectual meaning with an inner sense of meaning it. My main proposition is that, after he had come thus to *mean* it, Luther's message (in the first form of his early lectures) did contain a genuine Renaissance attitude. But since a renaissance emerges *against* something, it is necessary to discuss briefly those elements of the dogma which to Luther and his contemporaries were ideological alternatives, and which he restated, rejuvenated, or repudiated in his early lectures.

Our problem centers around the contribution of religious dogma and practice to the sense of identity of an age. All religions assume that a Higher Identity inhabits the great unknown; men of different eras and areas give this Identity a particular appearance or configuration from which they borrow that part of their identity which we may call *existential*, since it is defined by the relation of each soul to its mere existence. (In this context we should not be sidetracked by such monastic-ascetic techniques as those that systematically diminish man's sense of an individual identity; for they may be rather a supreme test of having a pretty firm one.) The particular Christian combination of a Higher Identity in the form of a Personal Maker of an absolutist moral bent, and a father figure who became more human in heaven as he became more totalitarian on earth was, we suggest, gradually robbing medieval man of just that existential identity which religion owed him.

As was pointed out in the Prologue, the matter is never strictly a religious one, even though the medieval Church could claim a monopoly on official ideologies. The question always involves those events, institutions, and individuals which actually influence the world-image at a given time in such a way that the identity needs of individuals are vitally affected, whether such influence is or is not quite conscious, generally intended, officially sanctioned, or specifically enforced. The problem is a psychohistorical one, and I can do no more than suggest it. There are two sides to it: what makes an ideology *really* effective at a given historical moment? and what is the nature of its effects on the individuals involved?

Consider for a brief moment certain great names of our time, which prides itself on a dominant identity enhanced by scientific truth. Darwin, Einstein, and Freud—omitting Marx, who was a conscious and deliberate ideological craftsman—would certainly deny that they had any intention of influencing, say, the editorials, or the vocabulary, or the scrupulosity of our time in the ways in which they undoubtedly did and do. They could, in fact, refute the bulk of the concepts popularly ascribed to them, or vaguely and anonymously derived from them, as utterly foreign to their original ideas, their methodology, and their personal philosophy and conduct. Darwin did not intend to debase man to an animal; Einstein did not preach relativism; Freud was neither a philosophical pansexualist nor a moral egotist. Freud pointed squarely to the psychohistorical problem involved when he said that the world apparently could not forgive him for having revised the image of man by demonstrating the dependence of man's will on unconscious motivation, just as Darwin had not been forgiven for demonstrating man's relationship to the animal world, or Copernicus for showing that our earth is off-center. Freud did not foresee a worse fate, namely that the world can absorb such a major shock by splintering it into minor half-truths, irrelevant exaggerations, and brilliant distortions, mere caricatures of the intended design. Yet somehow the shock affects the intimate inner balance of many, if not all, contemporary individuals, obviously not because great men are understood and believed, but because they are felt to represent vast shifts in man's image of the universe and of his place in it—shifts which are determined concomitantly by political and economic developments. The tragedy of great men is that they are the leaders and yet the victims of ideological processes.

From time to time, a great institution tries to monopolize, to stabilize, and to master the ideological process. The Church was such an institution. I shall try to reformulate from this point of view some of the main ideological influences which affected Luther's observances and studies.

Christianity, like all great movements, had its heroic era, repeatedly appealed to as a mythical justification, but rarely recaptured in earnest.

What is known of the early Christians of the Paulinian era creates the impression that they lived in the kind of clean and clear atmosphere which exists only after a catastrophic storm. This storm, of course, was Christ's passion. He had died for all men. To his followers, for a while, the merry-go-round of destruction and restoration which characterizes man's cycle of war and peace, festivals and carnivals, intoxication and remorse, had come to rest. The legend of Christ conveyed that total presence and absolute transcendence which is the rarest and the most powerful force among men. A few simple words had once more penetrated the disguises and pretenses of this world, words which at one and the same time were part of the language of the child, the language of the unconscious, and the language of the uncorrupted core of all spiritual tradition. Once again the mortal vulnerability of the individual soul had become the very backbone of its spiritual strength; the very fragility of a new beginning promised to move mountains. Death, fully accepted, became the highest identity on earth, superseding the need for smaller identities, and assuring at least one unquestionable equality for poor and rich, sick and healthy, ignorant and erudite. The disinherited (disinherited in earthly goods, and in social identity) above all desired to hear and rehear those words which made their inner world, long stagnant and dead, reverberate with forgotten echoes; this desire made them believe that God, from somewhere in the outer spaces, spoke through a chosen man on a definable historical occasion. Because the savior used the biological parable of a sonship of God, they believed in a traceable divine descendance of the son. But alas, having hardly made a God out of the son, they brought the Father down to a level where He seems much too human—for such a son.

The early Christians could be brothers and sisters, eating together without murderous envy, and together partaking of Him Who had commanded them to do so. They were able to ignore obsessive laws of observance, and improvise ritual and conduct as faith seemed to suggest—for had not the Son's uncorrupted self-sacrifice been accepted as valid by the Father of all fathers? History was dead. They could ignore the horizontal of worldly organization, that exchange of bewildering different currencies, all dirty from too much handling, and forever mutually contradictory in exchange value, forever cheating somebody, and most often everybody; they could concentrate on the vertical which connects each man's soul with the higher Identity in heaven, bringing down the currency of charity, and taking faith back up to Him. Occasionally in world history, communities like the early Christians have existed, and do exist, like a field of flowers, even though no one would mistake the single member for a lily, as St. Paul did not. What gave them, as a community, a glow greater than the sum of their individual selves was the identity of knowing transcendence: "We know, therefore we are—in eternity." St. Paul said to them, as if he were speaking to a garden of children: "You may all prophesy one by one, that all may learn, and all may be comforted." [1] Such identity, vulnerable as it seems, is indestructible in its immediate conviction, which carries within it a sense of reality common to good proselytizers and good martyrs.

I saw a small and transient example of the gaiety of *Agape* only

two decades ago, in a small pueblo in our Southwest. Though ex-
communicated by the Roman Church for an act of collective disobedience, the pueblo was preparing for a religious holiday, I think
Easter. The men were mending the adobe walls of the church, the
young people formed a chain to hand buckets of water from the
brook, and the women, dressed in gay colors, were scrubbing and
washing the church. Where the altar had been, an elder sat, wrin-
kled, shrewd, and dignified; he was the oldest and the newest priest,
and was supervising the construction of a madonna, an enormous
ball of colorful cloth topped by a tiny crowned head. Somewhere
on her global bosom there lay a tiny pink baby doll. Instead of
candles this goddess was surrounded by magnificent cornstalks. One
could not help feeling that the concordant gaiety which bound these
people together in the improvisation of a religion, combining the
best of the old and the new, was a response to having been freed
from the supervision of the law. In ignoring the excommunication
they gained a gay energy from the historical vacuum. Some, of
course, sulked and worried in their houses; and in the background
was the absent priest, who was being sacrificially murdered by the
proceedings.

Those early Christians did play havoc with the organized world,
the horizontal relation of things and events in space and time. Un-
historically, unhierarchically, and unconditionally, they treated as of
no substance or avail the Jewish identity of patriarchal law, the
Roman identity of world-citizenship, and the Greek identity of
body-mind harmony. All human order was only of this world,
which was coming to a foreseeable end.

Christianity also had its early organizational era. It had started as a
spiritual revolution with the idea of freeing an earthly proletariat
for victory in another world after the impending withering of this
one. But as always, the withering comes to be postponed; and in the
meantime, bureaucracies must keep the world in a state of prepared-
ness. This demands the administrative planning and the theoretical
definition of a double citizenship: one vertical, to take effect *when;*
and one horizontal, always in effect *now.* The man who first conceived of and busily built the intersection of the horizontal and the
vertical was St. Paul, a man converted out of a much too metro-
politan identity conflict between Jewish rabbi, Roman citizen, and

Greek philosopher not to become an empire-builder and doctrine-former. His much-traveled body reached Rome only to be beheaded; but his organizational testament merged with that of Christ's chosen successor, the sturdy Peter, to eventually establish in the capital of the horizontal empire of Rome a permanent anchorage and earthly terminal for all of man's verticals. (Luther, in his first theological restatements, was identifying with Paul's evangelical identity: he did not know, until it was to be foisted on him, how much he was preparing to identify with Paul's managerial fervor, his ecclesiastic identity, as well.)

The sacrifice, in whose blood the early gnostic identity had flourished, was gradually sacrificed to dogma; and thus that rare sublimation, that holiday of transcendence, which alone had been able to dissolve the forces of the horizontal, was forfeited. Philosophically and doctrinally, the main problem became the redefinition of the sacrifice so that its magic would continue to bind together, in a widening orbit, not only the faith of the weak and the simple, but also the will of the strong, the initiative of the ambitious, and the reason of the thinking. In each of these groups, also, the double citizenship meant a split identity: an eternal, always impending, one, and one within a stereotyped hierarchy of earthly estates. For all of these groups an encompassing theology had to be formulated and periodically reformulated.

The philosophers thus had their task set out for them: the theoretical anchoring of the vertical in the horizontal in such a way that the identities of the horizontal would remain chained to each other in a hierarchical order which would continue to receive its values and its style from the Church. To maintain itself, an ideological monopoly must assure all the stereotyped roles it creates, from the bureaucratic and ceremonial center to the militant and defensive outposts on the periphery, a sense of invigorating independence, without weakening their common bond to the centralized source of a common Super-Identity. The Roman Church, more than any other church or political organization, succeeded in making an ideological dogma—formulated, defended, and imposed by a central governing body—the exclusive condition for *any* identity on earth. It made this total claim totalitarian by using terror. In this case (as in others) the terror was not always directly applied to quivering bodies; it

was predicted for a future world, typically in such a way that nobody could quite know whom it would hit, or when. That a man
has or may have done something mortally bad, something which
may or may not ruin his eternal after-condition, makes his status
and inner state totally dependent on the monopolists of salvation,
and leaves him only the identity of a potential sinner. As in the case
of all terror, the central agency can always claim not to be responsible for the excessive fervor of its operatives; in fact, it may claim
it has dissuaded its terrorists by making periodic energetic pronouncements. These, however, never reach the lowly places where
life in the raw drives people into being each others' persecutors,
beginning with the indoctrination of children.

One philosophical problem, then, involved the definition of the
vertical's earthly anchorage in the Church, its unseen destination in
heaven, and the kind of traffic it would bear back and forth. This
is the question of man's identity in the hidden face of God, and of
God's in the revealed face of man; it includes the possibility of ever
receiving an inkling of mutual recognition as through a glass darkly,
or the shadow of a smile. The philosophers did not shirk concrete-
ness and substantiality; and all the concepts we will mention must
be understood to be as thing-like as we can conceive them to be:
who is man in this world of things? what equipment does he have
to approach God in the hope of making contact, to be heard and
perhaps to be given a message? Who is God? and where, and what
equipment does He use to partake in life on earth, for the sake of
whatever investment He may have in it? The idea that Christ had
been divinity become mortal and had returned to be next to and in
God again became dogma only centuries after his death, at which
time the question became involved in the nascent scientific curiosity
(then guided entirely by philosophy) which called for answers combining gnostic immediacy with philosophic speculation, and with
naturalist observation; all within a framework of obedience to the
Church's dogma.

Plato's Absolute Good, the world of pure ideas, was for thinking
people the strongest contender to the idea of a personal god; its
pole was the Absolute Bad, the world of special appearances and
worldly involvements. Christianity defended itself, as it absorbed
them, against Platonism and Aristotelianism; thus, questions of the

relatively greater identity and of the differential initiative of the two worlds became paramount. Does he who learns to recognize the more real also become more real—and more virtuous into the bargain? And who has the initiative in the matter? Is God waiting for our moves, or is He moving us? Do we have the leeway of some initiative? if so, how do we know of it and learn to use it—and when do we forfeit it?

It has been said that Descartes's "I think, therefore I am" marked the end of medieval philosophy, which began with St. Augustine, who saw in man's ability to think the proof not only of God's existence, but also of God's grace. Augustine thought that man's "inner light" is the realization of the *infusio caritatis*, so that we may speak of a *caritative* or *infused identity*. It is precisely because Augustine centered all his theology in faith that Luther called him the greatest theologian since the apostles and before Luther. Augustine (as Luther, later) made no concession about the completeness of *perditio*, man's total lostness, nor is he less relentlessly convinced that only God has Being by Himself. "Things," he says, "are and are not; they are because from God they derive existence; they are not because they only *have* being, they *are* not being. . . . they exist not all at once, but by passing away and succeeding, they together complete the universe, whereof they are a portion." [2] Man, without grace, would obviously be no different: he, too, passes away. Without grace, the identity of man is also one of the mere succession of men. But God gave him a mind and a memory, and thus the rudiment of an identity.

These things do I within, in that vast court of my memory. For there are present within me, heaven, earth, sea, and whatever I could think on therein, besides what I have forgotten. There also meet I with myself, and recall myself, and when, where, and what I have done, and under what feelings. There be all which I remember, either on my own experience or other's credit. Out of the same store do I myself with the past continually combine fresh and fresh likenesses of things which I have experienced, or, from what I have experienced, have believed: and thence again infer future actions, events and hopes, and all these again I reflect on, as present. . . . Sure I am that in it Thou dwellest, since I have remembered Thee ever since I learnt Thee, and there I find Thee, when I call Thee to remembrance. [3]

In spite of Augustine's pessimistic statements about man's total perdition, then, he does seem to be rather glad to meet himself face to face in his own memory. Nonetheless, it is a gift of God's *caritas* that he *can* thus meet himself, for, as Paul said: "Who maketh thee to differ from another? and what hast thou that thou didst not receive?" [4] To look at himself in his own memory without being grateful to God would be narcissism—what Augustine calls *praesumptio* which, together with *superbia*, constitutes man's greatest sin: egomania. For man forfeited all free will when he was born human, and thus sick in origin (*morbus originis*). Because of Christ's sacrifice, he is able to receive through baptism redemption from the sins of previous generations; but he is still burdened with *concupiscentia*, with the "touchwood, the tinder, of sin" (*fomes peccati*). He is only a *homo naturalis*, but does have the chance that his mind might be recreated by the infusion of God's grace, and that he might become a *homo spiritualis*.

To Augustine, *concupiscentia* was covetousness, and thus libido, which is not sin, but only the stuff sin is made of; it becomes sin through man's *consensus*. By a free act of love, God can give man the ability *not* to identify with his own drives. But should man sin, there is still God's *misericordia indebita*, his pity, which is available even to the undeserving. Thus, whatever we are and become, what we can do and will do, is all a gift from God: *Ex Deo nobis est, non ex nobis*. But for all his renunciation of free will, Augustine shows a pathway up the vertical whose waysigns are *fruitio* and *perfectio*. His theology, compared with those that followed, is a maternal one; in it the wretched human being is forever reassured that, because of Christ's sacrifice, he is born with a chance in life; growth, and fruition, and possible perfection are open to him; and he may always expect his share, and more, of the milk of grace.

St. Augustine saved the Church from Platonism by embracing and converting it; St. Thomas did the same with the Aristotelianism which re-emerged in the middle ages, intellectually ornamented by the medical and mystical Arabs and Jews. Platonism, the orientation toward the Idea, was, through St. Thomas' work, augmented by a new orientation toward the facts and forces of Nature. God, the *prima veritas* and the primary good, was shown to reveal Himself in His creation as the prime Planner and Builder. He was the *causa causans;* although man was only a *causa secunda*, he could feel necessary both as a planned part of this created world, and as its contemplator and theorist.

Aristotle had left Plato intact, but complemented him: God was the *sola gratia*, and it remained of prime importance to distinguish between *quod est ex gratia* and *quod est ex libero arbitrio*—that which originates in God's love, and that which man can accomplish with his God-given reason and free will. God was the only Being which, "being to all beings the cause of their being," was His own necessity. But it is clear that Aristotle permitted reason and will a greater leeway; they were active participants in the "creativity of creatures," which gave man's identity an independent method of self-verification. In theological terms, this process was one of reading God's goodness from the *ordo* which he had manifested in the world. Man could practise his power of observation by contemplating forms and similarities, images and ideas; he could establish causalities and eventually translate them into experiments, and thus become God's assistant planner and mover. In St. Augustine the currency which passed along the vertical between the two worlds was faith and love. St. Thomas added the currency of perceived form and order. God's message was perceivable in the *ordo divina;* man's equipment included the ability to perceive order; and there was prescribed order in the inner formability of man. So that he can negotiate among all these orders, man is given a number of organs: intuitive vision; perception on the basis of faith; and recognition *per rationem rationalem.* Man's reason, in turn, is given a high enough place in the order of things so that even matters of good and bad can, and in fact, must, be reasoned out. This may lead to no more than a *certitudo conjecturae;* but at any rate, St. Thomas reserves a place for active and reasonable conjecture where before there was room for only faith and hope. In this philosophy man as a contemplator acquires a new identity, that of a "theorist." We may, therefore, speak of Thomism as centering in a *rational identity:* the identity verified by a divine order perceived by reason.

It is clear that through Thomism theology acquired as its own those Aristotelian strivings for observation and speculation which became dominant in the Renaissance. But man's equipment for observation and reason still needed divine encouragement to give it the *perseverantia* to utilize the *cooperatio* between the two worlds.

A greater synthesis between Antiquity and Christianity, Reason and Faith, could not be conceived; its immediate results were a dignified piety, immaculate thought, and an integrated cosmology well-suited to the hierarchic and ceremonial style of the whole era. Luther's question however, was whether, in this synthesis, problems of conscience are not drawn into the sphere of reason, rather than reason being incorporated into faith.

St. Thomas, an architectural thinker and himself an expression of the *ordo* in which he recognized God's message, was also representative of the highest expression of the medieval identity: the grandiose as well as minute *stylization* which characterized the cathedrals, built for eternity, and the ceremonies, which allegorized God's order in the microcosm of special occasions. Ceremonialism permits a group to behave in a symbolically ornamental way so that it seems to represent an ordered universe; each particle achieves an identity by its mere interdependency with all the others. In ceremonial stylization, the vertical and the horizontal met; the Church's genius for hierarchic formulization spread from the Eucharist to the courts, the market places, and the universities, giving the identity of medieval man an anchor of colors, shapes, and sounds. The medieval ceremonialist also tried to place man in a symbolic and allegoric order, and in the static eternity of estates and castes, by drawing up minute and detailed laws of conduct: thus man partook of a gigantic as well as a minute order by giving himself ceremonial identities set apart by extravagantly differentiated roles and costumes.

It must be added, however, that active self-perpetuation and self-verification in the ceremonial microcosms were restricted to small groups of ecclesiastic and secular aristocracies. The masses could participate only as onlookers, as the recipients of a reflection of a reflection. This parasitic ceremonial identity lost much of its psychological power when the excessive stylization of the ruling classes proved to be a brittle defense against the era's increasing dangers; the plague and syphilis, the Turks, and the discord of popes and princes. At the same time, the established order of material and psychological warfare (always so reassuring a factor in man's sense of borrowed godliness) was radically overthrown by the invention of gunpowder and of the printing press.

The daily intellectual and religious life to which Luther was exposed in college and monastery was stimulated by three isms:

the great philosophical antithesis of realism and nominalism; and religious mysticism.

Realism was the assumption of a true substantive existence of the world of ideas. Its quite unphilosophical alliance with the fetichistic adoration of relics (messengers from the other world, like fragments of meteors from the skies) could not be illustrated better than by the fact that St. Thomas, immediately after his death, was boiled by his confreres so that they could sever, by one industrial act, the perishable flesh from the pile of negotiable bones. Realistic thought had little influence on Luther, the dogmatist; but it dominated the *Zeitgeist* which often emerged in Luther's more informal utterances, especially in its alliance with demonism. We know Luther to have been a lifelong addict of demonic thought, which he managed to keep quite separate from his theological thought and his scientific judgment. The devil's behind maintained a reality for him which—because his intellect and his religious intuition seemed to function on different planes—could be said to verge on the paranoid were it not at the same time representative of a pervading medieval tendency. As Huizinga puts it:

Now, it is in the domain of faith that realism obtains, and here it is to be considered rather as the mental attitude of a whole age than as a philosophic opinion. In this larger sense it may be considered inherent in the civilization of the Middle Ages and as dominating all expressions of thought and of the imagination. . . .[5]

All realism, in the medieval sense, leads to anthropomorphism. Having attributed a real existence to an idea, the mind wants to see this idea alive, and can only effect this by personifying it. In this way allegory is born. It is not the same thing as symbolism. Symbolism expresses a mysterious connection between two ideas, allegory gives a visible form to the conception of such a connection. Symbolism is a very profound function of the mind, allegory is a superficial one. It aids symbolic thought to express itself, but endangers it at the same time by substituting a figure for a living idea. The force of the symbol is easily lost in the allegory. . . .[6]

The Church, it is true, has always explicitly taught that sin is not a thing or an entity. But how could it have prevented the error, when everything concurred to insinuate it into men's minds? The primitive instinct which sees sin as stuff which soils or corrupts, which one should, therefore, wash away, or destroy, was strengthened by the extreme systematizing of sins, by their figurative representation, and even by the penitentiary technique of the Church itself. In vain did Denis the Carthusian remind the people that it was but for the sake of comparison that he calls sin a fever, a cold and corrupted humour—popular thought undoubtedly lost sight of the restrictions of dogmatists.[7]

The following passage gives us the medieval background for some of Luther's occasional preoccupation with bodily zones and modes:

> The infusion of divine grace is described under the image of the absorption of food, and also of being bathed. A nun feels quite deluged in the blood of Christ and faints. All the red and warm blood of the five wounds flowed through the mouth of Saint Henry Suso into his heart. Catherine of Sienna drank from the wound in His side. Others drank of the Virgin's milk, like Saint Bernard, Henry Suso, Alain de la Roche.
>
> Now, whereas the celestial symbolism of Alain de la Roche seems artificial, his infernal visions are characterized by a hideous actuality. He sees the animals which represent the various sins equipped with horrible genitals, and emitting torrents of fire which obscure the earth with their smoke. He sees the prostitute of apostasy giving birth to apostates, now devouring them and vomiting them forth, now kissing them and petting them like a mother.[8]

Huizinga's analysis prepares us for the issue of indulgences. Realism, just as it served to give supernatural reality to the "dirt" on earth, also gave monetary substance to grace itself, establishing the vertical as a canal system for that mysterious substance of supreme ambivalence which both the unconscious and mysticism alternately designate as gold and as dirt. The idea of a heavenly treasure of the works of supererogation was an ancient one; but the capitalist interpretation of a reserve which the Church can dispose of by retail was officially formulated only in 1343 by Clement VI, who established the dogma that the wide distribution of the treasure would lead to an increase in merit—and thus to continued accumulation of the treasure. In this dogma realism took a form which Luther eventually fought in his opposition to the cash-and-carry indulgences which were supposed to instantly affect the condition of a soul in purgatory—the way a coin can immediately be heard as it drops into the collector's box.

The dangers to man's identity posed by a confused realism allied with a popular demonology are obvious. The influences from the other world are brought down to us as negotiable matter; man is able to learn to master them by magical thinking and action. But momentary victories of magic over an oppressive superreality do

not, in the long run, either develop man's moral sense or fortify
a sense of the reality of his identity on this globe.

The systematic philosophical content of German mysticism is
small, indeed, and Luther did not read Tauler, the most systematic
mystic, until after he had established the basic tenets of his own
theology. Tauler was the exponent of an ism which is one of the
constant, if extreme, poles of spiritual possibilities. For Tauler, God
begins where all categories and differentiations end (*on allen under-
scheit*); he is the Unborn Light (*ein ungeschaffen Licht*). To reach
him, one must be able to develop the *raptus*, the rapt state of complete passivity in which man loses his name, his attributes, and his
will. He must achieve something for which only the German language has a proper word—*Gelassenheit*, meaning a total state of
letting things be, letting them come and go. This includes also the
all-Christian condition of accepting total guiltiness, but without
excessive remorse or melancholy. Thus, returning to one's inner
darkness and nebulousness (*nebulas et tenebras*) one becomes ready
for the *Einkehr*, the homecoming to the *Seelengrund*, the ground
and womb of spiritual creation. Here is the meeting-ground for the
wedding (*das Hochgezeit*), and God becomes, for an instant,
mightily active; his coming is as quick as a glance (*in einem snellen
Blicke*) which cuts through all the ways of the world (*ueber alle
die Wise und die Wese in einem Blicke*). But mind you, this ray
of light from God's eye does not penetrate to him who attempts to
look at God; it comes only to one who is in a state of total receptivity, free of all striving.[9]

We are here confronted with a system which retreats far behind
the gnostic position, and far below the trust position of infancy.
It is the return to a state of symbiosis with the matrix, a state of
floating unity fed by a spiritual navel cord. We may call it the
passive identity. Its clear parallel with, and its differentiation as
German mysticism from, other Western or Eastern systems must
not occupy us here. Luther adored it from afar (he wrote a preface
to Tauler's works); but he was intellectually and temperamentally
unfit for it, and somehow afraid of it.

The great common sense identity based on the view that things
are things, and ideas, ideas, was mainly established by Occam; his

influence helped to change the meaning of the term *realism* into "things as they are." Occamism was eagerly ideologized at a time when the empire of faith was threatening to fall apart into all-too-concrete, all-too-human entities: a God with the mind of a usurer, a lawyer, and a police chief; a family of saints, like holy aunts and uncles, with whom people made deals, instead of approaching the distant Father; a Church that had become a state, and a Pope who was a warring prince; priests who had lost their own awe and failed to inspire it in other people, and thus became more contemptible as they became only too understandable; observances which at the earthly end of the vertical were measured in hard cash, and at the other, in aeons of purgatory.

Occam, or at any rate Occamism, severed the vertical from the horizontal. One might almost say it made parallels out of them. Such entities as God, soul, or spirit were not considered to be matters accessible to the mind down here. God has no ascertainable attributes and does not underlie any generalities which we can "think." We cannot know His intentions or His obligations: his *potentia is absoluta*. He has *infinita latitudo*, and there is no way of obliging or coercing Him by developing the right disposition, be it ever so saintly. All we can hope is that when the judgment comes we will prove acceptable to Him, and that He will grant us an *extenuatio legis*. All we can do is to obey the Church (which Occam disobeyed) and be reasonable (*ratio recta spes*), for we can assume that even God's laws are subject to logic. Gerson, the famous French Occamist, who was one of Luther's favorite authors and whose pastoral writings were obligatory reading for all student priests, even suggested that one could expect God not to be too unreasonable in His decisions on judgment day.

As to this world, single things do have a concrete and immediate reality, as man's intuitive knowledge clearly perceives. But a symbol of a thing is nothing but *flatus vocis*, a burst of verbal air. Ideas, or universals, do not exist, except in *significando*, in the mental operations by which we give them meaning. We have no right to attribute to them the quality of thingness, and then to proceed to increase their quantity as our fancy might lead us to do: *Non est ponenda pluralitas sine necessitate* is the famous sentence which establishes the law of parsimony, a law which sharpened the search of the natural sciences, and now hounds psychology with its demand to reduce man, too, to a model of a minimal number of forces and mechanisms.

All in all, then, Occam's nominalism is a medieval form of skepticism and empiricism which antedates the philosophy of enlightenment. Some historians attribute to Occam operations of thought mature enough to antedate the mathematics of Descartes. But one can well see why, to some Catholic thinkers, Occamist became an adjective worse than Pelagian. And, in many ways, Occam was an abortive Luther. He, too, called the Pope an Antichrist; he, too, supported the princes' supremacy over the Curia; he, too, was attracted by the absolutism of an earlier form of Christianity, which was forever embarrassing to the Church: Franciscan communism. But Occam was at heart a pragmatic philosopher; and although Luther's own shrewdness appreciated Occam's practical scepticism, it was Occam's demonstration that the vertical could not be approached at all by way of the horizontal which impressed Martin. Occam showed that faith as an individual experience had been lost in all the cathedral building and hierarchy arranging, in all the ceremonializing of life and formalizing of thought. The dream of a predictable vertical anchored in an orderly horizontal was failing the most faithful, and leaving the faithless to the overwhelming dangers of the day.

In contrast to these medieval trends of thought, what did the Renaissance man think of his relative reality on this planet?

First of all, he recovered man's identity from its captivity in the eleventh heaven. He refused to exist on the periphery of the world theater, a borrowed substance subject to God's whims. He was anthropocentric, and existed out of his own substance—created, as he somewhat mechanically adds, by God. This substance was his executive center. His geographic center, because of his own efforts, turned out to be peripheral to the solar system: but what did lack of cosmic symmetry matter, when man had regained a sense of his own center? Ficino, one of the prime movers of the Platonic Academy of Lorenzo the Magnificent's Florence, made this clear. The soul of man, he says, "carries in itself all the reasons and models of the lower things that it recreates as it were of its own. It is the center of all and possesses the forces of all. It can turn to and penetrate this without leaving that, for it is the true connection of things.

Thus, it can rightly be called the center of nature." [10] And Pico della Mirandola, the author of *On the Dignity of Man* (1494) celebrated the "highest and most marvelous felicity of man! . . . To him it is granted to have whatever he chooses, to be whatever he wills. On man when he came to life, the Father conferred the seeds of all kinds and the germs of every way of life. . . . Who would not admire this chameleon?" [11]

The human theater of life, according to this humanist school, is circumscribed for each by the power of that specific endowment which in him happens to be blessed with the gift of workmanship, be he painter or sculptor, astronomer, physician, or statesman. For Leonardo, it was the trained, intent eye, the "knowing how to see," which was "the natural point," in which "the images of our hemisphere enter and pass together with those of all the heavenly bodies. . . . in which they merge and become united by mutually penetrating and intersecting each other." "These are the miracles . . . forms already lost, mingled together in so small a space, it can recreate and reconstitute." [12] Michelangelo found this center in the hand which, guided by intellect, can free the conception "circumscribed in the marble's excess." [13]

This view again anchors the human identity in the hierarchy of organs and functions of the human body, especially insofar as the body serves (or is) the mind. Renaissance sensuality (in contrast to the medieval alternation of asceticism and excess) tried to make the body an intuitive and disciplined tool of reality; it did not permit the body to be sickened with sinfulness, nor the mind to be chained to a dogma; it insisted on a full interplay between man's senses and intuitions and the world of appearances, facts, and laws. As Leonardo put it: "Mental things which have not gone through the senses are vain and bring forth no truth except detrimental." [14] But this implies disciplined sensuality, *"exact fantasy,"* and makes the verification of our functioning essence dependent on the meeting between our God-given mental machinery and the world into which God has put us. We need no proof of His identity nor of ours as long as, at any given time, an essential part of our equipment and a segment of His world continue to confirm each other. This is the law of operating inside nature.

Ficino strained this point of view to its ideological limit; his statement in many ways has remained the ideological test and limit of our own world image: "Who could deny," he says, "that man possesses as it were almost the same genius as the Author of the heavens? And who could deny that man could somehow also make the heavens, could he only obtain the instruments and the heavenly material?" [15]

It cannot escape those familiar with psychoanalytic theory that the Renaissance is the ego revolution *par excellence*. It was a large-scale restoration of the ego's executive functions, particularly insofar as the enjoyment of the senses, the exercise of power, and the cultivation of a good conscience to the point of anthropocentric vanity were concerned, all of which was regained from the Church's systematic and terroristic exploitation of man's proclivity for a negative conscience. Latin Christianity in Martin's time tended to promise freedom from the body at the price of the absolute power of a negative external conscience: negative in that it was based on a sense of sin, and external in that it was defined and redefined by a punitive agency which alone was aware of the rationale of morality and the consequences of disobedience. The Renaissance gave man a vacation from his negative conscience, thus freeing the ego to gather strength for manifold activity. The restoration of ego vanity to a position over superego righteousness, also established an ideological Utopia which found expression in Ficino's statement. Renaissance man was free to become what Freud called a god of protheses, and the question of how to dispose of this god's bad conscience came to occupy not only theology, but also psychiatry.

Nietzsche, Luther's fellow-Saxon, prided himself on being the belated German spokesman of the Renaissance and Europe's gay moralist. Wrongly informed about Luther's trip to Rome and believing his ninety-five theses to have been a German peasant's revolt against the Renaissance, Nietzsche blamed on Luther's untimely interference the failure of the Medici to imbue the papacy with a Renaissance spirit mature enough to completely absorb medieval spirituality. Nietzsche felt that Luther had forced the Church into the defensive instead, and had made it develop and reinforce a reformed dogma, a mediocrity with survival value. Erasmus, also, four hundred and fifty years before Nietzsche, had blamed Luther for ruining the dreams of Humanism. It is true that Luther *was* completely blind to the visual splendor and the sensual exquisiteness of the Renaissance, just as he was furiously suspicious of Erasmus' intellectuality: *"Du bist nicht fromm,"* he wrote to him. "You do not know what true piety is." [16] And although for a few years Luther occupied the stage of history with some of the exhibitionistic grandeur of a Renaissance man, there is no doubt that he concluded his life in an obese provinciality.

Yet one could make a case that Martin, even as he hiked back to Erfurt, was preparing himself to do the dirty work of the Renaissance, by applying some of the individualistic principles immanent in the Renaissance to the Church's still highly fortified homeground —the conscience of ordinary man. The Renaissance created ample leeway for those in art and science who had their work confirmed by its fruits, that is, by aesthetic, logical, and mathematical verification. It freed the visualizer and the talker, the scholar and the builder—without, however, establishing either a truly new and sturdy style of life, or a new and workable morality. The great progress in pictorialization, verbalization, and material construction left, for most of the people, something undone on an inner frontier. We should not forget that on his deathbed Lorenzo the Magnificent, who died so young and so pitifully soon after he had withdrawn to the country to devote the rest of his life to the "enjoyment of leisure with dignity," sent for Savonarola. Only the most strongly principled among Lorenzo's spiritual critics would do as his last confessor. Ficino, who in his youth addressed his students as "beloved in Plato," became a monk in his forties; Pico, who wrote *On the Dignity of Man* when he was a mere youth, died in his early thirties a devout follower of Savonarola, and considering a monastic life. These were all men who somehow had loved women, or at any rate their own maleness, too much; altogether womanless men, like Leonardo and Michelangelo, found and recognized the defeat of the male self in grandiose ways. Surely existential despair has never been represented more starkly than in the Sistine man facing eternal damnation, nor essential human tragedy with more dignity than in Michelangelo's Pieta. One must review the other Madonnas of the Renaissance (della Robbia's, del Sarto's, Raphael's) who are shown with the boy Jesus making a gay and determined effort to stand on his own feet and to reach out for the world, to appreciate Michelangelo's unrealistic and unhistorical sculpture—an eternally young mother holding on her lap the sacrificial corpse of her grown and aged son. A man's total answer to eternity lies not in what he says at any one period of his life, but in the balance of all his pronouncements at all periods. Psychologically speaking, Renaissance man contained within himself the same contradictions which are the burden of all mortals. History ties together whatever new ideological formulations most fitly correspond to new conquests over matter, and lets the men drop by the wayside.

Luther accepted for his life work the unconquered frontier of tragic conscience, defined as it was by his personal needs and his superlative gifts: *"Locus noster,"* he said in the lectures on the Psalms, *"in quo nos cum Deo, sponsas cum sponsa, habitare debet . . . est conscientia."* [17] Conscience is that inner ground where we and God have to learn to live with each other as man and wife. Psychologically speaking, it is where the ego meets the superego; that is, where our self can either live in wedded harmony with a positive conscience or is estranged from a negative one. Luther comes nowhere closer to formulating the auditory threat, the voice of wrath, which is internalized in a negative conscience than when he speaks of the "false Christ" as one whom we hear expostulate *"Hoc non fecisti,"* [18] "Again, you have not done what I told you"— a statement of the kind which identifies negatively, and burns itself into the soul as a black and hopeless mark: *conscientia cauterisata.*

Hans' son was made for a job on this frontier. But he did not create the job; it originated in the hypertrophy of the negative conscience inherent in our whole Judaeo-Christian heritage in which, as Luther put it: "Christ becomes more formidable a tyrant and a judge than was Moses." [19] But the negative conscience can become hypertrophied only when man hungers for his identity.

We must accept this universal, if weird, frontier of the negative conscience as the circumscribed *locus* of Luther's work. If we do, we will be able to see that the tools he used were those of the Renaissance: fervent return to the original texts; determined anthropocentricism (if in Christocentric form); and the affirmation of his own organ of genius and of craftsmanship, namely, the voice of the vernacular.

3

After his return from Rome, Martin was permanently transferred to the Wittenberg monastery. Some say that he was pushed out by the Erfurt Augustinians, some, that he was pulled to Wittenberg by Staupitz's influence. The fact is that his friend John Lang had to go, too; a few years later, Luther's influence over the whole province was so great that he was able to appoint Lang prior back at Erfurt.

Martin's preaching and teaching career started in earnest in Wittenberg, never to be interrupted until his death. He first preached to his fellow-monks (an elective job), and to townspeople who audited his intramural sermons. He became pastor of St. Mary's. As a professor, he lectured both to monks enrolled in advanced courses, and to the students in the university. Forced to speak his mind in public, he realized the rich spectrum of his verbal expression, and gained the courage of his conflicted personality. He learned to preach to the heart and to lecture to the mind in two distinct styles. His sermons were for the uplift of the moment; in his lectures, he gradually and systematically developed as a thinker.

Luther the preacher was a different man from Martin the monk. His posture was manly and erect, his speech slow and distinct. This early Luther was by no means the typical pyknic, obese and round-faced, that he became in his later years. He was bony, with furrows in his cheeks, and a stubborn, protruding chin. His eyes were brown and small, and must have been utterly fascinating, judging by the variety of impressions they left on others. They could appear large and prominent or small and hidden; deep and unfathomable at one time, twinkling like stars at another, sharp as a hawk's, terrible as lightning, or possessed as though he were insane. There was an intensity of conflict about his face, which might well impress a clinician as revealing the obsessive character of a very gifted, cunning, and harsh man who possibly might be subject to states of uncontrolled fear or rage. Just because of this conflicted countenance, Luther's warmth, wit, and childlike candor must have been utterly disarming; and there was a total discipline about his personality which broke down only on rare occasions. It was said about Luther that he did not like to be looked in the eye, because he was aware of the revealing play of his expression while he was trying to think. (The same thing was said of Freud; and he admitted that his arrangement for the psychoanalytic session was partially due to his reluctance "to be stared at.")

Martin's bearing gradually came to contradict the meekness demanded of a monk; in fact, his body seemed to be leaning backward so that his broad forehead was imperiously lifted toward the sky; his head sat on a short neck, between broad shoulders and over a powerful chest. Some, like Spalatin, the elector's chaplain and advisor, admired him unconditionally; others, like the elector himself, Frederic the Wise, felt uncomfortable in his presence. It is said that Luther and the elector, who at times must have lived only a short distance from him and to whose cunning diplomacy and militant protection he would later owe his survival, "personally never met" to converse, even though the elector often heard him preach —and on some occasions, preach against him and the other princes.

As a preacher and lecturer, Luther combined a command of quotations from world literature with a pervading theological sincerity. His own style developed slowly out of the humanistic preoccupation with sources, the scholastic love of definitions, and the medieval legacy of (to us, atrocious) allegory. He almost never became fanciful. In fact, he was soon known for a brusqueness and a folksy directness which was too much for some of his humanist friends, who liked to shock others in more sophisticated ways: but Luther, horrors! was one who "meant it." It could not have endeared him to Erasmus that of all the animals which serve preachers for allegories and parables, Luther came to prefer the sow; and there is no doubt but that in later years his colorful earthiness sometimes turned into plain porcography. Nervous symptoms harassed his preaching; before, during or after sermons he was on occasion attacked by dizziness. The popular German term of dizziness is *Schwindel*, a word which has a significant double meaning, for it is also used for the fraudulent acts of an impostor. And one of his typical nightmares was that he was facing a congregation, and God would not send him a *Konzept*.

But I think the psychiatrist misjudges his man when he thinks that endogenous sickness alone could have kept Luther from becoming a well-balanced (*ausgeglichen*) creature when his preaching brought him success. After all, he was not a Lutheran; or, as he said himself, he was a mighty bad one. On the frontier of conscience, the dirty work never stops, the lying old words are never done with, and the new purities remain forever dimmed. Once Luther had started to come into his own as a preacher, he preached lustily, and at times compulsively, every few days; when traveling, he preached in hospitable churches and in the marketplace. In later years when he was unable to leave his house because of sickness or anxiety, he would gather wife, children and house guests about him and preach to them.

To Luther, the inspired voice, the voice that means it, the voice that really communicates in person, became a new kind of sacrament, the partner and even the rival of the mystical presence of the Eucharist. He obviously felt himself to be the evangelical giver of a substance which years of suffering had made his to give; an all-embracing verbal generosity developed in him, so that he did not wish to compete with professional talkers, but to speak to the people so that the least could understand him: "You must preach," he said, "as a mother suckles her child." No other attitude could, at the time, have appealed more to members of all classes—except Luther's preaching against taxation without representation which, in 1517, made him a national figure. By then, he had at his command the newly created machinery of communication. Within ten years thirty printers in twelve cities published his sermons as fast as he or the devoted journalists around him could get manuscripts and transcripts to them. He became a popular preacher, especially for students; and a gala preacher for the princes and nobles.

Luther the lecturer was a different man from either preacher or monk. His special field was Biblical exegesis. He most carefully studied the classical textbooks (*Glossa, Ordinaria, and Lyra*), and his important predecessors among the Augustinians; he also kept abreast of the humanist scholars of his time and of the correctives provided by Erasmus's study of the Greek texts and Reuchlin's study of the Hebrew texts. He could be as quibbling a linguist as any scholasticist and as fanciful as any humanist. In his first course of lectures he tries the wings of his own thoughts; sometimes he bewilders himself, and sometimes he looks about for companions, but finally he soars his own lonesome way. His fascinated listeners did not really know what was happening until they had a national scandal on their hands, and by that time Luther's role had become so political and ideological that his early lectures were forgotten and were recovered only in the late nineteenth and early twentieth centuries. Because of Luther's habit of telescoping all of his theological prehistory into the events of 1517, when he became a celebrity, it has only been recognized in this century that his theology was already completed in outline when he burst into history. Then it became politics and propaganda; it became Luther as most of us know him.

But we are interested here in the beginnings, in the emergence of Martin's thoughts about the "matrix of the Scriptures." Biblical exegesis in his day meant the demonstration—scholarly, tortured, and fanciful—of the traditional assumption that the Old Testament was a prophecy of Christ's life and death. The history of the world was contained in the Word: the book of Genesis was not just an account of creation, it was also a hidden, an allegorical, index of the whole Bible up to the crowning event of Christ's passion. Exegesis was an ideological game which permitted the Church to reinterpret Biblical predictions of its own history according to a new theological line; it was a high form of intellectual and linguistic exercise; and it provided an opportunity for the display of scholastic virtuosity. There were rules, however; some education and some resourcefulness were required to make things come out right.

The medieval world had four ways of interpreting Biblical material: literally (*literaliter*), which put stress on the real historical meaning of the text; allegorically (*allegorice*), which viewed Biblical events as symbolic of Christian history, the Church's creation, and dogma; morally (*tropologice*), which took the material as figurative expression of proper behavior for a man of faith; and anagogically (*anagogice*), which treated the material as an expression of the life hereafter. Luther used these techniques for his own purposes, although he always tried to be sincere and consistent; for example, he felt that the demand for circumcision in the Old Testament foretold his new insight that outer works do not count; but this interpretation also expresses the idea that the covenant of circumcision stressed humility by its attack on the executive organ of male vainglory. Luther's ethical search gradually made him discard the other categories of exegesis and concentrate on the moral one: *tropologicem esse primarium sensum scripturae*.[20] The scriptures to him became God's advice to the faithful in the here and now.

The Book of Psalms was the subject of the first series of lectures given by the new *lector bibliae* in the academic year 1513–14. Tradition suggested that King David the Psalmist ought to be interpreted as an unconscious prophet whose songs prefigured what Christ would say to God or to the Church, or what others would say to or about Christ. Our point here is to establish the emergence of Lutherisms from the overripe mixture of neoplatonic, sacramental, mystical, and scholastic interpretations; but we must remember that the personal conflict and the theological heresy on which we will focus were firmly based in what was then scholarly craftsmanship and responsible teaching. Nothing could make this more clear than the fact that no eyebrows were raised at what Martin said: and that as far as he was concerned, what he said was good theology and dedicated to the service of his new function within the Church. Furthermore, despite the impression early Lutherisms give, Luther maintained in his sermons and in his lectures a disciplined dedication to his metier, and allowed his personality expression only in matters of divine conviction. When he discussed a certain depth of contrition in his lectures, he could confess simply, "I am very far from having reached this myself"; [21] but on the day he was to leave for Worms to face the Emperor, he preached in the morning without mentioning his imminent departure for that historical meeting.

His series of lectures, at the rate of one lecture a week, extended over a two-year course. Luther took the job of being a professor rather unprofessionally hard. He meticulously recorded his changes of mind, and accounted for insights for which he found the right words only as he went along with editorial honesty. "I do not yet fully understand this," [22] he would tell his listeners. "I did not say that as well the last time as I did today." *Fateamur nos proficere scribendo et legendo*,[23] he pleaded: We must learn to become more proficient as we write and read. He does not try to hide his arbitrariness ("I simply rhymed the abstract and the concrete together"),[24] or an occasional tour de force: "All you can do with a text that proves to have a hard shell is to bang it at a rock and it will reveal the softest kernel (*nucleum suavissimum*)." [25] For these words he congratulated himself by marks on the margins. It is obvious that his honesty is a far cry from the elegant arbitrariness of the scholastic divines, and their stylized methods of rationalizing gaps between faith and reason. Luther's arbitrariness is part of a working lecture in which both rough spots and polish are made apparent. The first lectures on the Psalms impress one as being a half-finished piece of work; and Luther's formulations fully matured only in the lectures on Paul's Epistles to the Romans (1515–16). But concerned as we are here with the solution of an extended identity crisis rather than with a completed theology, we will restrict ourselves to the first emergence of genuine Lutherisms in the lectures on the Psalms.

4

Rather dramatic evidence exists in Luther's notes on these lectures for the fact that while he was working on the Psalms Luther came to formulate those insights later ascribed to his revelation in the tower, the date of which scholars have tried in vain to establish with certainty. As Luther was reviewing in his mind Romans 1:17, the last sentence suddenly assumed a clarity which pervaded his whole being and "opened the door of paradise" to him: "For therein is the righteousness of God revealed from faith to faith: as it is written, *The just shall live by faith*." The power of these words lay in a new perception of the space-time of life and eternity. Luther saw that God's justice is not consigned to a future day of judgment based on our record on earth when He will have the "last word." Instead, this justice is in us, in the here and now; for, if we will only perceive it, God has given us faith to live by, and we can perceive it by understanding the Word which is Christ. We will discuss later the circumstances leading to this perception; what interests us first of all is its relation to the lectures on the Psalms.

In a remarkable study published in 1929, Erich Vogelsang demonstrated that the insights previously attributed exclusively to Luther's revelation in the tower, and often ascribed to a much later time, appear fully and dramatically early in these lectures. Whether this means, as Vogelsang claims, that the revelation really "took place" while Luther was occupied with the lectures, that is, late in the year 1513, is a theological controversy in which I will not become involved. My main interest is in the fact that at about the age of thirty —an important age for gifted people with a delayed identity crisis— the wholeness of Luther's theology first emerges from the fragments of his totalistic reevaluations.

Vogelsang's study is remarkable because he weeds out of Luther's text statements which are, in fact, literal quotations from older scholars; Vogelsang thus uncovers the real course and crescendo of Luther's original remarks. Moreover, he studies usually neglected dimensions of the original text, dimensions which are not visible in the monumental Weimar Edition. For instance, there is the "archeological" dimension—the layers of thought to be seen in the preparatory notes for the lectures, in the transcripts of the lectures, and in later additions written or pasted into the text. Vogelsang studied the kinds of paper and ink used, noted variations in handwriting, and analyzed the fluctuating personal importance attached by Luther himself to various parts of his notes, indicated by underscorings and by marginal marks of self-applause. Vogelsang discovered the path of a spiritual cyclone which cut right through the texts of the lectures on the Psalms: "When Luther, in the *Psalmenkolleg* faces the task of offering his listeners an *ex professo* interpretation of the passage, *in justitia tua libera me* [and deliver me in thy righteousness], this task confronts him with a quite personal decision, affects him like a clap of thunder, and awakes in him one of the severest temptations, to which he later could think back only with trembling for the duration of his life." [26]

This much was acknowledged by old Luther: "When I first read and sang in the Psalms," he said, "*in iustitia tua libera me*, I was horror-stricken and felt deep hostility toward these words, God's righteousness, God's judgment, God's work. For I knew only that *iustitia dei* meant a harsh judgment. Well, was he supposed to save me by judging me harshly? If so, I was lost forever. But *gottlob*, when I then understood the matter and knew that *iustitia dei* meant the righteousness by which He justifies us through the free gift of Christ's justice, then I understood the *grammatica*, and I truly tasted the Psalms." [27]

Vogelsang finds interesting bibliographical and graphological evidence of Luther's struggle. "In the whole *Dresdener Psalter*," he writes, "there is no page which bears such direct witness to personal despair as does the *Scholie* to Psalm 30:1 [Psalm 31 in the King James' version]. He who has trained his ear in steady dealings with these lectures here perceives a violence and passion of language scarcely found anywhere else. The decisive words, *in justitia tua libera me*, Luther jumps over in terror and anxiety, which closes his ear to the singularly reassuring passage, 'Into thine hand, I commit my spirit' [Psalm 31:5, King James version]." [28] Remember what Scheel said about Martin's *tentatio* during his first Mass: that he seemed blind to the reassuring passage which referred to Christ as the mediator, and preferred to test the rock bottom of his despair, "because there was no real faith." Vogelsang continues: "He immediately proceeds with 'Have mercy upon me, O Lord,' (the hand-writing here is extremely excited and confused; he adds a great number of underscorings) and prays with trembling conscience in the words of the sixth Psalm [Psalm 7, King James version]— '*Ex intuitu irae dei*.' And even as the text of the 31st Psalm is about to call him out of his temptation with the words '*in te speravi Domine*,' ['But I trusted in Thee, O Lord'] he deflects the discussion only more violently back to the words of the sixth Psalm." [29]

Although Vogelsang does not make a point of it, it cannot escape us that these psalms are expressions of David's accusations against his and (so he likes to conclude) the Lord's enemies; in them David vacillates between wishing the wrath of God and the mercy of God upon the heads of his enemies. There are other passages in Psalm 31 which Luther ignores, besides those which Vogelsang mentioned: "Pull me out of the net that they had laid privily for me: for thou art my strength"; [30] and "I have hated them that regard lying vanities: but I trust in the Lord." [31] Luther probably had enemies at the time in Erfurt. But there was another enemy who, "regarding lying vanities," had "privily laid a net" for Martin; had not his father, thwarted in his vain plans for his son, put a curse on his son's spiritual life, predicted his temptations, predicted, in fact, his coming rebellion? In Martin's struggle for justification, involv-ing the emancipation of his obsessive conscience from his jealous father and the liberation of his thought from medieval theology, this new insight into God's pervading justice could not, psycho-logically speaking, be experienced as a true revelatory solution without some disposition of his smouldering hate. We will come back to this point when we discuss Luther's identification with Christ; for the Psalmist's complaint about his enemies reminds us of the social setting of Christ's passion. He, too, was mockingly chal-lenged to prove his sonhood of God: "He trusted in God; let him deliver him now, if he will have him: for he said, I am the Son of God." [32]

When the lectures on the Psalms reached Psalm 71:2, Luther again faced the phrase, "Deliver me in thy righteousness," again preceded (Psalm 70) by "Let them be turned back for a reward of their shame that say, Aha, aha." But now his mood, his outlook, and his vocabulary had undergone a radical change.[33] He twice quotes Romans 1:17 (the text of his revelation in the tower) and concludes

"*Justitia dei . . . est fides Christi*": Christ's faith is God's righteousness. This is followed by what Vogelsang calls a dithyrambic sequence of new and basically "Protestant" formulations, a selection of which we will review presently. These formulations center in Luther's final acceptance of Christ's mediatorship, and a new concept of man's sonhood of God.

This was the breakthrough. In these lectures, and only in these, Luther quotes St. Augustine's account of his own awakening four times: in the very first lecture; in connection with the dramatic disruption caused by Psalm 31; and twice in connection with Psalm 71.

It seems entirely probable, then, that the revelation in the tower occurred sometime during Luther's work on these lectures. Alternatively, instead of one revelation, there may have been a series of crises, the first perhaps traceable in this manuscript on the Psalms, the last fixed in Luther's memory at that finite event which scholars have found so difficult to locate in time.

The finite event seems to be associated in Luther's mind with a preceding period of deep depression, during which he again foresaw an early death. The reported episode has been viewed with prejudice because of its *place* of occurrence. Luther refers to a *Secretus locus monachorum, hypocaustum,* or *cloaca;* that is, the monks' secret place, the sweat chamber, or the toilet. According to Scheel, this list originates from one transcript of a table-talk of 1532, when Luther is reported to have said "*Dise Kunst hatt mir der Spiritus Sanctus auff diss Cl. eingeben*": the holy spirit endowed me with this art on the Cl.[34] Rorer, whom the very critical Scheel considers the most reliable of the original reporters, transcribes Cl. as cloaca. Nevertheless, Scheel dismisses this interpretation; and indeed, no other reported statement of Luther's has made mature men squirm more uncomfortably, or made serious scholars turn their noses higher in contemptuous disbelief. The psychiatrist concedes that Cl. does refer to the toilet; but, of all people, he haughtily concludes that after all, it is not relevant *where* important things happen.

This whole geographic issue, however, deserves special mention exactly because it *does* point up certain psychiatric relevances. First of all, the locality mentioned serves a particular physical need which hides its emotional relevance only as long as it happens to function smoothly. Yet, as the psychiatrist himself points out,

Luther suffered from lifelong constipation and urine retention. Leaving the possible physical causes or consequences of this tendency aside, the functions themselves are related to the organ modes of retention and elimination—in defiant children most obviously, and in adults through all manner of ambivalent behavior. There can be little doubt that at this particular time, when Martin's power of speech was freed from its infantile and juvenile captivity, he changed from a highly restrained and retentive individual into an explosive person; he had found an unexpected release of self-expression, and with it, of the many-sided power of his personality.

Those who object to these possibly impure circumstances of Martin's spiritual revelation forget St. Paul's epileptic attack, a physical paroxysm often accompanied by a loss of sphincter control, and deny the total involvement of body and soul which makes an emotional and spiritual experience genuine. Scholars would prefer to have it happen as they achieve their own reflected revelations—sitting at a desk. Luther's statement that he was, in fact, sitting somewhere else, implies that in this creative moment the tension of nights and days of meditation found release throughout his being—and nobody who has read Luther's private remarks can doubt that his total being always included his bowels. Furthermore, people in those days expressed much more openly and conceptualized more concretely than we do the emotional implications (and the implication in our emotions) of the primary bodily functions. We permit ourselves to understand them in a burlesque show, or in circumstances where we can laugh off our discomfort; but we are embarrassed when we are asked to acknowledge them in earnest. Then we prefer to speak of them haughtily, as though they were something we have long left behind. But here the suppressed meaning betrays itself in the irrational defensiveness; for what we leave behind, with emotional repudiation, is at least unconsciously associated with dirt and feces. St. Paul openly counted all the glittering things which he had abandoned for Christ "but dung."

A revelation, that is, a sudden inner flooding with light, is always associated with a repudiation, a cleansing, a kicking away; and it would be entirely in accord with Luther's great freedom in such matters if he were to experience and to report this repudiation in frankly physical terms. The cloaca, at the "other end" of the bodily self, remained for him sometimes wittily, sometimes painfully, and sometimes delusionally alive, as if it were a "dirt ground" where one meets with the devil, just as one meets with God in the *Seelengrund*, where pure being is created.

The psychiatric relevance of all this is heightened by the fact that in later years, when Luther's freedom of speech occasionally deteriorated into vulgar license, he went far beyond the customary gay crudity of his early days. In melancholy moods, he expressed his depressive self-repudiation also in anal terms: "I am like ripe shit," he said once at the dinner table during a fit of depression (and the boys eagerly wrote it down), "and the world is a gigantic ass-hole. We probably will let go of each other soon." [35] We have no right to overlook a fact which Luther was far from denying: that when he, who had once chosen silence in order to restrain his rebellious and destructive nature, finally learned to let himself go, he freed not only the greatest oratory of his time, but also the most towering temper and the greatest capacity for dirt-slinging wrath.

The problem is not how extraordinary or how pathological all this is, but whether or not we can have one Luther without the other. We will return to this question in conclusion. In the meantime, what we know of Martin's autocratic conscience, and what we begin to know of his tempestuous temperament, will stand us in good stead as we see the lecturer find his balance and his identity in the act of lecturing, and with them, some new formulations of man's relation to God and to himself.

In what follows, themes from Luther's first lectures are discussed side by side with psychoanalytic insights. Theological readers will wonder whether Luther saved theology from philosophy only to have it exploited by psychology; while psychoanalysts may suspect me of trying to make space for a Lutheran God in the structure of the psyche. My purposes, however, are more modest: I intend to demonstrate that Luther's redefinition of man's condition—while part and parcel of his theology—has striking configurational parallels with inner dynamic shifts like those which clinicians recognize in the recovery of individuals from psychic distress. In brief, I will try to indicate that Luther, in laying the foundation for a "religiosity for the adult man," displayed the attributes of his own hard-won adulthood; his renaissance of faith portrays a vigorous recovery of his own ego-initiative. To indicate this I will focus on three ideas:

the affirmation of voice and word as the instruments of faith; the new recognition of God's "face" in the passion of Christ; and the redefinition of a just life.

After 1505 Luther had made no bones about the pernicious influence which "rancid Aristotelianism" had had on theology. Scholasticism had made him lose faith, he said; through St. Paul he had recovered it. He put the problem in terms of organ modes, by describing scholastic disputations as *dentes* and *linguae:* the teeth are hard and sinister, and form words in anger and fury; the tongue is soft and suavely persuasive. Using these modes, the devil can evoke purely intellectual mirages (*mira potest suggere in intellectu*).[36] But the organ through which the word enters to replenish the heart is the ear (*natura enim verbi est audiri*),[37] for it is in the nature of the word that it should be heard. On the other hand, faith comes from listening, not from looking (*quia est auditu fides, non ex visu*).[38] Therefore, the greatest thing one can say about Christ, and about all Christians, is that they have *aures perfectas et perfossas:* [39] good and open ears. But only what is perceived at the same time as a matter *affectionalis* and *moralis* as well as intellectual can be a matter sacred and divine: one must, therefore, hear before one sees, believe before one understands, be captivated before one captures. *Fides est "locus" animae:* [40] faith is the seat, the organ of the soul. This had certainly been said before; but Luther's emphasis is not on Augustinian "infusion," or on a nominalist "obedience," but, in a truly Renaissance approach, on a self-verification through a God-given inner "apparatus." This *locus*, this apparatus, has its own way of seeking and searching—and it succeeds insofar as it develops its own *passivity*.

Paradoxically, many a young man (and son of a stubborn one) becomes a great man in his own sphere only by learning that deep passivity which permits him to let the data of his competency speak to him. As Freud said in a letter to Fliess, "I must wait until it moves in me so that I can perceive it: *bis es sich in mir ruehrt und ich davon erfahre.*" [41] This may sound feminine, and, indeed, Luther bluntly spoke of an attitude of womanly conception—*sicut mulier in conceptu.*[42] Yet it is clear that men call such attitudes and modes feminine only because the strain of paternalism has alienated us from them; for these modes are any organism's birthright, and all our partial as well as our total functioning is based on a metabolism of passivity and activity. Mannish man always wants to pretend that he made himself, or at any rate, that no simple woman bore him, and many puberty rites (consider the rebirth from a kiva in the American Southwest) dramatize a new birth from a spiritual mother of a kind that only men understand.

The theology as well as the psychology of Luther's passivity is that of man in the *state of prayer*, a state in which he fully means what he can say only to God: *Tibi soli peccavi*, I have sinned, not in relation to any person or institution, but in relation only to God, to *my* God.

In two ways, then, rebirth by prayer is passive: it means surrender to God the Father; but it also means to be reborn *ex matrice scripturae nati*,[43] out of the matrix of the scriptures. "Matrix" is as close as such a man's man will come to saying "mater." But he cannot remember and will not acknowledge that long before he had developed those wilful modes which were specifically suppressed and paradoxically aggravated by a challenging father, a mother had taught him to touch the world with his searching mouth and his probing senses. What to a man's man, in the course of his development, seems like a passivity hard to acquire, is only a regained ability to be active with his oldest and most neglected modes. Is it coincidence that Luther, now that he was explicitly teaching passivity, should come to the conclusion that a lecturer should feed his audience as a mother suckles her child? Intrinsic to the kind of passivity we speak of is not only the memory of having been given, but also the identification with the maternal giver: "the glory of a good thing is that it flows out to others." [44] I think that in the Bible Luther at last found a mother whom he could acknowledge: he could attribute to the Bible a generosity to which he could open himself, and which he could pass on to others, at last a mother's son.

Luther did use the words *passiva* and *passivus* when he spoke Latin, and the translation *passive* must be accepted as correct. But in German he often used the word *passivisch*, which is more actively passive, as passific would be. I think that the difference between the old modalities of *passive* and *active* is really that between *erleben* and *handeln*, of being in the state of *experiencing* or of *acting*. Meaningful implications are lost in the flat word *passivity*—among them the total attitude of living receptively and through the senses, of willingly "suffering" the voice of one's intuition and of living a *Passion:* that total passivity in which man regains, through considered self-sacrifice and self-transcendence, his active position in the face of nothingness, and thus is saved. Could this be one of the psychological riddles in the wisdom of the "foolishness of the cross?"

To Luther, the preaching and the praying man, the measure in depth of the perceived presence of the Word was the reaction with a total affect which leaves no doubt that one "means it." It may seem paradoxical to speak of an affect that one could not thus mean; yet it is obvious that rituals, observances, and performances do evoke transitory affects which can be put on for the occasion and afterward hung in the closet with one's Sunday clothes. Man is able to ceremonialize, as he can "automatize" psychologically, the signs and behaviors that are born of the deepest reverence or despair. However, for an affect to have a deep and lasting effect, or, as Luther would say, be *affectionalis* and *moralis*, it must not only be experienced as nearly overwhelming, but it must also in some way be affirmed by the ego as valid, almost as chosen: one means the affect, it signifies something meaningful, it is significant. Such is the relative nature of our ego and of our conscience that when the ego regains its composure after the auditory condemnation of the absolutist voice of conscience we mean what we have learned to believe, and our affects become those of positive conscience: faith, conviction, authority, indignation—all subjective states which are attributes of a strong sense of identity and, incidentally, are indispensable tools for strengthening identity in others. Luther speaks of matters of faith as experiences from which one will profit to the degree to which they were intensive and expressive (*quanto expressius et intensius*). If they are more *frigidus,* however, they are not merely a profit missed, they are a terrible deficit confirmed: for man without intense convictions is a robot with destructive techniques.

It is easy to see that these formulations, once revolutionary, are the commonplaces of today's pulpits. They are the bases of that most inflated of all oratorical currency, credal protestation in church and lecture hall, in political propaganda and in oral advertisement: the protestation, made to order for the occasion, that truth is only that which one means with one's whole being, and lives every moment. We, the heirs of Protestantism, have made convention and pretense out of the very sound of meaning it. What started with the German *Brustton der Ueberzeugung*, the manly chestiness of conviction, took many forms of authoritative appeal, the most recent one being the cute sincerity of our TV announcers. All this only indicates that Luther was a pioneer on one of our eternal inner frontiers, and that his struggle must continue (as any great man's must) exactly at that point where his word is perverted in his own name.

Psychotherapists, professional listeners and talkers in the sphere of affectivity and morality know only too well that man seldom really knows what he really means; he as often lies by telling the truth as he reveals the truth when he tries to lie. This is a psychological statement; and the psychoanalytic method, when it does not pretend to deliver complete honesty, over a period of time reveals approximately what somebody really means. But the center of the problem is simply this: in truly significant matters people, and especially children, have a devastatingly clear if mostly unconscious perception of what other people really mean, and sooner or later royally reward real love or take well-aimed revenge for implicit hate. Families in which each member is separated from the others by asbestos walls of verbal propriety, overt sweetness, cheap frankness, and rectitude tell one another off and talk back to each other with minute and unconscious displays of affect—not to mention physical complaints and bodily ailments—with which they worry, accuse, undermine, and murder one another.

Meaning it, then, is not a matter of credal protestation; verbal explicitness is not a sign of faith. Meaning it, means to be at one with an ideology in the process of rejuvenation; it implies a successful sublimation of one's libidinal strivings; and it manifests itself in a liberated craftsmanship.

When Luther listened to the scriptures he did not do so with an unprejudiced ear. His method of making an unprejudiced approach consisted of listening both ways—to the Word coming from the book and to the echo in himself. "Whatever is in your disposition," he said, "that the word of God will be unto you." [45] Disposition here means the inner configuration of your most meant meanings. He knew that he meant it when he could say it: the spoken Word was the activity appropriate for his kind of passivity. Here "faith and word become one, an invincible whole." *"Der Glawb und das Worth wirth gantz ein Ding und ein unuberwintlich ding."* [46]

Twenty-five times in the Lectures on the Psalms, against once in the Lectures on the Romans, Luther quotes two corresponding passages from Paul's first Epistle to the Corinthians. The first passage:

22. For the Jews require a sign, and the Greeks seek after wisdom;

23. But we preach Christ crucified, unto the Jews a stumblingblock, and unto the Greeks foolishness;

25. Because the foolishness of God is wiser than men; and the weakness of God is stronger than men.[47]

This paradoxical foolishness and weakness of God became a theological absolute for Luther: there is not a word in the Bible, he exclaimed, which is *extra crucem*, which can be understood without reference to the cross; and this is all that shall and can be understood, as Paul had said in the other passage:

1. And I, brethren, when I came to you, came not with excellency of speech or of wisdom, declaring unto you the testimony of God.

2. For I determined not to know any thing among you, save Jesus Christ, and him crucified.

3. And I was with you in weakness, and in fear, and in much trembling.[48]

Thus Luther abandoned any theological quibbling about the cross. He did not share St. Augustine's opinion that when Christ on the cross exclaimed *Deus meus, quare me derelequisti,* He had not been really abandoned, for as God's son and as God's word, He *was* God. Luther could not help feeling that St. Paul came closer to the truth when he assumed an existential paradox rather than a platonic fusion of essences; he insists on Christ's complete sense of abandonment and on his sincere and active premeditation in visiting hell. Luther spoke here in passionate terms very different from those of medieval adoration. He spoke of a man who was unique in all creation, yet lives in each man; and who is dying *in* everyone even as he died *for* everyone. It is clear that Luther rejected all arrangements by which an assortment of saints made it unnecessary for man to embrace the maximum of his own existential suffering. What he had tried, so desperately and for so long, to counteract and overcome he now accepted as his divine gift—the sense of utter abandonment, *sicut jam damnatus,*[49] as if already in hell. The worst temptation, he now says, is not to have any; one can be sure that God is most angry when He does not seem angry at all. Luther warns of all those well-meaning (*bone intentionarii*) religionists who encourage man "to do what he can": to forestall sinning by clever planning; to seek redemption by observing all occasions for rituals, not forgetting to bring cash along to the limit of their means; and to be secure in the feeling that they are as humble and as peaceful as "it is in them to be." Luther, instead, made a virtue out of what his superiors had considered a vice in him (and we, a symptom), namely, the determined search for the rock bottom of his sinfulness: only thus, he says, can man judge himself as God would: *conformis deo est et verax et justus.*[50] One could consider such conformity utter passivity in the face of God's judgment; but note that it really is an active self-observation, which scans the frontier of conscience for the genuine sense of guilt. Instead of accepting some impersonal and mechanical absolution, it insists on dealing with sincere guilt, perceiving as "God's judgment" what in fact is the individual's own truly meant self-judgment.

Is all this an aspect of personal adjustment to be interpreted as a set of unconscious tricks? Martin the son, who on a personal level had suffered deeply because he could not coerce his father into approving his religiosity as genuine, and who had borne with him the words of this father with an unduly prolonged filial obedience, assumes now on a religious level a volitional role toward filial suffering, perhaps making out of his protracted sonhood the victory of his Christlikeness. In his first Mass, facing the altar—the Father in heaven—and at the same time waiting to face his angry earthly father, Martin had "overlooked" a passage concerning Christ's mediatorship. Yet now, in finding Christ in himself, he establishes an inner position which goes beyond that of a neurotic compromise identification. He finds the core of a praying man's identity, and advances Christian ideology by an important step. It is clear that Luther abandoned the appreciation of Christ as a substitute who has died "for"—in the sense of "instead of"—us; he also abandoned the concept of Christ as an ideal figure to be imitated, or abjectly venerated, or ceremonially remembered as an event in the past. Christ now becomes the core of the Christian's identity: *quotidianus Christi adventus,*[51] Christ is today here, in me. The affirmed passivity of suffering becomes the daily Passion and the Passion is the substitution of the primitive sacrifice of others with a most active, most masterly, affirmation of man's nothingness—which, by his own masterly choice, becomes his existential identity.

The men revered by mankind as saviors face and describe in lasting words insights which the ordinary man must avoid with all possible self-deception and exploitation of others. These men prove their point by the magic of their voices which radiate to the farthest corner of their world and out into the millennia. Their passion contains elements of choice, mastery, and victory, and sooner or later earns them the name of King of Kings; their crown of thorns later becomes their successor's tiara. For a little while Luther, this first revolutionary individualist, saved the Saviour from the tiaras and the ceremonies, the hierarchies and the thought-police, and put him back where he arose: in each man's soul.

Is this not the counterpart, on the level of conscience, to Renaissance anthropocentrism? Luther left the heavens to science and restricted himself to what he could know of his own suffering and faith, that is, to what he could mean. He who had sought to dispel the angry cloud that darkened the face of the fathers and of The Father now said that Christ's life *is* God's face: *qui est facies patris.*[52] The Passion is all that man can know of God: his conflicts, duly faced, are all that he can know of himself. The last judgment is the always present self-judgment. Christ did not live and die in order to make man poorer in the fear of his future judgment, but in order to make him abundant today: *nam judicia sunt ipsae passiones Christi quae in nobis abundant.*[53] Look, Luther said at one point in these lectures, (IV, 87) how everywhere painters depict Christ's passion as if they agreed with St. Paul that we know nothing but Christ crucified.[54] The artist closest to Luther in spirit was Dürer, who etched his own face into Christ's countenance.

The characteristics of Luther's theological advance can be compared to certain steps in psychological maturation which every man must take: the internalization of the father-son relationship; the concomitant crystallization of conscience; the safe establishment of an identity as a worker and a man; and the concomitant reaffirmation of basic trust.

God, instead of lurking on the periphery of space and time, became for Luther "what works in us." The way *to* Him is not the effortful striving toward a goal by "doing what you can"; rather, His way is what moves from inside: *via dei est, qua nos ambulare facit*.[55] God, now less of a person, becomes more personal for the individual; and instead of constituting a threat to be faced at the end of all things, He becomes that which always begins—in us. His son is therefore always reborn: *"ita et nos semper oportet nasci, novari, generari"*: It therefore behooves us to be reborn, renovated, regenerated.[56] To "do enough" means always to begin: *"Proficere est nihil aliud nisi semper incipere."* [57] The intersection of all the paradoxes of the vertical and the horizontal is thus to be found in man's own divided nature. The two *regna*, the realist sphere of divine grace and the naturalist sphere of animality, exist in man's inner conflicts and in his existential paradoxes: *"Die zwo Personen oder zweierlei ampt,"* [58] the two personalities and the two callings which a Christian must maintain at the same time on this earth.

It does not matter what these two personalities "are." Theologians, philosophers, and psychologists slice man in different ways, and there is no use trying to make the sections coincide. The main point to be made here is Luther's new emphasis on man in *inner* conflict and his salvation through introspective perfection. Luther's formulation of a God known to individual man only through the symbolism of the Son's Passion redefined the individual's existence in a direction later pursued in both Kierkegaard's existentialism and Freud's psychoanalysis—methods which lead the individual systematically to his own borders, including the border of his religious ecstasies.

Let us rephrase somewhat more psychologically what we have just put in theological terms. What we have referred to as the negative conscience corresponds in many ways to Freud's conceptualization of the pressure put by the superego on the ego. If this pressure is dominant in an individual or in a group, the whole quality of experience is overshadowed by a particular sense of existence, an intensification of certain aspects of subjective space and time. Any fleeting moment of really bad conscience can teach us this, as can also, and more impressively, a spell of melancholy. We are then strangely constricted and paralyzed, victims of an inner voice whispering sharply that we are far from that perfection which alone will do when the closely impending, but vague and unpredictable, doom arrives; in spite of that immediacy, we are as yet sinners, not quite good enough, and probably too far gone. Any temporary relief from this melancholy state (into which Luther, at the height of his worldly success, sank more deeply than ever before) is only to be had at the price of making a painful deal with the voice, a deal which offers the hope that maybe soon we will find the platform for a new start; or maybe at the hour of trial we will find that according to some unknown scale we will prove barely but sufficiently acceptable, and so may pass—pass into heaven, as some proud minds have asked, by just *getting by?* In the meantime, our obsessive scrupulosity will chew its teeth out and exercise its guts on the maybe-soons, the already-almosts, the just-a-bit-mores, the not-yet-quites, the probably-next-times. Not all minds, of course, naturally exercise themselves in this way; but everybody does it to some degree, and almost anybody can be prevailed upon to participate by an ideological system which blocks all exits except one, that one adorned with exactly matching symbols of hope and despair, and guarded by the system's showmen, craftsmen, and torturers.

To some individuals, however, such a state becomes, for personal reasons, habitual: from these people the religionists in any field are recruited. Whole peoples may elaborate this potential state into a world image. William James remarked that the Latin races seem to be able more easily to split up the pressure of evil into "ills and sins in the plural, removable in detail," while the Germanic races tend to erect one "Sin in the singular, and with a capital S . . . ineradicably ingrained in our natural subjectivity, and never to be removed by any piecemeal operation." [59] If this is true, climate may have much to do with it: the more decided retreat of the sun to the danger point of disappearance in the Nordic winter, the protracted darkness and the fatal cold which last over periods long enough to convey a sense of irretrievability or at any rate to enforce a totalistic adjustment to such a possibility. Just because Luther's periodic states of melancholy repeatedly forced him to accept despair and disease as final, and death as imminent, he may have expressed in his pessimistic and philosophically most untenable concepts (such as the total predestination of individual fate, independent of personal effort) exactly that cold rock bottom of mood, that utter background of blackness, which to Northern people is the condition of spring:

> *Der Sommer ist hart fuer der Tuer*
> *Der Winter ist vergangen*
> *Die zarten Blumen gehn herfuer;*

Der das hat angefangen
Der wird es auch vollenden.

This only says that winter is gone and summer is at the door, and that the flowers are coming up; and that Whoever has begun such a process will surely complete it.

A predominant state of mind in which the ego keeps the superego in victorious check can reconcile certain opposites which the negative conscience rigidly keeps separate; ego-dominance tends to be holistic, to blend opposites without blunting them. In his state of personal recovery, Luther (like any individual recovering from an oppressive mental state) had recourse to massive totalisms from which he derived the foundation stones for a new wholeness. The whole person includes certain total states in his balances: we are, Luther proclaimed, totally sinners (*totus homo peccator*) and totally just (*totus homo justus*), always both damned and blessed, both alive and dead. We thus cannot strive, by hook or by crook, to get from one absolute stage into another; we can only use our God-given organs of awareness in the here and now to encompass the paradoxes of the human condition. Psychologically speaking, this means that at any given moment, and in any given act or thought, we are codetermined to a degree which can never become quite conscious by our drives *and* by our conscience. Our ego is most powerful when it is not burdened with an excessive denial of our drives, but lets us enjoy what we can, refute what we must, and sublimate according to our creativity—always making due allowance for the absolutism of our conscience, which can never be appeased by small sacrifices and atonements, but must always remain part of the whole performance. Luther thus said in his terms what Freud formulated psychologically, namely, that only on the surface are we ever entirely driven *or* completely just; in our depths we are vain when we are most just, and bad conscience can always be shown to be at work exactly when we are most driven by lust or avarice. But this same inner psychological condition saves God (theologically speaking) from that impossible characteristic for which Martin had not been able to forgive him, namely, that of being The Father only in certain especially meritorious moments, rather than for all eternity, as he should be. To the ego, eternity is always now.

Luther's strong emphasis on the here and now of the spiritual advent, and on the necessity of always standing at the beginning, (*semper incipere*) is not only a platform of faith, it is akin to a time-space quality dominating the inner state which psychoanalysts call "ego-strength." To the ego the past is not an inexorable process, experienced only as preparation for an impending doom; rather, the past is part of a present mastery which employs a convenient mixture of forgetting, falsifying, and idealizing to fit the past to the present, but usually to an extent which is neither unknowingly delusional nor knowingly dishonest. The ego can resign itself to past losses and forfeitings and learn not to demand the impossible of the future. It enjoys the illusion of a present, and defends this most precarious of all assumptions against doubts and apprehensions by remembering most easily chains of experiences which were alike in their unblemished presentness. To the healthy ego, the flux of time sponsors the process of identity. It thus is not afraid of death (as Freud has pointed out vigorously); it has no concept of death. But it *is* afraid of losing mastery over the negative conscience, over the drives, and over reality. To lose any of these battles is, for the ego, living death; to win them again and again means to the ego something akin to an assumption that it is causing its own life. In theological terms, *creaturae procedunt ex deo libere et voluntarie et non naturaliter:* [60] what lives, proceeds from God freely and voluntarily, not naturally, that is, not by way of what can be explained biologically.

Luther's restatements about the total sinfulness and the total salvation which are in man at any given time, can easily be shown to be alogical. With sufficient ill will they can be construed as contrived to save Martin's particular skin, which held together upswings of spiritual elations and cursing gloominess, not to speak of lusts for power and revenge, women, food, and beer. But the coexistence of all these contradictions has its psychologic—as has also the fury of their incompatibility. Martin's theological reformulations imply a psychological fact, namely, that the ego gains strength *in practice*, and *in affectu* to the degree to which it can accept at the same time the total power of the drives and the total power of conscience—*provided* that it can nourish what Luther called *opera manum dei,*[61] that particular combination of work and love which alone verifies our identity and confirms it. Under these conditions, apparent submission becomes mastery, apparent passivity the release of new energy for active pursuits. We can make negative conscience work for the aims of the ego only by facing it without evasion; and we are able to manage and creatively utilize our drives only to the extent to which we can acknowledge their power by enjoyment, by awareness, and through the activity of work.

If the ego is not able to accomplish these reconciliations, we may fall prey to that third inner space-time characterized by the dominance of what Freud called the *id*. The danger of this state comes from what Freud considered biological instincts which the ego experiences as beneath and outside itself while at the same time it is intoxicated by them. Dominance by the id means that time and space are arranged in one way—toward wish fulfillment. We know only that our tension rises when time and circumstances delay release and satisfaction, and that our drivenness is accelerated when opportunities arise. The self-propelled will tends to ignore all that has been learned in the past and is perceived in the present, except to the extent to which past and present add fuel to the goal-directedness of the wish. This id-intoxication, as Luther formulated so knowingly, can become total poisoning especially when it is haughtily denied.

Some monastic methods systematically descend to the frontiers where all ego dangers must be faced in the raw—where an overweening conscience is appeased through prayer, drives tamed by asceticism, and the pressure of reality is itself defeated by the self's systematic abandonment of its identity. But true monasticism is a late development and is possible only to a mature ego. Luther knew why he later said that nobody under thirty years of age should definitely commit himself to it.

Luther's redefinitions of work have probably been more misunderstood than any other of his formulations, except, naturally, those pertaining to sex. In both these sensitive areas, theory and practice have become completely separated. In trying to decide what a great man meant by his original formulations, it is always good to find out what he was talking *against* at the time, or what previous overstatement he was trying to correct, for greatness is based on an excessive restatement of some previous overstatement, usually made by others, often by the master himself. To the extent that the restatement momentarily sharpens our perception of our own frontiers, it will live, even though the concepts themselves become the focus of the next period's overstatement. When Luther spoke about works and work, he was speaking against a climate of opinion which, in matters of religion, asked a man how much he had done of what there was in him (or in his pocketbook) to do. When Luther spoke against works, he spoke against holy busywork which has nothing whatsoever to do with the nature or the quality of devoted craftsmanship.

Luther felt that the Christianity of his time had forgotten St. Paul's and Christ's Christianity and had reverted to "Jewish, Turkish, and Pelagian" notions, particularly in putting so much emphasis on the fulfillment of prescribed rituals. We need only remember his own obsession in Rome with the collection of free and not so free coupons to heaven to know what he meant. He later caricatured this attitude: "He runs to St. James, Rome, Jerusalem, here, there; prays to St. Brigit, this, that; fasts today, tomorrow; confesses here, there; asks this one, that one—and yet does not find peace." [62] He considered this a regression to "the law" in Judaism, in which he felt there was an excess of righteousness expressed in meticulous observances. In the obsessive fulfillment of detailed rituals, as he knew only too well, the negative conscience takes over, dividing every minute of the day into a miniature last judgment. The small self-salvations thus gained come to count as virtue—a virtue which has no time for faith and leaves not a moment's peace to others, if it can help it. Much is in the language here, in English as well as German: those who *do* what is right (*richtig*) think that they *are* right (*recht*) and claim that they *have* the right to lord it over others (*rechthaben*).

Against this inner psychic sequence Luther, in accord with his whole new space-time configuration, re-emphasized the spirit in which a thing is done from the start for its own sake. Nobody is just, he said, because he does just works; the works are just *if* the man is just: *quia justus, opera justa*. As he says in one of his teutonic restatements of a biblical saying: "What would it avail you, if you did do miracles, and strangled all the Turks (*alle Turcken erwurgkist*) and yet would sin against love?" [63]

In matters of sex and work misquotation is easy. Even Nietzsche misunderstood Luther in the matter of work, claiming that exercise and practice are every bit as necessary for good work as is faith, and often are the forerunners of faith. Nietzsche was writing against

Schopenhauer's asceticism and pessimism at the time, and was intent on reinstating will and action as prime virtues. He ignored the fact that Luther was against works, but very much for work; and that he sanctified even such activities as piling up manure, washing babies, and cleaning up the house, if they were done with faith.

As far as Luther's attitude toward his own work is concerned, only when he was able to make speaking his main occupation could he learn to know his thoughts and to trust them—and also trust God. He took on the lectures, not with pious eagerness, but with a sense of tragic conflict; but as he prepared and delivered them, he became affectively and intellectually alive. This is not works; it is work, in the best sense. In fact, Luther made the verbal work of his whole profession more genuine in the face of a tradition of scholastic virtuosity. His style indicates his conviction that a thing said less elegantly and meant more truly is better work, and better craftsmanship in communication.

There is a psychological truth implicit in Luther's restatement. People with "well-functioning egos" do good work if they can manage to "mean" the work (for whatever reason or for whoever's sake) which they must do. This is not always easily arranged, by any means, and we should not be too glib with the term "strong ego." Many individuals should not do the work which they are doing, if they are doing it well at too great inner expense. Good work it may be in terms of efficiency; but it is also bad works. The point is, not how efficiently the work is done, but how good it is for the worker in terms of his lifetime within his ideological world. The work's individual goodness will be reflected in some technical goodness which is more than the sum of mastered procedures. In his insistence on the importance of the spirit of work Luther antedated Marx; but, of course, neither politically nor economically did he foresee progress as a new dimension of ideology, although he helped to make man free for it. His was a craftsman's point of view; and he considered one craft as good a way to personal perfection as another; but also as bad a potential lifelong prison as another.

We live always in all three space-times; certain alternations of emphases differentiate us from one another. We are all alternately driven and conscience-stricken some of the time; but usually we manage to live in a dominant ego space-time, despite the world-image which totalitarian powers of spirit, sword, or dollar may continuously try to impose on us. Each historical period has its lacunae of identity and of style; each best of all possible worlds has its tensions and crazes which attest to its peculiar excesses of drivenness and constriction. Man never lives entirely in his time, even though he can never live outside it; sometimes his identity gets along with his time's ideology, and sometimes it has to fight for its life. But it is only when an overwhelming negative conscience like Martin's is linked with the sensitivity and the power-drive of a Luther that a new positive conscience arises to sow ideological seeds into fresh furrows of historical change. And perhaps all such fresh starts have in common the ego qualities which I have tried to circumscribe in this discussion.

Luther's theology contains an unsolved personal problem which is more accessible to psychoanalysis than is the theology itself. This unsolved personal problem becomes obvious later, when the suddenly changed course of his life endangers the identity which he had won as a lecturer and preacher; and even more obvious when the crisis of middle age brings to the fore again that inner store of self-hate, and that murderous intolerance of disobedience which in the lectures on the Psalms had been relatively balanced—within Luther's identity as a lecturer.

God himself thus joins the benevolent paternal images. Luther interprets Psalm 102:13, "Thou shalt arise, and have mercy upon Zion," in these words: "This arising, this standing up, means the sweetest and most gracious becoming human on the part of God, for here He has come to us so that He may lift us up to Himself." [64]

The study of Luther's earliest lectures shows that in his self-cure from deep obsessive struggles he came, almost innocently, to express principles basic to the mastery of existence by religious and introspective means. As he stated in his notes for the lectures on Romans, in which he came much closer to perfection as a professor and to clarity as a dogmatist: "Perfect self-insight is perfect humility; perfect humility is perfect knowledge; perfect knowledge is perfect spirituality." [65] At the same time Luther crowns his attempt to cure the wounds of this wrath by changing God's attributes: instead of being like an earthly father whose mood-swings are incomprehensible to his small son, God is given the attribute of *ira miseri-cordiae*—a wrath which is really compassion. With this concept, Luther was at last able to forgive God for being a Father, and grant Him justification.

Only a very independent mind could thus restate the principles of pre-Roman Christianity; and only a righteously simple man could delude himself into believing that if he let the Roman Church live, she would let him preach. This self-deception had not ended when Luther nailed the ninety-five theses on the church door in Witten-berg—not a defiant gesture in itself, but rather scholastic routine. But circumstances, to be recounted in the concluding chapter, used his theory of the spiritual negligibility of works as the backbone of an economic revolt. All of Northern Germany jumped at the op-portunity to limit Roman taxation on what seemed like sound theological grounds; in the argument, the Germans began to hear the voice that argued, and it sounded like the kind of voice they had long been waiting for.

Luther grew elatedly into his role of reformer. How he thus changed identities—he who had denied his father's wish that he should become a secular leader by choosing monastic silence instead —we can only sketch. It is clear, however, that the negative con-science which had been aggravated so grievously by Martin's pater-nalistic upbringing had only waited (as such consciences always do) for an opportunity to do to others in some measure what had been done to him.

VII

Faith and Wrath

THE REVEALING notes and commentaries which Luther jotted down during his early thirties, when he was primarily a lecturer and preacher, were somehow buried in stacks of manuscripts. They were recognized for what they were only around the turn of the present century by determined and lucky scholars searching the royal libraries of Germany and the Vatican. Luther's own manuscript of the lectures of the Romans had to be "detected" in the Royal Library in Berlin, an "anonymous" exhibit in full view in a glass case. To such an extent had Luther permitted his prehistoric days to disappear behind the events of 1517. An interesting parallel is the late discovery in an antique book store in Nazi Germany of Freud's letters to Fliess, which contain the evidence for his intellectual as well as his personal involvement in the origins of his thought; Freud had wished and had assumed them to be destroyed, and only grudgingly consented to their preservation.

The importance of Luther's early lectures lies in the fact that they bear witness not only to the recovery of his ego, but also to a new theology conceived long before he suddenly became famous as a pamphleteer in the controversy over indulgences. To the Catholic scholar, his theological innovations seem pitiful, mere vulgarized fragments of the order he disavowed; to the Protestant, his theology is powerful and fundamentally new. The historical psychologist, however, can only question how efficacious an ideology is at a given historical moment. Obviously, when this monk spoke up he presented in his words and in his bearing the image of man in whom men of all walks of life were able to recognize in decisive clarity something that seemed right, something they wanted, they needed to be. Whatever theological rationale unified Luther's teachings as an evangelist was transcended by his influence on men in his own and in other reformers' churches, in his and in other countries, and even on the Catholic Church's own Counter Reformation.

There are a number of conflicting historical views about Luther's importance for the great movement called the Reformation. These views, strongly tinged by partisanship, attest to his original leadership or suggest that his was merely an adroitly timed episode on the order of Wycliffe's or Huss's; they affirm a divine providence in his survival and ascendance, or maintain that luck, in the form of his adversaries' fatal hesitation, permitted him to complete his rebellion when according to the criteria of his time he had forfeited his life to the stake many times over. He is revered as a voice of genuine inspiration, or made out to be the tool of a conspiracy of crude economic forces which were in need of a bit of evangelical polish. Be all this as it may, Luther was the herald of the age which was in the making and is—or was—still our age: the age of literacy and enlightenment, of constitutional representation, and of the freely chosen contract; the age of the printed word which at least tried to say what it meant and to mean what it said, and provided identity through its very effort.

It is true, of course, that both Wycliffe in England and Huss in Bohemia had focused with fanatic affront on holy issues which had been widely argued about even by dignitaries and writers within the Church for more than a century before Martin's birth: the entrusting of the sacraments, especially confession, to priests with dirty ears; the administering of the Mass by equally dirty hands; the extortion by the same hands of money, at first as an adjunct to, but then increasingly as a substitute for, that contrition which it was a priest's job to insist upon; and finally, the problem of all problems, the infallibility of the foreign and distant Roman papacy whose sanction lifted these priests and their performances above all earthly criticism. Wycliffe, a hundred years before Luther's birth, had translated the Bible into the English of his contemporaries, so that they could hear the original Word freed from its captivity by the Roman monopolists. Huss, in turn, had objected to the adoration of images and the emphasis on works; with a more decidedly nationalist flair, he had likewise translated the Bible into the Czech vernacular, insisting, as Luther would, that he would have to be *shown* that he was wrong from the *Book*.

Literacy, and a conscience speaking the mother tongue—these pillars of our present-day identity had long been in the building. But Gutenberg had, as it were, waited for Luther; and the new technique of mass communication was thus available to Luther's theological performance, which so attracted the charisma, the personality cult, of a nation. It would be fatal to underestimate the degree to which the future always belongs to those who combine a universal enough new meaning with the mastery of a new technology. The Church, however, whose influence had already been impaired by the development of national monarchies elsewhere, clung to its fateful investment in the German nation which because of its position in the center of Europe held then, as it still holds, the balance between the great isms of the world.

As we discuss a few of the events which brought Luther to prominence, we cannot hope to retell what the history books and the movies have told and retold, or give consistent historical meaning to the dogmatic moralism, the diplomatic corruption, or the popular foolery which this young monk outshouted and outprinted for a few historical moments. Nor can we in any way try to do justice to the relation within Luther between his continued inner conflicts and his public leadership. We can only outline what we are reasonably competent to perceive, namely, the step from Martin's identity crisis to that crisis of middle-age which occurs when an original man first stops to realize what he has begun to originate in others.

Here are a few dates:

EVENTS OF LUTHER'S THIRTIES AND FORTIES

1513–16	Started lecturing at the age of thirty, and delivered the great trilogy on the Psalms, Romans, and Galatians.
1517	Nailed the ninety-five theses against indulgences on the door of the Castle Church in Wittenberg.
1518	Appealed the Pope's Bull threatening excommunication.
1520	Publicly burned the Bull. Wrote his great pamphlets, culminating in *On the Freedom of a Christian Man*.
1521	Appeared before the Diet at Worms. Imperial ban. Hid on the Wartburg.
1522	New Testament published in German.

1525   Pamphlet against the peasants. Marriage.
1526   Son Hans born.
1527   Sickness and depression. *A Mighty Fortress.*
1546   Death at the age of sixty-three.

The matter of indulgences set off the time bomb which had been ticking in Luther's heart. The Church had, over the centuries, developed a system of high spiritual finance, made tangible in the imagery of accrued credit in heaven, and a kind of universal community chest. Some saints, it was claimed, had amassed a credit of salvation far above their personal needs; the Church had naturally been entrusted with its distribution among the deserving. There was some abundance available within this Catholic system, but there was no salvation whatsoever outside its monopoly. Gradually the transactions within the system—the dealings of the employees with each other, and their dealings with the masses of customers—became increasingly dominated by ideas of earthly cash. The most pitiful display of this commercialization was the number of small coins dropped in sundry boxes by the masses of the poor, at first as an accessory to ritual observance, then in the assumption that the money itself had a direct magic influence through the Church's vertical line on the accounting above.

The Jubilee of 1500 provided an excuse for a worldwide campaign to increase the number of indulgences. The money so raised was to help complete St. Peter's as an anchor for the vertical, outshining the capitol of any merely horizontal empire. Indulgences were collected by expert friars, who were sometimes accompanied by agents of banking houses to whom some of the pious money was already owed, and for purposes other than those advertised in the campaign. Still, Luther typically did not raise his voice about indulgences until the campaign made itself felt in his home town and electoral province.

His own archbishop, Albrecht von Brandenburg, used the Jubilee collection to pay his personal debts, and this with the Pope's permission. Brandenburg had borrowed the money which he had to pay to the Pope for the insignia of his third archbishopric from the Augsburg house of Fugger. The Pope permitted the Fuggers to repossess this money by taking out of the indulgence boxes half of the still warm coins which the people had dropped in them to save themselves from some temporal penance, and the souls of their loved ones from centuries in purgatory. When one collecting party, headed by an especially unprincipled salesman, Tetzel, approached the borders of Electoral Saxony, both Luther and his Elector pricked up their ears.

The Elector was through with taxation without representation. He had previously kept in his own treasury the sums donated by people in Wittenberg who had viewed the Electoral relic collection expecting to gain spiritually from its radiation. The Elector was damned if he was going to release this money to pay the overhead of the agency in Rome. The money he collected was going to be applied to *his* pride, the University of Wittenberg. There is no evidence that Luther was either a party to this diversion of pious funds into his own institution or that he objected to it. But he was highly incensed at the limitless promises made by Tetzel, a Dominican at that, to Luther's constituents who were flocking over the border to participate in the fun as well as in the gain of the noisy campaign. Tetzel had, in certain cases, dispensed with confession altogether, and was distributing sealed letters of credit for sins as yet contemplated; even worse, he suggested that potential purchasers of indulgences could go to confessors of their own choosing, so that they could avoid those who might maintain a too pronounced austerity in the time of the Jubilee. This was too much; it undercut the psychological conditions for individual piety on the part of Luther's Wittenberg constituents.

Furthermore, Luther also came to realize the incompatibility of principle between his own teachings and preachings and the monetary habits and images of the organization in whose name he spoke. As he always did in decisive moments, he acted without seeking the counsel of those who might have restrained him; his entry into the monastery is an earlier example of this behavior, and his marriage is a later one. His closest friends were unaware of the fact that on the day before All Souls, when masses of people came to see the Elector's relics spread out on the castle square as if at a country fair, he had nailed the ninety-five theses on the door of the castle church. This was a custom generally used whenever one wished to invite the public disputation of a controversy. It usually neither touched the populace, nor reached the higher-ups. This time, however, Luther had a copy of the Latin text delivered to the archbishop, from whom he intended to get an answer over and above private disputation. But the answer came from elsewhere, from everywhere. The German translation of the theses evoked an immediate, wide, and emphatic echo: from the general public, who were anti-Italian and patriotic; from the dispossessed, who were anticapitalist and equalitarian; from the petty plutocrats, who were antimonopolistic; from the princes, who were particularist and territorial; from the educated, who were anticlerical and secularist; and from the knights, who were Teutonic and anarchistic. From all of these groups came encouragement so personal and folksy that it can be rendered in American only as "Atta boy, Monk!" The response of the educated, including Erasmus and Dürer, was what it has remained over the centuries: "When Luther, in his immense manly way, swept off by a stroke of his hand the very notion of a debit and credit account kept with individuals by the Almighty, he stretched the soul's imagination and saved theology from puerility." [1]

The explosiveness of the popular response immediately warned both Luther and the Church that many kinds of rebellious desires had been ignited by this one issue of alien taxation. There were moments in the following months when Luther seemed ready to recant, and when the Pope made amazing concessions by publicly "clarifying" some of the excessive claims for the papal power of divine intercession which had been made, implied, or not denied by his operatives. But Luther and the Pope acted mostly like animals who withdraw when they hear the echoes of their own growls, then are emboldened by the other's withdrawal, and soon find themselves irrevocably engaged. There is no retreat once blood is drawn. A year after the theses had been published, Luther wrote to the Pope: "Most blessed Father, I offer myself prostrate at the feet of your Holiness, with all that I am and have. Quicken, slay, call, recall, approve, reprove, as may seem good to you. I will acknowledge your voice as the voice of Christ, residing and speaking in you. If I have deserved death I will not refuse to die." [2] Yet, summoned to Rome, he refused to go; as a matter of fact, the Elector refused to let him go, having been told by the Emperor "to take good care of that monk." Soon, however, Luther began to refer to the Pope as "Antichrist"; to the Pope Luther was the "child of Satan."

Luther once again promised submission to the Pope; but then he used a legalistic excuse to break his promise of silence, and entered into public debate with the experienced Eck, who cornered him into statements which amounted to an outspoken heretical doubt in the God-givenness of the Roman Pope's supremacy in Christendom. Although (or perhaps because) he had shown himself inferior to Eck in the disputation itself, Luther began to play to the gallery, and to develop and enjoy a certain showmanship. The point of no return was soon reached; Luther preached open revolt, even suggesting that it would be entirely in order "to wash our hands in the blood" of cardinals and popes.[3] I will not quote from the rhetoric, so boring in its monotonous excess, which this once quiet and tortured monk released against the "sink of the Roman Sodom." It is enough to say that on July 10, 1520, he wrote to Spalatin: "I have cast the die . . . I will not reconcile myself to them in all eternity."[4] A few days later, the Pope published a bull threatening Luther's excommunication. Knowing that there was no way to avoid this ultimatum, Luther openly attacked specific fundamentals previously assailed by Wycliffe and Huss: the sacraments of penance and of baptism, and finally of the Eucharist itself. His views on theological matters were an applied extension of his earlier lectures, but about 1520 he appeared in an entirely new role: as a German prophet and ideological leader. He published a trilogy of pamphlets in German, the titles of which are like fanfares: *An den christlichen Adel Deutscher Nation* (*To the Christian Nobility of German Nationality*); *Ueber die Babylonische Gefangenschaft der Kirche* (*On the Babylonian Captivity of the Church*); and *Von der Freiheit eines Christenmenschen* (*About the Freedom of a Christian*).

The three prehistoric lectures on the Psalms, Romans, and Galations had developed a new vertical, a new theology of the praying man, rediscovering the passion of Christ in each man's inner struggles. These three pamphlets of 1520 outlined a new horizontal, a civic reformation in which such prayer could exist. We will mention only his claims for the equality of all Christians; for every Christian's priesthood, prepared for by baptism, and confirmed by his receptivity for the Word of the Scriptures; and for the necessity for elected councils as the true representation of all the faithful. It must interest us that he urged the postponement of monastic vows until the age of thirty—the age when sexual drive has passed its peak, when identity is firmly established, and when man's ideological pliability comes to an end. The Pope pronounced his ban in September, 1520. Luther took the Pope's Bull out by one of the

Wittenberg gates and burned it, together with other printed works. The students loved it. Rarely have young people been in on such decisive events as the students and faculty of that frontier University of Wittenberg. The next day, Luther announced that nobody could be saved except by following him out of the Church of Rome.

Luther was gladder about this pyrotechnic deed, he told Staupitz, than about anything he had said in his whole life. Even as hearing his own words had previously inspired his convictions, seeing the fire he set seems to have inflamed his rebelliousness. From this time on, the struggle set in between the Word and the Deed, between the method of persuasion and the method of fire. Every one of his words aroused his countrymen to deeds; every one of their deeds made him reaffirm: "By the Word the world has been vanquished, by the Word the Church has been saved, by the Word it will again be put in order, and the Antichrist . . . will fall without violence." [5] His verbosity could inspire chorales apt (as Goethe remarked) to lift heart and roof; but the heartlifting would persistently be matched by the roof-destroying. Almost before he knew it, Luther uttered words of violence which to him no doubt were often nothing more than poems of wrath; but to his followers, his words were tantamount to acts which obliged and justified concrete deeds.

The occasion of his most decisive oratory is the most famous moment of his life. Books and movies which have depicted his appearance before the Diet in Worms have more often than not adjusted the historical setting to fit the eternal quality of his words: a large hall, a dignified audience, and the sonorous resonance of his voice. It is too bad that history has not yet recognized the drama inherent in the rare clear voice which transcends both the anxiety within the speaker and the tense bedlam of the surrounding scene. Gettysburg should remind us how to visualize an unrehearsed historic scene; although in Worms they did crowd in to see and hear the featured speaker.

Luther had been warned not to appear, in spite of his Imperial passport. He was guided into town by a bodyguard of robber barons, and at the first brief session could hardly speak for fright or discomfort. But friends, beer in the evening, and a night's sleep restored him, and in the morning his voice was clear. In his native German he spoke those words of conscience which were a new kind of revelation achieved on the inner battlefield. At Worms Luther faced ostracism and death, not for the sake of an established creed or ties of ancestry and tradition; he did so because of *personal* convictions, derived from inner conflict and still subject to further conflict. The conscience he spoke of was not an inner sediment of a formalized morality; it was the best a *single man* between heaven, hell, and earth could know. If Luther did not really say the words which became most famous: "Here I stand," legend again rose to the occasion; for this new credo was for men whose identity was derived from their determination to stand on their own feet, not only spiritually, but politically, economically, and intellectually. No matter what happened afterward—and some terrible and most terribly petty things did occur because of it—Luther's emphasis on individual conscience prepared the way for the series of concepts of equality, representation, and self-determination which became in successive secular revolutions and wars the foundations not of the dignity of some, but of the liberty of all.

True, Luther did not really contemplate armed rebellion: "Had I desired to foment trouble, I could have brought great bloodshed upon Germany. Yea, I could have started such a little game at Worms that the Emperor would not have been safe. But what would it have been? A fool's game. I left it to the Word." [6] And he would soon so act as to deserve to be called a great reactionary. Historical dialectics refuses to acknowledge the principle that a great revolutionary's psyche may also harbor a great reactionary; but psychological dialectics must assume it to be possible, and even probable.

The new Emperor, only twenty-one years of age, and obviously stirred by the proceedings, reaffirmed *his* identity: "I am descended from a long line of Christian emperors. . . . a single friar who goes counter to all Christianity for a thousand years must be wrong . . . I will have no more to do with him." [7] He put a ban on the monk. But the Elector arranged for Luther to be kidnapped and taken to a secret hideout on the Wartburg, only a mile from Eisenach and the Cottas.

After his father's house, this castle was Luther's most fateful residence. He was still a monk, committed to obedience, prayer, and celibacy; but at the castle he was without monastery or observances, without brethren or prior. From his window he could see the wide world, now (as messages conveyed) full of his name, and full of sinister threats. That world needed his leadership as much as he, so abruptly awakened to action, was ready to assume leadership. But at the very moment of his readiness, he was forced back into anonymity and inactivity, forced to read his own obituaries written by mourning friends whom he could have joined in reform and revolution.

Deprived of institutional routine, he was prey to the ego's double threat: the id within him, and the mob around him. His letters from the Wartburg frankly reveal how the mature man, grown beyond his tortured attempt at monasticism and abruptly blocked in his development as a leader, was tormented by desire. His enjoyment of food and beer under his immobile circumstances aggravated his tendency to be constipated, which in turn increased his demonological preoccupation with the lower parts of the body. All the *tentationes* from which he had fled as a young man into the monastery obsessed him as a grown man and the potential leader of a nation. His lust for power turned into furious anger with himself, with his circumstances, and with the devil. Much has been said about his hallucinations; but what would he have done without the devil, without being able to lump the grotesque and embarrassing paradoxes of his condition into one personalized creature—not invented by him, but confirmed by tradition (black dog and all) and thus "real" enough to permit a degree of hallucinatory projection, and, above all, now and then a superhuman temper tantrum? Luther on the Wartburg apparently at times suffered from something akin to a prison psychosis, which brought out in somewhat spectacular fashion those elements of unresolved infantile conflict which later, when he could not blame prison walls for his exposure to "the devil," turned into spells of brooding melancholy.

But despite his laments in the form of confessions to his friends (and this orator, as others of his kind, was also a colossal crybaby) he worked and could work. Under these conditions he wrote his pamphlet *On Monastic Vows*, the one which he prefaced with a letter to his father. The pamphlet stated as a general principle what the father had predicted for this particular son, namely, that the sexual instinct is essentially insurmountable, and, except in the case of rare and naturally celibate individuals, should not be subjected to attempts at suppression lest they poison the whole person. Marriage, he said, is the answer. Nevertheless, the father had been wrong because God alone could be right; and only Martin could have found this out—by becoming a monk.

He also began translating the New Testament from Erasmus's Greek version into German. It became his and his nation's most complete literary achievement. All the facets of a many-sided personality and all the resources of a rich vernacular were combined to create a language not intended as poetry for the few, but as inspiration in the life of the people. As Nietzsche put it: "The masterpiece of German prose is, appropriately enough, the masterwork of Germany's greatest preacher: the Bible so far has been the best German book. Compared with Luther's Bible, almost everything else is 'literature,' that is, a thing which has not grown in Germany and has not grown, and does not grow, into German hearts as the Bible has done." [8] Jacob Grimm, a scholar considered to be the founder of German linguistics, said that the later flowering of German literature would have been unthinkable without Luther's work. "Because of its almost miraculous purity and because of its deep influence, Luther's German must be considered the core and the fundament of the new German language. Whatever can be said to have nursed this language, whatever rejuvenated it so that a new flowering of poetry could result—this we owe to nobody more than to Luther." [9] Almost literally thunderstruck in the choir, this man translated the Lord's Prayer so that most Germans came to feel that Christ conceived it in German; and beside his diatribes of hate and blasphemous filth, wrote lyrics which have the power and the simplicity of folksong.

"Ein Woertlein kann ihn faellen": a tiny word can topple the devil. Luther's muteness was more than cured. The cultivation of national vernaculars was part of the growing nationalism; it was also part of the verbal Renaissance, one of the principles of which was that man, to reaffirm his identity on earth, needed to be able to say what is most worth saying in his native tongue. At any rate, language was the means by which Luther became a historical force in Ranke's sense; that is, "a moral energy. . . . which dares to penetrate the world in free activity." [10] Or, as Luther put it: "God bestows all good things; but you must take the bull by the horns, you must do the work, and so provide God with an opportunity and a disguise." [11]

Here, in a way, our story ends. We could leave to mass psychology and political philosophy what mankind made of Luther's insights and doctrines; and we could ascribe to endogenous processes or to early aging the residual conflicts which marred the further development of Luther's personality. But a completed identity is only one crisis won.

Luther's letters from the Wartburg indicate the psychological setting for his future actions: having openly challenged Pope and Emperor and the universal world order for which they both stood, and having overcome his own inhibitions in order to express this challenge effectively, he now fully realized not only how ravenous his appetites were, and how rebellious his righteousness, but also how revolutionary were the forces which he had evoked in others. He was again moved to universal action by provincial events; Wittenberg and Erfurt, so he was informed, were falling to pieces. The friars had disbanded and married; even worse, they and the students, supported by a mob and led by Luther's friends, had planlessly changed such procedures as the holy Mass, destroyed sacred images, and banned music from the churches. Here, then, was initiated revolutionary puritanism—that strange mixture of rebellious individualism, aesthetic asceticism, and cruel righteousness which came to characterize much of Protestantism. Luther could hardly recognize what he had generated. Against all command or advice, he hurried to Wittenberg and for a week preached daily, with power, restraint, and humor. If one destroyed everything which one *might* abuse, he said, why, one would have to abolish women and wine too. How he got away with this last remark in the capital of Saxon beer brewing, I do not know; but he did make his point. He also made his first enemies among his own friends, who began to call him a reactionary.

The development of Luther's personal and provincial life, on the one hand, and of the general social dislocation, rebellion, and evolution, on the other, now took on a combination of naive eagerness, unconscious irony, and righteous frightfulness fit for a drama of Shavian dimensions. The Augustinian monastery in Wittenberg, abandoned by the friars, was turned over by the Elector to Luther's personal use. After his marriage it was shared by his wife, a former nun, and their children—certainly an ironic architectural setting for the first Lutheran parsonage. Then, just as he was about to settle down, his revolutionary poetry came home to roost. The peasants rose up all over Germany. He had said about the priests and bishops: "What do they better deserve than a strong uprising which will sweep them from the earth? And we would smile did it happen." [12] He had said: "In Christendom . . . all things are in common and each man's goods are the other's, and nothing is simply a man's own." [13] He had said, "The common man has been brooding over the injury he has suffered in property, in body, and in soul. . . . If I had ten bodies . . . I would most gladly give all to death in behalf of these poor men." [14]

The peasants published a Manifesto of the Twelve Articles, and sent it to him.[15] Peasants had revolted before and had been massacred before; but this time they were speaking as a class with a leader and a book—a new identity. They spoke with simplicity and dignity: "seeing that Christ has redeemed and bought us all with the precious shedding of his blood, the lowly as well as the great," they promised each other to retreat only "if this is explained to us with arguments from the Scripture"—the divine, the only, constitution. Otherwise they demanded that each, for his work, receive "according to the several necessities of all." It is easy to agree today that they were as moderate in their demands as they were immoderate wherever violence sprang up. Luther had previously warned of such violence, and did so again in *An Earnest Exhortation for all Christians, Warning Them Against Insurrection and Rebellion*. He emphasized, in measured tones, that "no insurrection is ever right no matter what the cause . . . my sympathies are and always will be with those against whom insurrection is made." [16] He objected to the concept of political and economic freedom; spiritual freedom, he said was quite consistent with serfdom, and serfdom with the Scriptures. This, of course, corresponded to his medieval notions of the estate to which the individual is born; he wished to reform man's prayerful relation to God, not change his earthly estate. This dichotomy between man's spiritual freedom and his station in social life, which Luther subsequently tried to formulate convincingly, haunts Protestant philosophy to this day. For among the estates, the offices, and the callings which he defined as equally God-given and God-guided, he forgot to mention his own vocation of reformer and revolutionary. But he had burned the Bull publicly. He had called for rebellion; and his original Word-deed now left him far behind.

The peasants, as it were, quoted Martin back to Luther. He ad-

vised compromise, and he, Hans' son, found that he was being disobeyed and ignored. He could forgive neither the peasants for this,
nor later the Jews, whom he had hoped to convert with the help
of the Scriptures where the Church had failed to do so. In 1525 he
wrote his pamphlet *Against the Robbing and Murdering Hordes of
Peasants*, suggesting both public and secret massacres in words
which could adorn the gates of the police headquarters and concentration camps of our time. He promised rewards in heaven to those
who risked their lives in subduing insurrection. One sentence indicates the full cycle taken by this once beaten down and then dis-
obedient son: "A rebel is not worth answering with arguments, for
he does not accept them. The answer for such mouths is a fist that
brings blood from the nose." [17] Do we hear Hans, beating the residue
of a stubborn peasant out of his son?

Luther now went too far even for some members of his own family. One of his brothers-in-law asked him whether he wished to be
"the prophet of the overlords," and accused him of cowardice—an
accusation which was unfair. Luther wrote against the peasants when
they were advancing in his direction like a steamroller; and he refused
to flatter the princes when he needed them most. It makes him more
understandable, even if it does not make his immediate influence more
palatable, to realize that his excessive statements were always directed
against deliberate disobedience. Otherwise, he could be entirely
tolerant and express outright liberal views. He pleaded with the
princes to permit free discussion of sectarian views; and he established the principle for a clergyman "never to remain silent and
assent to injustice, whatever the cost." [18] If he did become the
prophet of the overlords, it was because he would not begin political
history anew as the leaderless enthusiasts wanted him to. In the long
run, one may fairly say that this reactionary established some of the
individualist and equalitarian imagery, and thus the ideological issues
for both the rightists and the leftists in the revolutions then to come.

In May, 1525, the peasants were massacred, first by superior
artillery, then by ferocious footsoldiers, in the battle of Franken-
hausen. All in all, 130,000 peasants were killed in that war. In June,
Luther wrote "all is forgotten that God has done for the world
through me. . . . Now lords, priests, and peasants are all against
me and threaten me with death." [19] But the Reformation was on its
way, and Luther was safe in Wittenberg, master of the empty mon-

astery and the recipient of an increased salary as professor and
pastor.

In July, he suddenly married and settled down in his parsonage.
He married, he said, because his father wanted him to, a statement
so incomprehensible to some that they think it must have been a
joke; yet his father, when he heard of Luther's hesitation, urged him
to continue the family name which was endangered by the death of
his brothers. And marriage was part of the belatedly manifest identification with his father which at this time, openly and secretly,
began to determine much of Luther's life. No doubt, also, he loved
children; he loved a combination of children and homemade music
most of all, so that again, one must assume some early happiness in
his own childhood. True, once settled in his domesticity and in his
fame, he said awful things in the children's presence, and not in
Latin, either. But this is just one aspect of his many-cornered mouth.
"*Homo verbosatus*," he called himself, leniently. A superior resiliency is suggested by the fact that despite having been a captive after
years of monastic abstinence and a virginal youth, he could at the
age of forty-five enter an apparently happy marriage. To be sure,
one finds in his remarks references to a kind of eliminative sexuality,
a need to get rid of bodily discharge which one could ascribe partially to a persistent preoccupation with the body's waste products.
This will be discussed presently. But here as elsewhere, he was, up
to a point, merely more frank and less romantic in expressing what
dominates the sexual urge of most ordinary men, and what, in refined men, leads to conflicts with their sense of propriety and personal affection. He also said deep, sweet, humorous, and novel things
about marriage.

In 1526, his son was born, and christened: Hans.

In this quiet after the storm, Luther again developed severe anxiety, this time protracted and bordering on a deep melancholia. How
can this be? asks the psychiatrist; wasn't Luther at the height of his
influence, happily married and out of the range of danger? He obviously had no reason to be sad again, sadder than ever; his "psychosis"
must have been endogenous, dictated by strictly biological changes
within him; so it would be foolish to look for meaningful reasons.
Our sociologist, in contrast to the psychiatrist, feels that Luther had
reason to be troubled far more than he was: "That he was able to

effect such a volte-face without being stricken in his conscience shows that he did not feel that he was betraying a principle which he felt to be fundamental." [20] The fact is that Luther, facing the full consequences of his oratory, stood before a new crisis which—and here his constitution helped to determine his symptoms—brought back his sadness in a new and incongruous context.

Luther, now a father himself, abnegated much of his postadolescent identity. This is (or was) a not uncommon phenomenon in Europe, and especially in Germany.[21] Except for a few more and more hypothetical Christians, Luther increasingly perceived man as a potentially dangerous child, if not a ravenous beast. The only safe men were the *Landeskinder*, the children of the petty principalities, whose head was the *Landesvater* (the father of the country), as all the heads of the tiny states and of their churches came to be called. In 1528, Luther expressed the opinion that Moses' commandment "Honor thy father," applied to these princes, and is, therefore, equivalent to an injunction against political rebellion.[22] Famous and infamous are his words: "The secular sword must be red and bloody, for the world will and must be evil" [23]—a statement plausible enough from the view of common sense, and from that of Luther's political philosophy which assumes that the prince in power is born to a singular function in the commonwealth. Since he is a Christian, he is subject to the same injunctions against a personal abuse of his calling, and to the same obligation to be guided by prayer, as is any other man in any other position; otherwise, as Luther admitted, he might "start a war over an empty nut." [24] But even then he must be obeyed, although under pronounced protest.

The ordinary man thus surrendered to ordinary princes, lost much of what Luther's early lectures had stood for. The same praying man whose soul Luther had emancipated from Roman authoritarianism was now obliged to accept the ruling family, the economic practice, and (so the law of territorial identity soon decreed) the religious creed which were dominant in his prince's domain. In Protestant states, Luther established Consistorial Councils as the governing religious bodies. These councils were headed by the prince in power, and were composed of two theologians and two jurists; they could imprison a man and exclude him from all work, decree his social boycott, and take away his civic rights. The Protestant Revolution thus led to a way of life in which a man's daily works, including his occupation, became the center of his behavioral orientation, and were rigorously regimented by the church-state. Such a condition Luther had once decried as "Mosaic law." Now he rationalized it: since a Christian man has not only a soul, but also a body living among other bodies, he must "resign himself to Moses" (*sich in Mosen schicken*).[25] Even praying man should take council not only with himself, but with the rulers, in order to be sure of perceiving all the signs of God's plan. This new face of a God, recognizable in prayer, in the Scriptures, *and* in the decisions of the *Landesvater*, became the orientation of a new class, and of a religiosity compliant to the needs of progress in the new, the mercantile, line of endeavor. In spite of having reacted more violently than anyone else against indulgences and against usury, Luther helped prepare the metaphysical misalliance between economic self-interest and church affiliation so prominent in the Western world. Martin had become the metaphysical jurist of his father's class.

This is the Luther known to most, and quoted most in sociological treatises of our time by authors from Weber [26] to Fromm.[27] These treatises quickly proceed from cursory biographic sketches of Luther to the Reformation at large, as personified in Calvin and Knox and institutionalized in the various Protestant sects. Tawney sharply contrasts Luther with Calvin, who, impressed in his youth with Luther's writings, was to be the real lawgiver of Protestantism:

Luther's utterances on social morality are the occasional explosions of a capricious volcano, with only a rare flash of light amid the torrent of smoke and flame, and it is idle to scan them for a coherent and consistent doctrine. . . . His sermons and pamphlets on social questions make an impression of naivete, as of an impetuous but ill-informed genius, dispensing with the cumbrous embarrassments of law and logic, to evolve a system of social ethics from the inspired heat of his own unsophisticated consciousness. It was partly that they were *pièces de circonstance*, thrown off in the storm of a revolution, partly that it was precisely the refinements of law and logic which Luther detested. . . . He is too frightened and angry even to feel curiosity. Attempts to explain the mechanism merely enrage him; he can only repeat that there is a devil in it, and that good Christians will not meddle with the mystery of iniquity. But there is a method in his fury. It sprang, not from ignorance, for he was versed in scholastic philosophy, but from a conception which made the learning of the schools appear trivial or mischievous.[28]

The younger Luther remained the personification of universal rebellion; but the older, the often "frightened and angry" Luther—his reformation remained a provincial one. His theology had announced a Secret Church of all the truly faithful whom only God could know; his reformation led to the all-powerful church-state. His doctrines included Predestination; but his reformation opened the future to petty-bourgeois optimism. His theology was based on the inner experience and the clear expression of meaning it; his influence, in the long run, furthered the humorless and wordy phraseology of "right thinking." His principal recourse was to the Scriptures as perceived in prayer; his own juristic habits made them a legal text rationalizing all kind of practical compromise. Only when other constitutions began to offer healthy competition to the Bible, guaranteeing the individual rights which Luther had helped secularize only against his will and intention, did Protestantism make its contribution to a way of life at times singularly free from terror. But with this contribution went developments for which moral philosophers like Kierkegaard, who saw in Luther the potentially truest religious figure since Christ and Paul, could not forgive him.

Hypersensitive Kierkegaard, another melancholy Dane, had to live in a Protestant monarchy which is one of the smallest and best-fed, best-natured, and most self-satisfied nations in the world, and does not easily betray the chronic melancholy underlying its mandatory happiness. Philosophically, Kierkegaard had to do again all that Luther had done; but he deliberately remained a philosopher without a country and without a family. "For a few years of his life," he wrote about Luther, "he was the salt of the earth; but his later life is not free of the staleness of which his tabletalks are an illustration: a man of God, who sits in small-bourgeois coziness, surrounded by admiring followers who believe that if he lets go of a fart, it must be a revelation, or the result of an inspiration. . . . Luther has lowered the standards of a reformer, and has helped create in later generations that pack, that damned pack of nice, hearty people, who would all like to play at being reformers. . . . Luther's later life has accredited mediocrity." [29] Kierkegaard blames two trends for this calamity, which now we can claim to understand better: first, that Luther spent himself in attacks on one high office and, in an increasingly personal fashion, on the office-holder, the Pope, thus diverting energy from the true object of reformatory fervor—the evil in man's soul; and secondly, that as a reformer, Luther was for-ever *against* something, and therefore was supported by those who (as Burckhardt also said pointedly) "would rather *not* have to do this or that any more" (*gerne einmal etwas nicht mehr wollen*).[30] "Luther," said Kierkegaard, "in a certain sense, made it too easy for himself. He should have known that the freedom for which he fought (and in this fight itself he was right) is apt to make life, the life of the spirit, immeasurably more strenuous than it had been before. If he had held to this, nobody would have held with him, and he would have been given the taste of the great Double-Danger. Nobody holds with another just to make his own life more strenu-ous." [31] As Kierkegaard saw it, Luther did not concentrate enough energy on the refinement of those introspective steps which he had outlined in the lectures on the Psalms; and he spent too much venom in a personal animosity and contrariness against his enemies and, above all, against the Pope. Luther, incidentally, was quite aware of his excessive vindictiveness; but he argued that at least he was not needling in a poisonous fashion, that he poked only with pigs' pokes which did not leave any wounds, and that, at any rate he was not as bad as the "*Koenig von Engellandt*" [32] [Henry VIII].

Is it not shocking, however, that even a Danish philosopher can think of no better simile than an anal one to criticize Luther's private verbosity? Luther would probably not have felt criticized; he had said himself, and proudly, that a wind in Wittenberg, if occasioned by him, could be smelled in Rome.

2

In January, 1527 (the littlest Hans was a suckling baby), Luther's lengthiest state of anxiety and depression commenced: a state in which Luther repeatedly requested his friends to reaffirm his justifi-cation of faith so that he could believe it himself. The most obvious reason for anxiety in the face of the upheavals which he had brought about Luther expressed in the words of an inner voice: "*Du bist allein Klug?!*" "You alone know everything? But what if you were wrong, and if you should lead all these people into error and into eternal damnation?" [33] Or as he tried to make the voice say half-humorously: "*Bistu allein des Heiligen Geistes Nestei blieben auf diese Zeit?* All this time the Holy Ghost has saved *you* as His nest egg?" [34] He was able to overcome this voice sometimes only by a kind of cosmic grandiosity, putting his teaching above the judgment of even the angels on the ground that, since he so deeply knew it to be right, it must be God's teaching and not his own. In his own support he quoted Galatians 1:8: "But though we, or an angel from heaven, preach any other gospel unto you than that which we have preached unto you, let him be accursed." This is preceded by 1:1: "Paul, an apostle, (not of men, neither by man, but by Jesus Christ. . . .)"

He proceeded to a formulation which does not, on the face of it, convey its fatal meaning; he said that his "judgment," in the sense of judiciousness, must also be God's "judgment" (*Gericht*) in the sense of justice. The justified thus becomes judge: whatever the theological rationale, it is obvious that the positive conscience, the good conscience of true indignation, without which there can be no true leadership or effective education, becomes the negative conscience for others, and in its self-increasing wrath must again become a bad, an "unjustified" conscience. This development, which we will sketch in conclusion, betrays, I believe, the fact that in Luther a partially unsuccessful and fragmentary solution of the identity crisis of youth aggravated the crisis of his manhood. The crisis of an ideological leader naturally emerges when he must recognize what his rebellion—which began with the application of a more or less disciplined phantasy to the political world in the widest sense—has done to the imagination, the sense of reality, and the conscience of the masses. The fact is that all walks of life, revolutionized but essentially leaderless, exploited Luther's reformation in all directions at once. They refused to let him, and a few people like him, settle down in parsonages as the representatives of the praying orientation in life, and otherwise accept the estate and occupation in which, as he claimed, God had placed them. The princes became more absolute, the middle-class more mercantile, the lower classes more mystical and revolutionary; and the universal reign of faith envisaged in Luther's early teachings turned into an intolerant and cruel, Bible-quoting bigotry such as history had never seen. As Tawney put it, "the rage of Luther . . . was sharpened by embarrassment at what seemed to him a hideous parody of truths which were both sacred and his own." [35]

In spite of all this, the psychiatrist feels it necessary to assume exclusively "endogenous" reasons for Luther's aggravated melancholy; he could and should have been an *ausgeglichener*, a well-balanced parson. I think that Kierkegaard again comes closer to the truth when he suggests, on the contrary, that Luther should have been a martyr. I mean psychological truth; for Luther somehow felt in need of martyrdom. He did create his own private martyrdom, and knew it. "Because Pope and Emperor could not get me down, there must be a Devil so that virtue will not languish without an enemy (*Ne virtus sine hoste elanguiscat*)." [36] He thus appointed the Devil (the "emperor from hell") as his executioner; in an increasingly personalized form the Devil increasingly persecuted him, "Christ's evangelist" and the "prophet of the Germans."

I will not claim that the clinical form which this martyrdom assumed in Luther's middle age, namely, a severe manic-depressive state, could have come about without a specific constitutional make-up. But I would point out, as I did in regard to Martin's identity crisis, the life-stage which provided the scene for this breakdown.

The *crisis of generativity* occurs when a man looks at what he has generated, or helped to generate, and finds it good or wanting, when his life work as part of the productivity of his time gives him some sense of being on the side of a few angels or makes him feel stagnant. All this, in turn, offers him either promise of an old age that can be faced with a sense of integrity, and in which he can say, "All in all, I would do this over again," or confronts him with a sense of waste, of despair. These alternatives are not entirely functions of the acute condition of this life-stage: previous stages also contribute their blessing or their curse, for the total span of a life is characterized by the hierarchy of all stages, from the first to the last. In view of Luther's relation to his father, it makes sense that his deepest clinical despair emerged when he had become so much of what his father had wanted him to be: influential, economically secure, a kind of superlawyer, and the father of a son named Hans.

Clinically, Luther's suffering began with cardiac symptoms accompanied by severe anxiety. "*Mein herz zappelt*," he said: "My heart quivers." [37] He broke out in severe sweats (his old "devil's bath,") and into severe fits of crying. He was sure that death was impending, and felt, in such fateful moments, without faith and justification. Above all, or below it all, he was depressed and deprived of all self-esteem: *Ora pro me misero et abjecto verme tristitiae spiritu bene vexato.*[38] Even when he was free from these acute attacks, he suffered from indigestion, constipation, and hemorrhoids; from kidney stones, which eventually caused him severe pain; and from an annoying *Ohrensausen*, or *sussurrus*, as he called it, a buzzing in his ears. This buzzing was originally caused by a chronic middle-ear infection; and it became the mediator between his physical and his mental torments, the weapon of his inner voice.

We must remember that the curative and revelatory Word of the Scriptures could enter Luther only through "the ear," as a combination of the capacity to hear and a receptivity for the perceived. Keeping the ear open for the entry of the Word was the Christian's creative passivity, and femininity. However, the voice now in Luther's ear was again the voice of the negative conscience: "*Was hastu gepredigt?*" it said—"What have you preached?" In vain did Luther tell his voice that he was a "doctor" and thus ordained to know; or that he had been forced by Staupitz to become a preacher, making his defense (as so many middle-aged men do) on the basis of unquestionable obligations of official status and position. *Mein befolen Ampt,* the position which I was ordered from above to occupy. It again became difficult to differentiate earthly law from divine grace, Moses from Christ. In this new confusion, Luther tried any number of desperate means. When his own prayer failed, he asked a friend literally to yell the Paternoster with a ringing voice (*mit hellen Worten*),[39] so that maybe the voice of God could be heard again. When "Christ comes and talks to you as if to a sinner and tortures you like Moses: 'What have you done?'—slay him to death. But when he talks to you as God does, and as a savior, prick up both ears."[40] In this statement he is obviously reassuring himself by recalling Staupitz's words after the anxiety attack in the procession; but Staupitz was gone with all the others from the monastery, and from his wrecked congregation.

To open his ear to the good Word and to music was only one of Luther's mental medicines. Faith, of course, came first; if that did not work, a towering rage might help; as a last resort, there was amorous thought. At other times he forced himself to eat ravenously, and to "keep the belly as full as the head." As though his lack of appetite was caused by a gnawing interior devil, he sent a chaser of food after him, or of beer (which was also supposed to flush out the kidney stones). There was also the anal affront, which he thought the devil feared most: "Note this down: I have shit in the pants, and you can hang them around your neck and wipe your mouth with it." [41] And finally, cosmic sarcasm: "*Sancte Sathana, ora pro me*": [42] Holy Satan, pray for me. These statements suggest that we should discuss those traits in Luther's make-up which reveal the active remnants of his childhood repressions. There is no triumph in showing that these remnants exist, even in a great man: we have come to take it for granted that any greatness also harbors massive conflict.

Martin's tortured attempt to establish silence, self-restraint, and submission to the Church's authority and dogma had led to rebellious self-expression. Among his retrospective remarks is this: "The only portion of the human anatomy which the Pope has had to leave uncontrolled is the hind end." [43] This extraterritoriality, however, was immediately recognized and monopolized by the devil: "A Christian should and could be gay," said Luther, "but then the devil shits on him." [44] It is all too easy to consider these and a great number of similar statements mere uncouthnesses typical of Luther's time or of himself. Some of them may not have been more than vulgar bantering, others an expression of the reformer's extraordinary ability to recognize the psychosomatic language of the body, and, as it were, to converse with and through his body. He would speak of "being in labor" when kidney stones made him swell up. When they had passed, he announced the elimination of Gargantuan quantities of fluid: eleven buckets at one time. That he could be bawdy as well as fanciful about all this is further evidence of the resilience with which, in more normal times, he kept together the many facets of his complicated psyche and of his bulky body. He obviously enjoyed hearty food and plenty of beer; when his total "inner condition" made him almost unable to eat, he would stubbornly gorge himself so as to deny the devil possession of his innards. He called this kind of eating "fasting," because he did it without pleasure and as a kind of ritual performance. In the same way, he obviously enjoyed, as did his contemporaries, the belching and farting which were the expression of a satisfied belly, until pain and constipation ruined this perspective of liberalization, too. But, no doubt, among all the anatomical territories involved, the hind end has a malignant dominance.

Luther often says outright things which in our era only Freud recognized are implicitly, symbolically, and unconsciously expressed in neurotic symptoms. A determined turn in his self-analysis brought

Freud to a dynamic understanding of the importance of the "other end" of the human anatomy, that factory of waste-products and odorous gases which is totally removed from our own observation and is the opposite of the face we show to the world. When Freud first discovered the unconscious relevance of all this, he was struck by the "obvious parallel with witchcraft" which sought to gain hellish influence over people from below and behind, by way of their excreta. "I am beginning to dream of an extremely primitive devil religion." [45] And indeed, demonology as well as psychiatry has every reason to consider in all their severity those matters of the bowels which in our enlightened day can become conscious only on the level of a bawdy joke: as long as you smile when you say that. The reformer, however, speaking of himself in the depth of his depression as fecal matter soon to be evacuated by the world-rectum, is so close to the language of the unconscious that with a less poetic mind he would seem close to a psychosis; while his coprophilic attacks on the Pope clearly became obsessional with him. At a time when his stature called for leadership, not continued pamphleteering, he made "*Furzesel*" (fartass) out of the family name Farnese, and had woodcuts made representing the Church as a whore giving rectal birth to a brood of devils. In its excess, Luther's obscenity expresses the needs of a manic-depressive nature which has to maintain a state of unrelenting paranoid repudiation of an appointed enemy on the outside in order to avoid victimizing and, as it were, eliminating itself.

I would like to suggest that this side of Luther was a kind of personalized profanity, which in some ways is the opposite of praying, for it uses the holiest names "in vain." Its tonal nature is explosive, its affect repudiative, and its general attitude a regressed, defiant obstinacy. It is the quickest way for many to find release from feeling victimized by the impudence of others, by the gremlins of circumstance, or by their own inanity. The degree of the release experienced, however, is in inverse relation to the frequency with which this means is employed: a chronic swearer is a bore, and obviously an unrelieved obsessive.

We have already quoted statements of Luther's which, like swearing, were shortcircuits of divinity and profanity: for example, his recommendation that one should kill the apparition of Jesus if it shows its questionable origin by talking like Moses. With some charity this comment could be considered starkly imaginative popular teaching. But that it really was a symptomatic part of a systematic obsession can be seen from this quotation:

For I am unable to pray without at the same time cursing. If I am prompted to say, "Hallowed be Thy name," I must add, "Cursed, damned, outraged be the name of papists." If I am prompted to say, "Thy Kingdom come," I must perforce add, "Cursed, damned, destroyed must be the papacy." Indeed, I pray thus orally every day and in my heart, without intermission.[46]

We must conclude, that Luther's use of repudiative and anal patterns was an attempt to find a safety-valve when unrelenting inner pressure threatened to make devotion unbearable and sublimity hateful—that is, when he was again about to repudiate God in supreme rebellion, and himself in malignant melancholy. The regressive aspects of this pressure, and the resulting obsessive and paranoid focus on single figures such as the Pope and the Devil, leave little doubt that a transference had taken place from a parent figure to universal personages, and that a central theme in this transference was anal defiance.

During childhood when man's ego is most of all a body-ego, composed of all pleasures and tensions experienced in major body regions, the alimentary process assumes in phantasy the character of a model of the self, nourished and poisoned, assimilating and eliminating not only substances, but also good and bad influences. Prayer and swearing can later take over these two aspects of an intrinsic ambivalence toward the personified forces behind reality: prayer can express the trustful modality of incorporation—expressed in the Latin *coram Deo*, in the presence of God, a phrase which Luther loved. *Coram* is a combination of *cum*, with, and *or*, mouth. Swearing can express the hateful mode of elimination, of total riddance.

This magical ambivalence is much aggravated in some cultures and classes by particular emphasis on bowel and bladder training. Such training obviously reveals magical superstitions about these primitive functions; the horror of the evacuated substances is eventually replaced by anxiety over the possible consequences for an individual's later character and performance should he not achieve early and complete mastery of his sphincters. Primitive superstitions, and the miners' attempts to anthropomorphize the fickle and dangerous bowels of the earth may, as we discussed earlier, have influenced little Martin's body concepts. We have also indicated the significance of the choice of the buttocks as the preferred place for corporal punishment: a safe place physiologically, but emotionally potentially dangerous, since punishment aggravates the significance of this general area as a battlefield of parental and infantile wills. The fear that his parents and teachers might ever completely subject him by dominating this area and thus gaining power over his will may have provided some of the dynamite in that delayed time bomb of Martin's rebellion, and may account for the excessiveness with which Luther, to the end, expressed an almost paranoid defiance, alternating with a depressed conception of himself.

We have no information concerning little Martin's cleanliness training: the times, at any rate in Mansfeld, may not have been too particular. Nonetheless, the period which marked the establishment of a dominant middle-class in Germany brought with it a cleanliness, a bathing, craze. It may well be, then, that little Martin was educated at a time when the combination of cleanliness, punctuality, and penuriousness first came to be considered necessary virtues of the mercantile, managerial, and professional class to which Hans so desperately wanted him to belong; his cleanliness training may have been intensified by this. We do not know. However, an appreciation of this era's prevalent personification of suppressed evil modalities can be gained from a study of the devils on medieval cathedrals and paintings. These devils sport overgrown organs. They are impudent enough to feel safe without trusting anybody. Naked yet shameless, they seem to enjoy having and using their bulging eyes and pointed ears, their teeth and lecherous tongues, their exposed behinds, their horns, and that phallic tail which betrays the satyr of old. They appear to be like caricatures of animals, but they certainly have nothing of the animal's innocence: they know exactly what they are doing, and intend to go ahead and do it anyway. They are nature, evil as only man can perceive it who for the sake of being moral must see that he is naked. Mark Twain once said that man's only great distinction in the universe is that he is the animal who blushes. He might have added that he never forgives those who first made him blush.

Luther used the folklore and the official superstition of his time to personify the dark side, the backside, of life as the devil, with whom he could argue, and confer, and whom, up to a point, he could dismiss. What we today explain as meaningful slips, he simply called the devil's work. When during a wedding somebody dropped the ring, he loudly told the devil to stay out of the ceremony. When he was disturbed, he would often be satisfied with recognizing that it was devil's work, and with a contemptuous air go to sleep. Every age has its interpretations which seem to take care of inner interference with our plans and with our self-esteem.

But, at the end, Luther lived with the devil on terms of a mutual obstinacy, an inability to let go of each other, as tenacious as his old fixation on his father and his later fixation on the Pope. Whether or not he thus merely participated in, or actually imparted, Protestantism's diabolical preoccupation, I do not know. Nor could I on theoretical grounds decide the question whether without this repudiative trend we would have had a better Luther—or no Luther at all. It may involve a mighty capacity for repudiation to affirm so mightily. All in all, our modern views of inner economics suggest that Luther's fixation on these matters absorbed energy which otherwise might have helped the old Luther to reaffirm with continued creativity the ideological gains of his youth; and if this energy had been available to him, he might have played a more constructive role in the mastery of the passions, as well of the compulsions, which he had evoked in others.

This is the other side of the medal. It is obvious I have charted the decline of a youth, and not the ascendance of a man. Another book would have to do that. Such a book would have to establish, in the terms of another level of the life-cycle, the grown man's victories over a new environment, partially his own creation, and over a new inner frontier overshadowed by a more biological sense of impending death. The comment made above that the tragedy of the ideological leader is that he exploits in all sincerity, only to have his sincerity exploited would have to be explored by someone sympathetic to this plight.

The systematic theological accomplishments of the man Luther are beyond the chosen topic of this book, and entirely outside my competence. I started this discussion by commenting on what is known of the family of his childhood; in conclusion, I must point to this man's extraordinary resiliency by again referring to his great capacity for love. He wrapped himself in the intimacy of marriage and parsonage, of friendship and teaching, with all the neediness of one who has little time left to bestow on others the things he must have received from his mother. A generous father, pastor, and host, Luther was as maternal as he probably was reckless in his all-embracing (and obese) nurturance. At his own table he occasionally indulged himself in belligerent preaching, which almost advocated anarchy to fight the papal order of things; he often teased his wife into a more or less bantering disputation (for example, by advocating bigamy in front of the listening flock of children and houseguests); and he made many a provocative and nasty statement. But he vigorously supported, by his example, the emergence of a fond and rich middle-class marriage and nursery, with immeasurably more intimacy and equality for husband and wife as well as parents and children than came out of the morose Calvinian reformation. One may fairly state that a certain simple hedonism was Luther's true goal and gift when he was not in acute conflict: "We know now," he wrote to a melancholy prince, "that we can be happy with a good conscience." He added: "No one knows how it hurts a young man to avoid happiness and to cultivate solitude and melancholy. . . . I, who have hitherto spent my life in mourning and sadness, now seek and accept joy whenever I can find it." [47] It is true that except for some markedly elated and moderately alcoholic periods his happiness was easily overshadowed by that inner voice which re-evoked in him the tragic feeling of any ideological leader: he had raised human consciousness to new heights, but he had also settled a personal account by provoking a public accounting, had treated the universe as a projected family and gotten away with it—to a point. In his personal and provincial life (and he probably was the most provincial of all universal leaders) he was and remained the prototype of a new man, husband, and father. Sir Thomas More was another such man, and, more consistent, died a martyr; but Luther had tasted deeper personal conflict and more revolutionary revelation, and at the end, he was not always himself. "When I am well again, I see it all nicely," he said. "*Ja, wenn Einer by ihm selb ist, sonst nit ehe:* Alas, if a fellow can only be at one with himself—it won't work otherwise."

VIII

Epilogue

To RELEGATE Luther to a shadowy greatness at the turbulent conclusion of the Age of Faith does not help us see what his life really stands for. To put it in his own words:

"I did not learn my theology all at once, but I had to search deeper for it, where my temptations took me." [1] "*Vivendo, immo moriendo et damnando fit theologus, non intelligendo, legendo, aut speculando*": [2] A theologian is born by living, nay dying and being damned, not by thinking, reading, or speculating.

Not to understand this message under the pretense of not wanting to make the great man too human—although he represented himself as human with relish and gusto—only means to protect ourselves from taking our chances with the *tentationes* of our day, as he did with his. Historical analysis should help us to study further our own immediate tasks, instead of hiding them in a leader's greatness.

I will not conclude with a long list of what we must do. In too many books the word "must" increases in frequency in inverse relation to the number of pages left to point out how what must be done might be done. I will try, instead, to restate a few assumptions of this book in order to make them more amenable to joint study.

When Luther challenged the rock bottom of his own prayer, he could not know that he would find the fundament for a new theology. Nor did Freud know that he would find the principles of a new psychology when he took radical chances with himself in a new kind of introspective analysis. I have applied to Luther, the first Protestant at the end of the age of absolute faith, insights developed by Freud, the first psychoanalyst at the end of the era of absolute reason; and I have mentioned seemingly incidental parallels between the two men. A few weightier connections must be stated in conclusion.

Both men endeavored to increase the margin of man's inner freedom by introspective means applied to the very center of his conflicts; and this to the end of increased individuality, sanity, and service to men. Luther, at the beginning of ruthless mercantilism in Church and commerce, counterpoised praying man to the philosophy and practice of meritorious works. Subsequently, his justification by faith was absorbed into the patterns of mercantilism, and eventually turned into a justification of commercialism by faith. Freud, at the beginning of unrestricted industrialization, offered another method of introspection, psychoanalysis. With it, he obviously warned against the mechanical socialization of men into effective but neurotic robots. It is equally obvious that his work is about to be used in furtherance of that which he warned against: the glorification of "adjustment." Thus both Doctor Luther and Doctor Freud, called great by their respective ages, have been and are apt to be resisted not only by their enemies, but also by friends who subscribe to their ideas but lack what Kierkegaard called a certain strenuousness of mental and moral effort.

Luther, as we saw, instituted a technique of prayer which eminently served to clarify the delineation of what we, to the best of our knowledge, really mean. Freud added a technique (totally inapplicable to people who do not really mean anything at all) which can make us understand what it means when we insist we mean what we, according to our dreams and symptoms, cannot mean deep down. As to prayer, Luther advocated an appeal to God that He grant you, even as you pray, the good intention with which you started the prayer: *ut etiam intentionem quam presumpsisti ipse tibi dat*. Centuries later Freud postulated an analogous rigor for genuine introspection, namely, the demand that one take an especially honest look at one's honesty.

Luther tried to free individual conscience from totalitarian dogma; he meant to give man credal wholeness, and, alas, inadvertently helped to increase and to refine authoritarianism. Freud tried to free the individual's insight from authoritarian conscience; his wholeness is that of the individual ego, but the question is whether collective man will create a world worth being whole for.

Luther accepted man's distance from God as existential and absolute, and refused any traffic with the profanity of a God of deals; Freud suggests that we steadfastly study our unconscious deals with morality and reality before we haughtily claim free will, or righteously good intentions in dealings with our fellowmen.

Luther limited our knowledge of God to our individual experience of temptation and our identification in prayer with the passion of God's son. In this, all men are free and equal. Freud made it clear that the structure of inner *Konflict*, made conscious by psychoanalysis and recognized as universal for any and all, is all we can know of ourselves—yet it is a knowledge inescapable and indispensable. The devoutly sceptical Freud proclaimed that man's uppermost duty (no matter what his introspective reason would make him see, or his fate suffer) was *das Leben auszuhalten:* to stand life, to hold out.

In this book I have described how Luther, once a sorely frightened child, recovered through the study of Christ's Passion the central meaning of the Nativity; and I have indicated in what way Freud's method of introspection brought human conflict under a potentially more secure control by revealing the boundness of man in the loves and rages of his childhood. Thus both Luther and Freud came to acknowledge that "the child is in the midst." Both men perfected introspective techniques permitting isolated man to recognize his individual patienthood. They also reasserted the other pole of existence, man's involvement in generations: for only in facing the helplessness and the hope newly born in every child does mature man (and this *does* include woman) recognize the irrevocable responsibility of being alive and about.

2

Let us consider, then, what we may call the metabolism of generations.

Each human life begins at a given evolutionary stage and level of tradition, bringing to its environment a capital of patterns and energies; these are used to grow on, and to grow into the social process with, and also as contributions to this process. Each new being is received into a style of life prepared by tradition and held together by tradition, and at the same time disintegrating because of the very nature of tradition. We say that tradition "molds" the individual, "channels" his drives. But the social process does not mold a new being merely to housebreak him; it molds generations in order to be remolded, to be reinvigorated, by them. Therefore, society can never afford merely to suppress drives or to guide their sublimation. It must also support the primary function of every individual ego, which is to transform instinctual energy into patterns of action, into character, into style—in short, into an identity with a core of integrity which is to be derived from and also contributed to the tradition. There is an optimum ego synthesis to which the individual aspires; and there is an optimum societal metabolism for which societies and cultures strive. In describing the interdependence of individual aspiration and of societal striving, we describe something indispensable to human life.

In an earlier book, I indicated a program of studies which might account for the dovetailing of the stages of individual life and of basic human institutions. The present book circumscribes for only one of these stages—the identity crisis—its intrinsic relation to the process of ideological rejuvenation in a period of history when organized religion dominated ideologies.

In discussing the identity crisis, we have, at least implicitly, presented some of the attributes of any psychosocial crisis. At a given age, a human being, by dint of his physical, intellectual and emotional growth, becomes ready and eager to face a new life task, that is, a set of choices and tests which are in some traditional way prescribed and prepared for him by his society's structure. A new life task presents a *crisis* whose outcome can be a successful graduation, or alternatively, an impairment of the life cycle which will aggravate future crises. Each crisis prepares the next, as one step leads to another; and each crisis also lays one more cornerstone for the adult personality. I will enumerate all these crises (more thoroughly treated elsewhere) to remind us, in summary, of certain issues in Luther's life; and also to suggest a developmental root for the basic human values of faith, will, conscience, and reason—all necessary in rudimentary form for the identity which crowns childhood.

The first crisis is the one of early infancy. How this crisis is met decides whether a man's innermost mood will be determined more by basic trust or by basic mistrust. The outcome of this crisis—apart from accidents of heredity, gestation, and birth—depends largely on the quality of maternal care, that is, on the consistency and mutuality which guide the mother's ministrations and give a certain predictability and hopefulness to the baby's original cosmos of urgent and bewildering body feelings. The ratio and relation of basic trust to basic mistrust established during early infancy determines much of the individual's capacity for simple faith, and consequently also determines his future contribution to his society's store of faith—which, in turn, will feed into a future mother's ability to trust the world in which she teaches trust to newcomers. In this first stage we can assume that a historical process is already at work; history writing should therefore chart the influence of historical events on growing generations to be able to judge the quality of their future contribution to history. As for little Martin, I have drawn conclusions about that earliest time when his mother could still claim the baby, and when he was still all hers, inferring that she must have provided him with a font of basic trust on which he was able to draw in his fight for a primary faith present before all will, conscience, and reason, a faith which is "the soul's virginity."

The first crisis corresponds roughly to what Freud has described as orality; the second corresponds to anality. An awareness of these correspondences is essential for a true understanding of the dynamics involved.

The second crisis, that of infancy, develops the infantile sources of what later becomes a human being's will, in its variations of willpower and wilfulness. The resolution of this crisis will determine whether an individual is apt to be dominated by a sense of autonomy, or by a sense of shame and doubt. The social limitations imposed on intensified wilfulness inevitably create doubt about the justice governing the relations of grown and growing people. The way this doubt is met by the grown-ups determines much of a man's future ability to combine an unimpaired will with ready self-discipline, rebellion with responsibility.

The interpretation is plausible that Martin was driven early out of the trust stage, out from "under his mother's skirts," by a jealously ambitious father who tried to make him precociously independent from women, and sober and reliable in his work. Hans succeeded, but not without storing in the boy violent doubts of the father's justification and sincerity; a lifelong shame over the persisting gap between his own precocious conscience and his actual inner state; and a deep nostalgia for a situation of infantile trust. His theological solution—spiritual return to a faith which is there before all doubt, combined with a political submission to those who by necessity must wield the sword of secular law—seems to fit perfectly his personal need for compromise. While this analysis does not explain either the ideological power or the theological consistency of his solution, it does illustrate that ontogenetic experience is an indispensable link and transformer between one stage of history and the next. This link is a psychological one, and the energy transformed and the process of transformation are both charted by the psychoanalytic method.

Freud formulated these matters in dynamic terms. Few men before him gave more genuine expression to those experiences which are on the borderline between the psychological and the theological than Luther, who gleaned from these experiences a religious gain formulated in theological terms. Luther described states of badness which in many forms pervade human existence from childhood. For instance, his description of shame, an emotion first experienced when the infant stands naked in space and feels belittled: "He is put to sin and shame before God . . . this shame is now a thousand times greater, that a man must blush in the presence of God. For this means that there is no corner or hole in the whole of creation into which a man might creep, not even in hell, but he must let himself be exposed to the gaze of the whole creation, and stand in the open with all his shame, as a bad conscience feels when it is really struck. . . ." [3] Or his description of doubt, an emotion first experienced when the child feels singled out by demands whose rationale he does not comprehend: "When he is tormented in *Anfechtung* it seems to him that he is alone: God is angry only with him, and irreconcilably angry against him: then he alone is a sinner and all the others are in the right, and they work against him at God's orders. There is nothing left for him but this unspeakable sighing through which, without knowing it, he is supported by the Spirit and cries 'Why does God pick on me alone?'" [4]

Luther was a man who would not settle for an easy appeasement of these feelings on any level, from childhood through youth to his manhood, or in any segment of life. His often impulsive and intuitive formulations transparently display the infantile struggle at the bottom of the lifelong emotional issue.

His basic contribution was a living reformulation of faith. This marks him as a theologian of the first order; it also indicates his struggle with the ontogenetically earliest and most basic problems of life. He saw as his life's work a new delineation of faith and will, of religion and the law: for it is clear that organized religiosity, in circumstances where faith in a world order is monopolized by religion, is the institution which tries to give dogmatic permanence to a reaffirmation of that basic trust—and a renewed victory over that basic mistrust—with which each human being emerges from early infancy. In this way organized religion cements the faith which will support future generations. Established law tries to formulate obligations and privileges, restraints and freedoms, in such a way that man can submit to law and order with a minimum of doubt and with little loss of face, and as an autonomous agent of order can teach the rudiments of discipline to his young. The relation of faith and law, of course, is an eternal human problem, whether it appears in questions of church and state, mysticism and daily morality, or existential aloneness and political commitment.

The third crisis, that of initiative versus guilt, is part of what Freud described as the central complex of the family, namely, the Oedipus complex. It involves a lasting unconscious association of sensual freedom with the body of the mother and the administrations received from her hand; a lasting association of cruel prohibition with the interference of the dangerous father; and the consequences of these associations for love and hate in reality and in phantasy. (I will not discuss here the cultural relativity of Freud's observations nor the dated origin of his term; but I assume that those who do wish to quibble about all this will feel the obligation to advance systematic propositions about family, childhood, and society which come closer to the core, rather than go back to the periphery, of the riddle which Freud was the first to penetrate.) We have reviewed the strong indications of an especially heavy interference by Hans Luder with Martin's attachment to his mother, who, it is suggested, secretly provided for him what Goethe openly acknowledged as his mother's gift—"*Die Frohnatur, die Lust zu fabulieren*": gaiety and the pleasure of confabulation. We have indicated how this gift, which later emerged in Luther's poetry, became guilt-laden and was broken to harness by an education designed to make a precocious student of the boy. We have also traced its relationship to Luther's lifelong burden of excessive guilt. Here is one of Luther's descriptions of that guilt: "And this is the worst of all these ills, that the conscience cannot run away from itself, but it is always present to itself and knows all the terrors of the creature which such things bring even in this present life, because the ungodly man is like a raging sea. The third and greatest of all these horrors and the worst of all ills is to have a judge." [5] He also said, "For this is the nature of a guilty conscience, to fly and to be terrified, even when all is safe and prosperous, to convert all into peril and death." [6]

The stage of initiative, associated with Freud's phallic stage of psycho-sexuality, ties man's budding will to phantasy, play, games, and early work, and thus to the mutual delineation of unlimited imagination and aspiration and limiting, threatening conscience. As far as society is concerned, this is vitally related to the occupational and technological ideals perceived by the child; for the child can manage the fact that there is no return to the mother as a mother and no competition with the father as a father only to the degree to which a future career outside of the narrower family can at least be envisaged in ideal future occupations: these he learns to imitate in play, and to anticipate in school. We can surmise that for little Martin the father's own occupation was early precluded from anticipatory phantasy, and that a life of scholarly duty was obediently and sadly envisaged instead. This precocious severity of obedience later made it impossible for young Martin to anticipate any career but that of unlimited study for its own sake, as we have seen in following his path of obedience—in disobedience.

In the fourth stage, the child becomes able and eager to learn systematically, and to collaborate with others. The resolution of this stage decides much of the ratio between a sense of industry or work completion, and a sense of tool-inferiority, and prepares a man for the essential ingredients of the ethos as well as the rationale of his technology. He wants to know the *reason* for things, and is provided, at least, with rationalizations. He learns to use whatever simplest techniques and tools will prepare him most generally for the tasks of his culture. In Martin's case, the tool was literacy, Latin literacy, and we saw how he was molded by it—and how later he remolded, with the help of printing, his nation's literary habits. With a vengeance he could claim to have taught German even to his enemies.

But he achieved this only after a protracted identity crisis which is the main subject of this book. Whoever is hard put to feel identical with one set of people and ideas must that much more violently repudiate another set; and whenever an identity, once established, meets further crises, the danger of irrational repudiation of otherness and temporarily even of one's own identity increases.

I have already briefly mentioned the three crises which follow the crisis of identity; they concern problems of intimacy, generativity, and integrity. The crisis of intimacy in a monk is naturally distorted in its heterosexual core. What identity diffusion is to identity—its alternative and danger—isolation is to intimacy. In a monk this too is subject to particular rules, since a monk seeks intentional and organized isolation, and submits all intimacy to prayer and confession.

Luther's intimacy crisis seems to have been fully experienced and resolved only on the Wartburg; that is, after his lectures had established him as a lecturer, and his speech at Worms as an orator of universal stamp. On the Wartburg he wrote *De Votis Monasticis*, obviously determined to take care of his sexual needs as soon as a dignified solution could be found. But the intimacy crisis is by no means only a sexual, or for that matter, a heterosexual, one: Luther, once free, wrote to men friends about his emotional life, including his sexuality, with a frankness clearly denoting a need to share intimacies with them. The most famous example, perhaps, is a letter written at a time when the tragicomedy of these priests' belated marriages to runaway nuns was in full swing. Luther had made a match between Spalatin and an ex-nun, a relative of Staupitz. In the letter, he wished Spalatin luck for the wedding night, and promised to think of him during a parallel performance to be arranged in his own marital bed.[7]

Also on the Wartburg, Luther developed, with his translation of the Bible, a supreme ability to reach into the homes of his nation; as a preacher and a table talker he demonstrated his ability and his need to be intimate for the rest of his life. One could write a book about Luther on this theme alone; and perhaps in such a book all but the most wrathful utterances would be found to be communications exquisitely tuned to the recipient.

Owing to his prolonged identity crisis, and also to delayed sexual intimacy, intimacy and generativity were fused in Luther's life. We have given an account of the time when his generativity reached its crisis, namely, when within a short period he became both a father, and a leader of a wide following which began to disperse his teachings in any number of avaricious, rebellious, and mystical directions. Luther then tasted fully the danger of this stage, which paradoxically is felt by creative people more deeply than by others, namely, a sense of *stagnation*, experienced by him in manic-depressive form. As he recovered, he proceeded with the building of the edifice of his theology; yet he responded to the needs of his parishioners and students, including his princes, to the very end. Only his occasional outbursts expressed that fury of repudiation which was mental hygiene to him, but which set a lasting bad example to his people.

3

We now come to the last, the integrity crisis which again leads man to the portals of nothingness, or at any rate to the station of *having been*. I have described it thus:

Only he who in some way has taken care of things and people and has adapted himself to the triumphs and disappointments adherent to being, by necessity, the originator of others and the generator of things and ideas—only he may gradually grow the fruit of these seven stages. I know no better word for it than ego integrity. Lacking a clear definition, I shall point to a few constituents of this state of mind. It is the ego's accrued assurance of its proclivity for order and meaning. It is a post-narcissistic love of the human ego—not of the self—as an experience which conveys some world order and some spiritual sense, no matter how dearly paid for. It is the acceptance of one's one and only life cycle as something that had to be and that, by necessity, permitted of no substitutions: it thus means a new, a different, love of one's parents. It is a comradeship with the ordering ways of distant times and different pursuits, as expressed in the simple products and sayings of such times and pursuits. Although aware of the relativity of all the various life styles which have given meaning to human striving, the possessor of integrity is ready to defend the dignity of his own life style against all physical and economic threats. For he knows that an individual life is the accidental coincidence of but one life cycle with but one segment of history; and that for him all human integrity stands or falls with the one style of integrity of which he partakes. The style of integrity developed by his culture or civilization thus becomes the "patrimony of his soul," the seal of his moral paternity of himself (". . . *pero el honor/Es patrimonio del alma*": Calderon). Before this final solution, death loses its sting.[8]

This integrity crisis, last in the lives of ordinary men, is a lifelong and chronic crisis in a *homo religiosus*. He is always older, or in early years suddenly becomes older, than his playmates or even his parents and teachers, and focuses in a precocious way on what it takes others a lifetime to gain a mere inkling of: the questions of how to escape corruption in living and how in death to give meaning to life. Because he experiences a breakthrough to the last problems so early in his life maybe such a man had better become a martyr and seal his message with an early death; or else become a hermit in a solitude which anticipates the Beyond. We know little of Jesus of Nazareth as a young man, but we certainly cannot even begin to imagine him as middle-aged.

This short cut between the youthful crisis of identity and the mature one of integrity makes the religionist's problem of individual identity the same as the problem of existential identity. To some extent this problem is only an exaggeration of an abortive trait not uncommon in late adolescence. One may say that the religious leader becomes a professional in dealing with the kind of scruples which prove transitory in many all-too-serious postadolescents who later grow out of it, go to pieces over it, or find an intellectual or artistic medium which can stand between them and nothingness.

The late adolescent crisis, in addition to anticipating the more mature crises, can at the same time hark back to the very earliest crisis of life—trust or mistrust toward existence as such. This concentration in the cataclysm of the adolescent identity crisis of both first and last crises in the human life may well explain why religiously and artistically creative men often seem to be suffering from a barely compensated psychosis, and yet later prove superhumanly gifted in conveying a total meaning for man's life; while malignant disturbances in late adolescence often display precocious wisdom and usurped integrity. The chosen young man extends the problem of his identity to the borders of existence in the known universe;

other human beings bend all their efforts to adopt and fulfill the departmentalized identities which they find prepared in their communities. He can permit himself to face as permanent the trust problem which drives others in whom it remains or becomes dominant into denial, despair, and psychosis. He acts as if mankind were starting all over with his own beginning as an individual, conscious of his singularity as well as his humanity; others hide in the folds of whatever tradition they are part of because of membership, occupation, or special interests. To him, history ends as well as starts with him; others must look to their memories, to legends, or to books to find models for the present and the future in what their predecessors have said and done. No wonder that he is something of an old man (a *philosophus*, and a sad one) when his age-mates are young, or that he remains something of a child when they age with finality. The name Lao-tse, I understand, means just that.

The danger of a reformer of the first order, however, lies in the nature of his influence on the masses. In our own day we have seen this in the life and influence of Gandhi. He, too, believed in the power of prayer; when he fasted and prayed, the masses and even the English held their breath. Because prayer gave them the power to say what would be heard by the lowliest and the highest, both Gandhi and Luther believed that they could count on the restraining as well as the arousing power of the Word. In such hope great religionists are supported—one could say they are seduced— by the fact that all people, because of their common undercurrent of existential anxiety, at cyclic intervals and during crises feel an intense need for a rejuvenation of trust which will give new meaning to their limited and perverted exercise of will, conscience, reason, and identity. But the best of them will fall asleep at Gethsemane; and the worst will accept the new faith only as a sanction for anarchic destructiveness or political guile. If faith can move mountains, let it move obstacles out of *their* way. But maybe the masses also sense that he who aspires to spiritual power, even though he speaks of renunciation, has an account to settle with an inner authority. He may disavow their rebellion, but he is a rebel. He may say in the deepest humility, as Luther said, that "his mouth is Christ's mouth"; his nerve is still the nerve of a usurper. So for a while the world may be worse for having had a vision of being better. From the oldest Zen poem to the most recent psychological formulation, it is clear that "the conflict between right and wrong is the sickness of the mind." [9]

The great human question is to what extent early child training must or must not exploit man's early helplessness and moral sensitivity to the degree that a deep sense of evil and of guilt become unavoidable; for such a sense in the end can only result in clandestine commitment to evil in the name of higher values. Religionists, of course, assume that because a sense of evil dominated them even as they combated it, it belongs not only to man's "nature," but is God's plan, even God's gift to him. The answer to this assumption is that not only do child training systems differ in their exploitation of basic mistrust, shame, doubt, and guilt—so do religions. The trouble comes, first, from the mortal fear that instinctual forces would run wild if they were not dominated by a negative conscience; and second, from trying to formulate man's optimum as negative morality, to be reinforced by rigid institutions. In this formulation all man's erstwhile fears of the forces and demons of nature are reprojected onto his inner forces, and onto the child, whose dormant energies are alternatively vilified as potentially criminal, or romanticized as altogether angelic. Because man needs a disciplined conscience, he thinks he must have a bad one; and he assumes that he has a good conscience when, at times, he has an easy one. The answer to all this does not lie in attempts to avoid or to deny one or the other sense of badness in children altogether; the denial of the unavoidable can only deepen a sense of secret, unmanageable evil. The answer lies in man's capacity to create order which will give his children a disciplined as well as a tolerant conscience, and a world within which to act affirmatively.

4

In this book we are dealing with a Western religious movement which grew out of and subsequently perpetuated an extreme emphasis on the interplay of initiative and guilt, and an exclusive emphasis on the divine Father-Son. Even in this scheme, the mother remains a counterplayer however shadowy. Father religions have mother churches.

One may say that man, when looking through a glass darkly, finds himself in an inner cosmos in which the outlines of three objects awaken dim nostalgias. One of these is the simple and fervent wish for a hallucinatory sense of unity with a maternal matrix, and a supply of benevolently powerful substances; it is symbolized by the affirmative face of charity, graciously inclined, reassuring the faithful of the unconditional acceptance of those who will return to the bosom. In this symbol the split of autonomy is forever repaired: shame is healed by unconditional approval, doubt by the eternal presence of generous provision.

In the center of the second nostalgia is the paternal voice of guiding conscience, which puts an end to the simple paradise of childhood and provides a sanction for energetic action. It also warns of the inevitability of guilty entanglement, and threatens with the lightning of wrath. To change the threatening sound of this voice, if need be by means of partial surrender and manifold self-castration, is the second imperative demand which enters religious endeavor. At all cost, the Godhead must be forced to indicate that He Himself mercifully planned crime and punishment in order to assure salvation.

Finally, the glass shows the pure self itself, the unborn core of creation, the—as it were, preparental—center where God is pure nothing: *ein lauter Nichts*, in the words of Angelus Silesius. God is so designated in many ways in Eastern mysticism. This pure self is the self no longer sick with a conflict between right and wrong, not dependent on providers, and not dependent on guides to reason and reality.

These three images are the main religious objects. Naturally, they often fuse in a variety of ways and are joined by hosts of secondary deities. But must we call it regression if man thus seeks again the earliest encounters of his trustful past in his efforts to reach a hoped-for and eternal future? Or do religions partake of man's ability, even as he regresses, to recover creatively? At their creative best, religions retrace our earliest inner experiences, giving tangible form to vague evils, and reaching back to the earliest individual sources of trust; at the same time, they keep alive the common symbols of integrity distilled by the generations. If this is partial regression, it is a regression which, in retracing firmly established pathways, returns to the present amplified and clarified.[10] Here, of course, much depends on whether or not the son of a given era approaches the glass in good faith: whether he seeks to find again on a higher level a treasure of basic trust safely possessed from the beginning, or tries to find a birthright denied him in the first place, in his childhood. It is clear that each generation (whatever its ideological heaven) owes to the next a safe treasure of basic trust; Luther was psychologically and ideologically right when he said in theological terms that the infant *has* faith if his community *means* his baptism. Creative moments, however, and creative periods are rare. The process here described may remain abortive or outlive itself in stagnant institutions—in which case it can and must be associated with neurosis and psychosis, with self-restriction and self-delusion, with hypocrisy and stupid moralism.

Freud has convincingly demonstrated the affinity of some religious ways of thought with those of neurosis.[11] But we regress in our dreams, too, and the inner structures of many dreams correspond to neurotic symptoms. Yet dreaming itself is a healthy activity, and a necessary one. And here too, the success of a dream depends on the faith one has, not on that which one seeks: a good conscience provides that proverbially good sleep which knits up the raveled sleeve of care. All the things that made man feel guilty, ashamed, doubtful, and mistrustful during the daytime are woven into a mysterious yet meaningful set of dream images, so arranged as to direct the recuperative powers of sleep toward a constructive waking state. The dreamwork fails and the dream turns into a nightmare when there is an intrusion of a sense of foreign reality into the dreamer's make-believe, and a subsequent disturbance in returning from that superimposed sense of reality into real reality.

Religions try to use mechanisms analogous to dreamlife, reinforced at times by a collective genius of poetry and artistry, to offer ceremonial dreams of great recuperative value. It is possible, however, that the medieval Church, the past master of ceremonial hallucination, by promoting the reality of hell too efficiently, and by tampering too successfully with man's sense of reality in this world, eventually created, instead of a belief in the greater reality of a more desirable world, only a sense of nightmare in this one.

I have implied that the original faith which Luther tried to restore goes back to the basic trust of early infancy. In doing so I have not, I believe, diminished the wonder of what Luther calls God's disguise. If I assume that it is the smiling face and the guiding voice of infantile parent images which religion projects onto the benevolent sky, I have no apologies to render to an age which thinks of painting the moon red. Peace comes from the inner space.

5

The Reformation is continuing in many lands, in the form of manifold revolutions, and in the personalities of protestants of varied vocations.

I wrote this book in Mexico, on a mirador overlooking a fishing village on Lake Chapala. What remains of this village's primeval inner order goes back to pre-Christian times. But at odd times, urgent church bells call the populace to remembrance. The church is now secular property, only lent to the Cura; and the priest's garb is legally now a uniform to be worn only in church or when engaged in such business as bringing the host to the dying. Yet, at night, with defensive affront, the cross on the church tower is the only neon light in town. The vast majority of the priest's customers are women, indulging themselves fervently in the veneration of the diminutive local madonna statue, which, like those in other communities, is a small idol representing little-girlishness and pure motherhood, rather than the tragic parent of the Savior, who, in fact, is little seen. The men for the most part look on, willing to let the women have their religion as part of women's world, but themselves bound on secular activity. The young ones tend toward the not too distant city of Guadalajara, where the churches and cathedrals are increasingly matched in height and quiet splendor by apartment houses and business buildings.

Guadalajara is rapidly turning into a modern city, the industrial life of which is dominated by the products and techniques of the industrial empire in the North; yet, the emphasis is on Mexican names, Mexican management. A postrevolutionary type of businessman is much in evidence: in his appearance and bearing he protests Mexican maleness and managerial initiative. His modern home can only be called puritan; frills and comforts are avoided, the lines are clean and severe, the rooms light and barren.

The repudiation of the old is most violently expressed in some of the paintings of the revolution. In Orozco's house in Guadalajara one can see beside lithographs depicting civil war scenes with a stark simplicity, sketches of vituperative defamation of the class he obviously sprang from: his sketches swear and blaspheme as loudly as any of the worst pamphlets of Martin Luther. In fact, some of the most treasured murals of the revolution vie with Cranach's woodcuts in their pamphleteering aimed at an as yet illiterate populace. But will revolutions against exploiters settle the issue of exploitation, or must man also learn to raise truly less exploitable men—men who are first of all masters of the human life cycle and of the cycle of generations in man's own lifespace?

On an occasional trip to the capital, I visit ancient Guanajuato where the university, a formidable fortress, has been topped by fantastic ornamental erections in order to overtower the adjoining cathedral which once dominated education. The cathedral wall bears this announcement about death, judgment, inferno, and eternal glory:

> La Muerta que es puerta de la Eternidad
> El Judicio que decidera la Eternidad
> El Infierno que es la habitacion de la desgraciada Eternidad
> La Gloria que es la masion de la feliz Eternidad

The area of nearby Lake Patzcuaro is dominated by an enormous statue erected on a fisherman's island. The statue depicts the revolutionary hero Morelos, an erstwhile monk, his right arm raised in a gesture much like Luther's when he spoke at Worms. In its clean linear stockiness and stubborn puritanism the statue could be somewhere in a Nordic land; and if, in its other hand, it held a mighty book instead of the handle of a stony sword, it could, for all the world, be Luther.

References

These standard works on and by Luther will be referred to by the following abbreviations:

Dok. = Otto Scheel, *Dokumente zu Luthers Entwicklung* (Tuebingen, J. C. B. Mohr, 1929).

Enders = E. L. Enders, *Martin Luthers Briefwechsel* (Frankfurt, 1884–1907).

L.W.W.A. = Martin Luther, *Werke* (Weimarer Ausgabe, 1883).

Reiter = Paul J. Reiter, *Martin Luthers Umwelt, Charakter und Psychose* (Kopenhagen, Leven & Munksgaard, 1937).

Scheel = Otto Scheel, *Martin Luther: Vom Katholizismus zur Reformation* (Tuebingen, J. C. B. Mohr, 1917).

TR = Luther's *Tischreden* (Weimarer Ausgaben).

PREFACE

1. Anna Freud, *The Ego and the Mechanisms of Defence*, translated from the German by Cecil Baines (New York, International Universities Press, 1946).
2. August Aichhorn, *Wayward Youth*, with a foreword by Sigmund Freud (New York, Viking Press, 1935).
3. Heinz Hartmann, *Ego Psychology and the Problem of Adaptation*, translated by David Rapaport (New York, International Universities Press, 1958). Also, "Notes on the Reality Principle," *The Psychoanalytic Study of the Child*, XI (New York, International Universities Press, 1956), 31–53.
4. David Rapaport, "Some Metapsychological Considerations Concerning Activity and Passivity," unpublished paper, 1953. Also, "The Theory of Ego Autonomy: A Generalization," *Bulletin of the Menninger Clinic*, 22 (1958), 13–35.
5. E. H. Erikson, "The Problem of Ego Identity," *Journal of the American Psychoanalytic Association*, 4 (1956), 56–121. I have presented some applications of the identity concept to study groups; see *Totalitarianism*, ed. by Carl J. Friedrich (Cambridge, Harvard University Press, 1954), 156–171; *New Perspectives for Research on Juvenile Delinquency* (Washington, D.C., Children's Bureau, U.S. Department of Health, Education and Wel-

fare, 1956), 1–23; and *Discussions on Child Development*, Proceedings of the Third Meeting of the Child Study Group, World Health Organization (London, Tavistock Publications, Ltd., 1956).

6. E. H. Erikson, "The First Psychoanalyst," *Yale Review*, XLVI (1956).
7. E. H. Erikson, "Freuds Psychoanalytische Krise," *Freud in der Gegenwart* (Frankfurt, Europaeische Verlagsanstalt, 1957).

CHAPTER I

1. *Soeren Kierkegaards efterladte Papirer*, ed. P. A. Heiberg (Cophenhagen, 1926), IX, 75. Cf. Eduard Geismar, "Wie urteilte Kierkegaard ueber Luther?" *Luther-Jahrbuch* X (1928), 18.
2. R. G. Collingwood, *The Idea of History* (New York, Oxford University Press, 1956), 226–27.
3. Ref. 1, Preface.
4. *Ibid.*, 177.
5. Heinz Hartmann, *Ego Psychology and the Problem of Adaptation.*
6. E. H. Erikson, "On the Nature of Clinical Evidence," *Evidence and Inference, The First Hayden Colloquium* (Cambridge, The Technology Press of M.I.T., 1958); also, "Daedalus," *Journal of the American Academy of Arts and Sciences Proceedings*, 87 (Fall, 1958).
7. Sigmund Freud, *New Introductory Lectures on Psychoanalysis*, translated by W. T. H. Sprott (New York, W. W. Norton & Co., 1933).
8. Sigmund Freud, *The Future of an Illusion*, translated by W. D. Robson-Scott (New York, Liveright Publishing Corp., 1949).
9. Karl Mannheim, *Utopia and Ideology* (New York, Harcourt Brace, 1949).

CHAPTER II

1. Scheel, II, 116.
2. *Dok.*, No. 533.
3. *Dok.*, No. 533.
4. Johannes Cochlaeus, *Commentaria de actis et scriptis Martini Lutheri* (Mainz, 1549).
5. Scheel, II, 117.
6. *Dok.*, No. 533.
7. P. Heinrich Denifle, *Luther in Rationalistischer und Christlicher Beleuchtung* (Mainz, Kirchheim & Co., 1904), p. 31.
8. Reiter, II, 99.
9. Reiter, II, 556.
10. Reiter, II, 240.
11. Preserved Smith, *The Life and Letters of Martin Luther* (New York, Houghton Mifflin & Co., 1911).
12. Preserved Smith, *Luther's Correspondence* (Philadelphia, The Lutheran Publication Society, 1913).
13. Preserved Smith, "Luther's Early Development in the Light of Psychoanalysis," *American Journal of Psychology*, XXIV (1913).
14. *Ibid.*, 362.
15. *Dok.*, No. 199.
16. *L.W.W.A.*, XXXIII, 507.
17. Scheel, I, 261.

18. Heinrich Boehmer, *Road to Reformation* (Philadelpia, Muhlenberg Press, 1946).
19. Leopold von Ranke, *History of the Reformation in Germany* (London, 1905).
20. Theodosius Harnack, *Luthers Theologie I* (1862); II (1886).
21. Hartmann Grisar, *Luther* (Freiburg, Herder Verlag, 1911).
22. Lucien Febvre, *Martin Luther, A Destiny* (London, J. M. Dent & Sons, Ltd., 1930), 18.
23. Denifle, Ref. 7, 77.
24. P. Heinrich Denifle, *Luther und Luthertum in der ersten Entwicklung* (Mainz, Kirchheim & Co., 1906), I, 774–75.
25. *Ibid.*
26. Reiter, II, 121.
27. R. Pascal, *The Social Basis of the German Reformation* (London, Watts & Co., 1933), 227.
28. Ernst Troeltsch, *The Social Teaching of the Christian Churches* (London, 1931).
29. Max Weber, *The Protestant Ethic and the Spirit of Capitalism* (London, 1948).
30. R. H. Tawney, *Religion and the Rise of Capitalism* (New York, Harcourt, Brace and Co., 1952).
31. Quoted in Heinrich Bornkamm, *Luther im Spiegel der deutschen Geistesgeschichte* (Heidelberg, Quelle und Meyer, 1955), 191.
32. *Dok.*, No. 209.
33. *Dok.*, No. 248.
34. Quoted in Bornkamm, Ref. 31, 330.
35. William James, *Varieties of Religious Experience* (Longmans, Green and Co., 1935), 199.
36. E. H. Erikson, "The Problem of Ego Identity," *Journal of the American Psychoanalytic Association*, 4 (1956), 56–121.
37. G. B. Shaw, Preface to *Selected Prose* (New York, Dodd, Mead and Co., 1952).
38. E. H. Erikson, "The First Psychoanalyst," *Yale Review*, XLVI (1956), 43.
39. Sigmund Freud, *The Interpretation of Dreams*, Complete Psychological Works of Sigmund Freud, Volumes IV and V (London, Hogarth Press, 1953).
40. *L.W.W.A.*, VII, 838.

CHAPTER III

1. *L.W.W.A.*, VIII, 574–75.
2. *L.W.W.A.*, VIII, 575.
3. R. H. Tawney, *Religion and the Rise of Capitalism*, 68.
4. Martin Luther, *Werke* (Erlanger Ausgabe), LIX, 324.
5. Julius Koestlin, *Martin Luther, Sein Leben und seine Schriften* (Berlin, Alexander Duncker, 1903), I, 48.
6. Reiter, I, 362.
7. Roland H. Bainton, *Here I Stand* (New York, Abingdon-Cokesbury Press, 1930), 23.
8. *TR*, II, No. 1559; *Cf.* Scheel, I, 11.
9. See the chapter on two American Indian Tribes in *Childhood and Society*.
10. Scheel, I, 20. *Dok.*, Nos. 406 and 430.

11. Luther's *Werke* (Erlanger Ausgabe), XL, 164.
12. *Dok.*, No. 417.
13. *L.W.W.A.*, XXXVIII, 338.
14. Reiter, I, 362.
15. Huizinga, *The Waning of the Middle Ages* (New York, Doubleday, 1956), 150.
16. *Ibid.*, 138.
17. *Ibid.*
18. *L.W.W.A.*, XXXVIII, 105.
19. Scheel, I, 229.
20. *TR*, IV, No. 4714.
21. *TR*, IV, No. 5024.
22. Scheel, I, 150-74.
23. *L.W.W.A.*, VIII, 573.
24. *L.W.W.A.*, VIII, 573-74.
25. *TR*, IV, No. 4707.
26. *Dok.*, No. 175.
27. Ernst Kris, *Psychoanalytic Explorations in Art*, Chapter 13, "On Inspiration" (New York, International Universities Press, 1952), 291-302.
28. Scheel, I, 259.
29. Robert Lifton, "Thought Reform of Chinese Intellectuals, a Psychiatric Evaluation," *Journal of Asian Studies*, XVI (November, 1956), 1.
30. Rupert E. Davies, *The Problem of Authority in the Continental Reformers* (London, The Epworth Press, 1946), 98.
31. *TR*, III, No. 3593.
32. Friedrich Nietzsche, *Zur Genealogie der Moral, Werke* (Stuttgart, Alfred Kroner, 1921), VII, 463.

CHAPTER IV

1. August Kubizek, *Young Hitler* (London, Allan Wingate, 1954).
2. *Ibid.*, 35.
3. *Ibid.*, 51-54.
4. *Ibid.*, 70-71.
5. *Ibid.*, 53.
6. H. R. Trevor-Roper, *The Last Days of Hitler* (New York, Macmillan Co., 1947), 57.
7. *Ibid.*, 78.
8. *Ibid.*, 54-55.
9. *Ibid.*, 57.
10. *Dok.*, No. 815.
11. Crane Brinton, *The Shaping of the Modern Mind* (New York, New American Library, 1953), 11-12.
12. I Cor. 13:12.
13. *L.W.W.A.*, XXXII, 328-29.
14. For a detailed clinical example, see "The Nature of Clinical Evidence," Ref. 6, Chapter I.
15. Rolf Ahrens, "Beitrag zur Entwicklung des Physiognomie- und Mimikerkennens," *Zeitschrift fuer experimentelle und angewandte Psychologie*, II, 3 (1954), 412-454; II, 4 (1954), 599-633. Also see Charlotte Buehler and H. Hetzer, "Die Reaktionen des Saeuglings auf das menschliche Gesicht," *Zeitschrift fuer Psychologie*, 132 (1934), 1-17; and R. A. Spitz and K. M.

Wolf, "The Smiling Response. A Contribution to the Ontogenesis of Social Relation," *General Psychological Monographs*, 24 (1946), 55–125.

16. René Spitz, "Hospitalism," *The Psychoanalytic Study of the Child*, Vol. I (New York, International Universities Press, 1945), 53–74.

17. *L.W.W.A.*, XLIX, 180.

18. *L.W.W.A.*, XI, 4201.

19. William James, Ref. 35, Chapter II, 40.

20. Quoted in Bornkamm, 284, Ref. 31, Chapter II, from *Predigt über Exod.* (*2 Mose*), 20.

21. Thomas Wolfe, *The Story of a Novel* (New York, Charles Scribner's Sons, 1936), 39.

CHAPTER V

1. Scheel, I, 260–61.

2. *Dok.*, No. 50.

3. Miguel de Unamuno, *Soledad*, translated by John Upton, *The Centennial Review* (Summer, 1958).

4. Lifton, Ref. 29, Chapter II, 149.

5. David Rapaport, Ref. 4, Preface, 12.

6. James Joyce, *A Portrait of the Artist as a Young Man* (New York, Viking Press, 1957), 410.

7. *L.W.W.A.*, XXX, 3, 530.

8. Scheel, II, 23–24.

9. *TR*, IV, No. 4174.

10. *TR*, III, No. 3556.

11. *TR*, IV, No. 4174.

12. I Cor. 11:28, 31.

13. I Cor. 10:17.

14. I Cor. 11:24.

15. *Childhood and Society*, 152.

16. I Cor. 2:25; Luke 22:20.

17. Mark 14:24; Matthew 26:28.

18. I Cor. 11:29–30.

19. *Dok.*, No. 508.

20. *Ibid.*, Nos. 46 and 508.

21. *L.W.W.A.*, VIII, 574.

22. *Dok.*, No. 162.

23. *Dok.*, No. 487.

24. *L.W.W.A.*, III, 549.

25. *L.W.W.A.*, I, 576.

26. *L.W.W.A.*, XXXI, 2, 230.

27 *TR*, I, No. 121.

28. *L.W.W.A.*, XX, 773.

29. Reiter, II, 543.

30. Joyce, *Portrait*, 409.

31. *L.W.W.A.*, XIV, 471.

32. *TR*, III, No. 3298.

33. *TR*, I, No. 508.

34. *L.W.W.A.*, II, 586.

35. *L.W.W.A.*, II, 586.

36. *L.W.W.A.*, IX, 215.

37. *L.W.W.A.*, XV, 559.
38. *L.W.W.A.*, VIII, 119.
39. *L.W.W.A.*, XL, 1, 221.
40. *Dok.*, No. 184.
41. *L.W.W.A.*, XXVII, 126.
42. Scheel, II, 124; Cf. *TR*, I, 644.
43. *Dok.*, No. 275.
44. *Dok.*, Nos. 230, 444, and 485.
45. *TR*, IV, No. 4868.
46. Elmer Carl Riessling, *The Early Sermons of Luther and Their Relation to the Pre-Reformation Sermon* (Grand Rapids, Zondervar Publishing House, 1935), 38.
47. *TR*, I, No. 526.

CHAPTER VI

1. I Cor. 14:31.
2. Anne Freemantle, *The Age of Belief* (New York, Mentor, 1954), 26–27.
3. *Ibid.*, 28, 33.
4. I Cor. 4:7.
5. Huizinga, Ref. 15, Chapter III, 204.
6. *Ibid.*, 205.
7. *Ibid.*, 219.
8. *Ibid.*, 199.
9. Wilhelm Link, *Das Ringen Luthers um die Freiheit der Theologie von der Philosophie* (Muenchen, Chr. Kaiser, 1940), 319–21; 324–25; 340.
10. Giorgio de Santillana, *The Age of Adventure* (Boston, Houghton Mifflin Company, 1957), 13–14.
11. Pico, "On the Dignity of Man," *The Renaissance Philosophy of Man*, ed. by E. Crosirer, P. O. Rinsteller, and J. H. Randall (Chicago, Phoenix Books, 1956), 225.
12. Santillana, *Age of Adventure*, 83–84.
13. *Ibid.*, 155.
14. *Ibid.*, 69.
15. *Ibid.*, 15.
16. Quoted by Preserved Smith, Ref. 11, Chapter II, 206.
17. *L.W.W.A.*, III, 593.
18. Erich Vogelsang, *Die Anfaenge von Luthers Christologie* (Berlin, De Gruyter Co., 1929), Ö. 89, fn. 1; Cf. *L.W.W.A.*, XL, 1, 562.
19. *Dok.*, No. 182; Cf. *L.W.W.A*, XL, 1, 562.
20. *L.W.W.A.*, III, 531.
21. *L.W.W.A.*, III, 134.
22. *L.W.W.A.*, III, 257; III, 14. Cf. Vogelsang, 6, fn. 2.
23. *L.W.W.A.*, IV, 330.
24. Vogelsang, 58, fn. 1.
25. *L.W.W.A.*, III, 12. Cf. Vogelsang, 26.
26. Vogelsang, 32.
27. *TR*, V, No. 5247.
28. Vogelsang, 32–33.
29. *Ibid.*, 33.
30. Psalms 31:4.
31. Psalms 31:6.

32. Matthew 27:43.
33. Vogelsang, 50–51.
34. *Dok.*, No. 238.
35. *TR*, V, No. 5537.
36. *L.W.W.A.*, III, 408.
37. *L.W.W.A.*, IV, 9, 18.
38. *L.W.W.A.*, III, 227, 28.
39. *L.W.W.A.*, II, 28, 13.
40. *L.W.W.A.*, III, 651.
41. Sigmund Freud, *The Origins of Psychoanalysis* (London, Imago Publishing Co. Ltd., 1954), 236.
42. Johannes Ficker, *Luthers Vorlesung ueber den Roemerbrief Herausg* (Leipzig, Die Scholien, 1930), 206.
43. *L.W.W.A.*, IV, 234.
44. *L.W.W.A.*, V, 149.
45. *L.W.W.A.*, IV, 511.
46. *L.W.W.A.*, IX, 639.
47. I Cor. 1:22–5.
48. I Cor. 2:1–3.
49. *L.W.W.A.*, III, 420.
50. *L.W.W.A.*, III, 289.
51. *L.W.W.A.*, XL/1, 537.
52. *L.W.W.A.*, IV, 147.
53. *L.W.W.A.*, IV, 330; *Cf.* Vogelsang, 103, fn. 1; and 108, fn. 1.
54. *L.W.W.A.*, IV, 87.
55. *L.W.W.A.*, III, 529; *Cf.* Vogelsang, 136, fn. 5.
56. *L.W.W.A.*, IV, 365.
57. *L.W.W.A.*, IV, 350.
58. *L.W.W.A.*, XXXII, 390.
59. James, Ref. 21, Chapter 10.
60. *L.W.W.A.*, IX, 45.
61. *L.W.W.A.*, III, 289.
62. *L.W.W.A.*, VI, 207.
63. I have mislaid this reference; but no fairminded reader will suspect me of having invented this quotation.
64. *L.W.W.A.*, I, 200–201.
65. *L.W.W.A.*, V, 85.

CHAPTER VII

1. James, *Varieties of Religious Experience*, 348.
2. Charles Beard, *Martin Luther and the Reformation in Germany* (London, Philip Green, 1896), 231.
3. *L.W.W.A.*, VIII, 203.
4. Enders, II, 432–33.
5. Enders, III, 73.
6. *Works of Martin Luther* (Philadelphia, A. J. Holman Co., 1916), II, 400.
7. Bainton, Ref. 7, Chapter III, 186.
8. Nietzsche, Ref. 32, Chapter III, VII, 216.
9. Jacob Grimm, *Vorrede zur Deutschen Grammatik*, 1, 1822, 11 (quoted in Bornkamm, Ref. 31, Chapter II, 176–77).

10. *Ibid.*, 40.
11. *L.W.W.A.*, XXX, 1, 436; translated by Gordon Rupp in *The Righteousness of God* (London, Hodder and Stoughton, 1953), 293.
12. *L.W.W.A.*, XXVIII, 142.
13. Will Durant, *The Reformation* (New York, Simon and Schuster, 1957), 378.
14. Ref. 6, IV, 206–207.
15. "The Twelve Articles," *ibid.*, IV, 210–16.
16. *Ibid.*, III, 211–12.
17. *L.W.W.A.*, XVIII, 386.
18. *L.W.W.A.*, XXVIII, 286.
19. Smith, Ref. 11, Chapter II, 165.
20. Pascal, Ref. 27, Chapter II, 178.
21. See the chapter on Hitler in *Childhood and Society*.
22. *L.W.W.A.*, III, 1, 70.
23. Pascal, 187.
24. *L.W.W.A.*, XXXI, 1, 196.
25. *L.W.W.A.*, IV, 274.
26. Max Weber, Ref. 29, Chapter II.
27. Erich Fromm, *Escape from Freedom* (New York, Rinehart and Co., 1941).
28. Tawney, Ref. 30, Chapter II, 88–89.
29. Kierkegaard, Ref. 1, Chapter I, XI, 44, No. 61.
30. Quoted in Bornkamm, Ref. 31, Chapter II, 57.
31. Kierkegaard, Ref. 1, Chapter I, X, 401, No. 559.
32. *L.W.W.A.*, X, 2, 237.
33. *L.W.W.A.*, VIII, 483.
34. *L.W.W.A.*, XXIII, 421.
35. Tawney, Ref. 30, Chapter II, 93.
36. *TR*, II, No. 1263.
37. *L.W.W.A.*, VIII, 482.
38. Enders, VI, 110.
39. Enders, VI, 298.
40. *TR*, II, No. 2655a.
41. *TR*, II, No. 1557.
42. *Ibid.*
43. Bainton, Ref. 7, Chapter III, 295.
44. *TR*, I, 522.
45. Freud, Ref. 41, Chapter VI, 189.
46. *L.W.W.A.*, XXX, 3, 470. Translation in Durant, Ref. 13, 418.
47. Preserved Smith, Ref. 11, Chapter II, 322.

CHAPTER VIII

1. *TR*, I, No. 352.
2. *L.W.W.A.*, V, 163.
3. *L.W.W.A.*, XIX, 216–17; translated in Rupp, Ref. 11, Chapter VIII, 108.
4. *L.W.W.A.*, V, 79; translated in Rupp, 107.
5. *L.W.W.A.*, XLIV, 504.
6. *L.W.W.A.*, IV, 602; translated in Rupp, 109.
7. Enders, V, 278–79.
8. E. H. Erikson, "Integrity," *Childhood and Society*.
9. Seng-ts'an, Hsin-hsin, Ming. Alan W. Watts, *The Way of Zen* (New York, Pantheon Books, 1957).

10. See Ernst Kris' concept of a regression in the service of the ego, *Psychoanalytic Explorations in Art* (New York, International Universities Press, 1952).
11. Freud, Ref. 8, Chapter L.

Index